河南大学教材建设基金资助项目

Computational Methods
计算方法

Zhihao Ge/ Chenmei Xu

葛志昊　徐琛梅　编著

河南大学出版社

郑州

图书在版编目(CIP)数据

计算方法＝Computational Methods：英文/葛志昊，徐琛梅编著. —郑州：河南大学出版社，2017.12
ISBN 978-7-5649-3054-7

Ⅰ.①计… Ⅱ.①葛… ②徐… Ⅲ.①计算方法－高等学校－教材－英文 Ⅳ.①O241

中国版本图书馆 CIP 数据核字(2017)第 307732 号

责任编辑 张雪彩
责任校对 王　贝
装帧设计 郭　灿

出版发行　河南大学出版社
　　　　　地址：郑州市郑东新区商务外环中华大厦 2401 号　邮编：450046
　　　　　电话：0371-86059701(营销部)　　　　　　　　　网址：www.hupress.com
排　　版　河南金河印务有限公司
印　　刷　北京虎彩文化传播有限公司
版　　次　2018 年 7 月第 1 版
印　　次　2018 年 7 月第 1 次印刷
开　　本　720mm×1000mm　1/16
印　　张　12.75
字　　数　229 千字
定　　价　32.00 元

(本书如有印装质量问题，请与河南大学出版社营销部联系调换)

Preface

With the rapid development of computer and computing methods, scientific computing, theory and experiment have become the three major means of modern scientific activities. Computing has become an important tool in the fields of physics, chemistry, life sciences, medicine, systems science, meteorology, aeronautics and astronautics, and so on. Therefore, computational methods have become a compulsory course in information and computing science, and also the core course of mathematics, applied mathematics, other science and engineering specialities.

Internationalization of personnel training is one of the important goals of higher education. In order to make the students of information and computing science accord with the international standards as soon as possible, we write the text book in English, so that the students can benefit from the following aspects: to enjoy the first-class foreign education resources in China; create an English environment for students to improve the ability of English, especially professional English; train students' ability of English thinking; improve the learning interest in mathematics. Students' international competition consciousness and comprehensive quality can be improved.

This book covers undergraduate students in information and computing science, as well as undergraduate and graduate students in mathematics and applied mathematics and other science and engineering. This book emphasizes both theoretical analysis and practice, which focuses on training the two aspects of capacity of theoretical analysis and practical application. All lectures need 72 hours, and mathematics and applied mathematics and other science and engineering can choose parts of the book according to the specific needs.

Zhihao Ge
2017.06

Contents

Chapter 1 Introduction ·· 1
   § 1.1   Numerical Computational Methods and Main Contents ············ 1
   § 1.2   Error ·· 7
   § 1.3   Stability Analysis of Numerical Methods ································ 12
   § 1.4   How to Avoid Error ·· 15
   Excises 1 ·· 16
Chapter 2 Interpolation and Polynomial Approximation ································ 18
   § 2.1   Introduction ·· 18
   § 2.2   Lagrange Interpolation Polynomial ·· 20
   § 2.3   Neville's Interpolating Formula ·· 26
   § 2.4   Newton Interpolation ·· 27
   § 2.5   Hermite Interpolation ·· 34
   § 2.6   Piecewise Polynomial Approximation ···································· 38
   § 2.7   Cubic Spline Interpolation ·· 42
   Excises 2 ·· 48
Chapter 3 Approximation Theory ·· 53
   § 3.1   Optimal Approximation ·· 53
   § 3.2   Optimal Approximation of Normed Linear Space ·················· 54
   § 3.3   Optimal Uniform Approximation Polynomial ························· 57
   § 3.4   Minimum Error to Zero-Chebyshev Polynomial ····················· 60
   § 3.5   Optimal Approximation of the Inner Product Space ·············· 64
   § 3.6   Optimal Square Approximation and Orthogonal Polynomials ······ 68
   § 3.7   Discrete Optimal Square Approximation and Least Square
           Method (L-S) ·· 75
   Excises 3 ·· 80
Chapter 4 Numerical Integration and Differentiation ···································· 83
   § 4.1   Introduction ·· 83
   § 4.2   Newton-Cotes Quadrature Formula ······································ 88

§4.3	Composite Numerical Integration	93
§4.4	Richardson Extrapolation and Romberg Integration	96
§4.5	Gaussian Quadrature	100
§4.6	Numerical Differentiation	109
Excises 4		111
Chapter 5	Solving Linear System of Equations	117
§5.1	Elementary Notions and Results of Linear Algebra	117
§5.2	Direct Methods for Solving Linear System of Equations	125
§5.3	Error of Gaussian Elimination	131
§5.4	Iterative Methods for Solving Linear Systems	132
§5.5	Conjugate Gradient Method	139
Excises 5		142
Chapter 6	Approximating Eigenvalues	147
§6.1	Linear Algebra and Eigenvalues	147
§6.2	The Power Method and the Inverse Power Method	148
§6.3	Householder's Method	152
§6.4	QR Algorithm	155
§6.5	Improved Power Method	156
Excises 6		157
Chapter 7	Numerical Solutions of Nonlinear Systems	160
§7.1	The Bisection Method	160
§7.2	Fixed Point Iterative Method	161
§7.3	Newton's Iteration Method	164
§7.4	Numerical Solutive for Nonlinear Systems of Equations	169
Excises 7		172
Chapter 8	Numerical Solutions of Ordinary Differential Equations	175
§8.1	Introduction	175
§8.2	Euler's Method	176
§8.3	Multistep Methods (I)	180
§8.4	Multistep Methods (II)	184
§8.5	Runge-Kutta Method	187
§8.6	Stiff Problem	189
§8.7	Numerical Solution for Boundary-value Problem	190
Excises 8		193
References		197

Chapter 1 Introduction

§1.1 Numerical Computational Methods and Main Contents

1.1.1 Introduction

a) The Earliest Example

It gives a sexagesimal numerical approximation of the length of the diagonal in a unit square (See Figure 1.1.1). Being able to compute square roots is extremely important, for instance, in carpentry and construction.

b) History

· The field of numerical analysis predates the invention of modern computers by many centuries.

· Linear interpolation was already in use more than 2000 years ago.

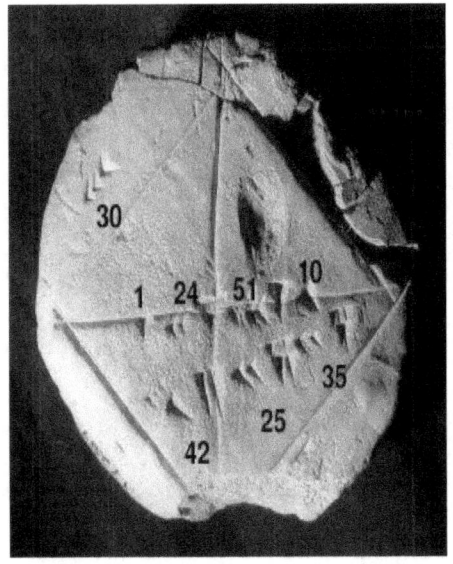

Figure 1.1.1 Sexagesimal numerical approximation

· Many great mathematicians of the past were preoccupied by numerical analysis, such as

Newton's method,

Lagrange interpolation polynomial,

Gaussian elimination,

Euler's method.

c) Applications

· Engineering.

· Physical sciences.

· In 21st century, the life sciences and even the arts have adopted many elements of scientific computations.

· Advanced numerical methods are essential in making numerical weather prediction feasible.

· Computing the trajectory of a spacecraft requires the accurate numerical solution of ordinary differential equations.

· Car companies use computer simulations of car crashes by partial differential equations numerically to improve the crash safety of their vehicles.

· Numerical analysis to calculate the value of stocks and so on.

· Airlines use sophisticated optimization algorithms to decide ticket prices, airplane and crew assignments and fuel needs. This field is also called operations research.

· Insurance companies use numerical programs for actuarial analysis.

d) How to Compute

In general, we need the following steps (See Figure 1.1.2).

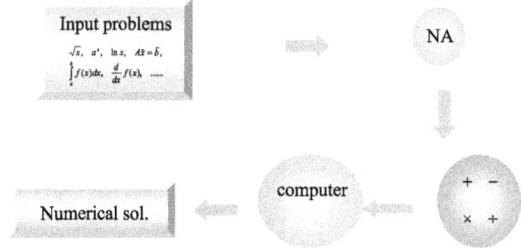

Figure 1.1.2 Computing in computer

Qin Jiushao Algorithm

$$P_n(x) = a_0 + a_1 x + a_2 x^2 + \cdots + a_n x^n.$$

Algorithm I

Let $S_0 = a_0$,

$S_k = S_{k-1} + a_k x_k, k = 1, 2, \cdots, n$.

Algorithm II (Qin Jiushao algorithm) (See Figure 1.1.3)

Let $S_n = a_n$,

$$S_{k-1} = a_{k-1} + x_k S_k, k = n, n-1, \cdots, 1.$$

1.1.2 Main Contents

· Interpolation.

· Approximation theory.

· Solving linear system of equations.

· Numerical integration and differential.

· Approximating eigenvalues.

· Numerical methods to nonlinear systems.

· Numerical solution to ordinary differential equations.

Next, we give some examples:

a) Numerical Methods to Nonlinear Systems

$$\begin{cases} f_1(x_1, x_2, \cdots, x_n) = 0, \\ f_2(x_1, x_2, \cdots, x_n) = 0, \\ \cdots\cdots \\ f_n(x_1, x_2, \cdots, x_n) = 0. \end{cases} \quad (1.1.1)$$

Denote $F(X) = 0$, **defined by**

$F: D \subset \mathbf{R}^n \to \mathbf{R}^n, X = (x_1, x_2, \cdots, x_n)^T.$

For example: Global Positioning System, GPS (See Figure 1.1.4).

(x, y, z, t) denotes the position of receiving point R on the earth, (x_i, y_i, z_i, t_i) is the position of satellite S_i (See Figure 1.1.5), then we have the following nonlinear systems:

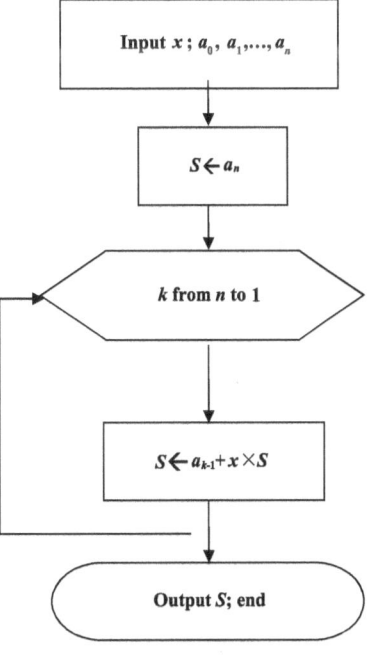

Figure 1.1.3 Qin Jiushao algorithm

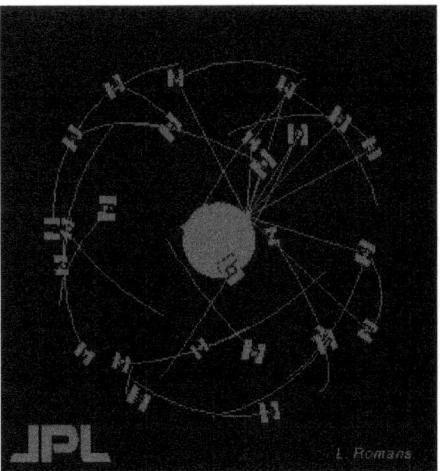

Figure 1.1.4 GPS

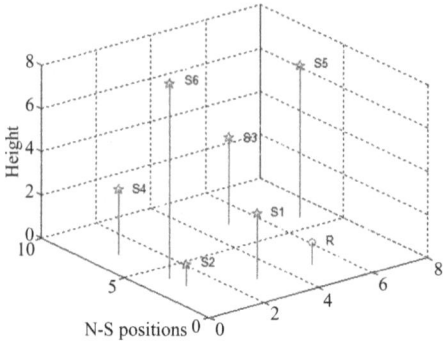

Figure 1.1.5 Positions of GPS

$$\begin{cases} \sqrt{(x-x_1)^2+(y-y_1)^2+(z-z_1)^2}-(t_1-t)\cdot c=0, \\ \sqrt{(x-x_2)^2+(y-y_2)^2+(z-z_2)^2}-(t_2-t)\cdot c=0, \\ \sqrt{(x-x_3)^2+(y-y_3)^2+(z-z_3)^2}-(t_3-t)\cdot c=0, \\ \sqrt{(x-x_4)^2+(y-y_4)^2+(z-z_4)^2}-(t_4-t)\cdot c=0, \\ \sqrt{(x-x_5)^2+(y-y_5)^2+(z-z_5)^2}-(t_5-t)\cdot c=0, \\ \sqrt{(x-x_6)^2+(y-y_6)^2+(z-z_6)^2}-(t_6-t)\cdot c=0. \end{cases}$$

b) Numerical Solution to Ordinary Differential Equations

For example: 1963, E. N. Lorenz gave the model:

$$\begin{cases} \dfrac{dx}{dt}=\sigma(y-x), \\ \dfrac{dy}{dt}=x(\rho-z)-y, \\ \dfrac{dz}{dt}=xy-\beta z \end{cases} \tag{1.1.2}$$

is called by **Lorenz model** (See Figure 1.1.6).

When $\sigma=10, \beta=8/3, \rho=28$, we have

Black line: x-axis, red line: y-axis, blue line: z-axis;

Length of step = pi/10.

c) Numerical Solution to Partial Differential Equations

For example: Car deforms (See Figure 1.1.7).

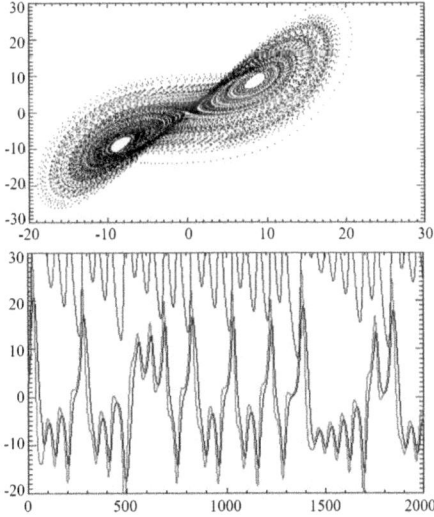

Figure 1.1.6 Lorenz model

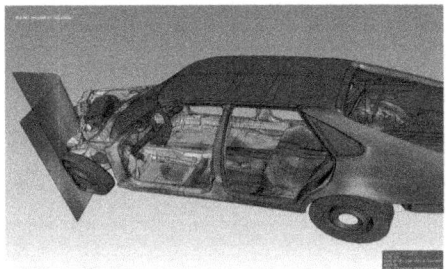

Figure 1.1.7 Car deforms

Visualization of how a car deforms in an asymmetrical crash using finite element analysis.

d) Numerical Integration

The integral $\int_a^b f(x)\,dx$ (See Figure 1.1.8).

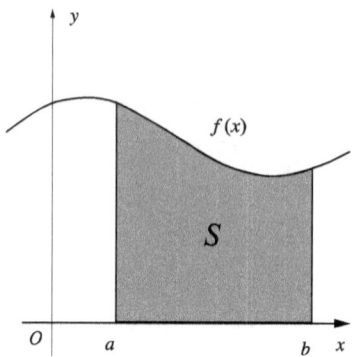

Figure 1.1.8 The integral

Rectangle rule (See Figure 1.1.9):

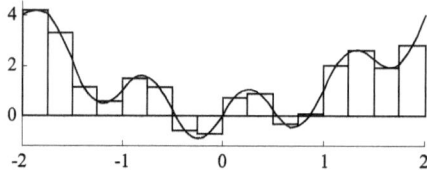

Figure 1.1.9 Rectangle rule

$$\int_a^b f(x)\,dx \approx (b-a)f\left(\frac{a+b}{2}\right).$$

Trapezoidal rule (See Figure 1.1.10):

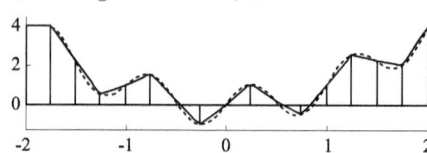

Figure 1.1.10 Trapezoidal rule

$$\int_a^b f(x)\,dx \approx (b-a)\cdot\frac{f(a)+f(b)}{2}.$$

§1.2 Error

1.2.1 Source & Classification

· Modeling error.

From the practical problem, we have to omit some factors so that we create a mathematical model.

· Measurement error.

· Truncation error.

To get the approximation number, one must chop, which result in truncation error.

Example 1.2.1 $\sin x = x - \dfrac{x^3}{3!} + \dfrac{x^5}{5!} - \dfrac{x^7}{7!} + \dfrac{x^9}{9!} + \cdots$.

If we take

$$\sin x \approx x - \dfrac{x^3}{3!} + \dfrac{x^5}{5!},$$

then

$$\left| \sin x - \left(x - \dfrac{x^3}{3!} + \dfrac{x^5}{5!} \right) \right| \leq \dfrac{x^7}{7!}.$$

· Round-off error.

1.2.2 Error and Significant Digits

1.2.2.1 Error

Definition 1.2.1 If x^* is an approximation to x, then the absolute error is $E(x) = x - x^*$, and the relative error is $E_r(x) = \dfrac{x - x^*}{x}$, provided that $x \neq 0$.

Example 1.2.2

(1) $x = 0.3000 \times 10$ and $x^* = 0.3100 \times 10$, the absolute error is 0.1, and the relative error is $0.3\dot{3}3\dot{3} \times 10^{-1}$.

(2) $x = 0.3000 \times 10^{-3}$ and $x^* = 0.3100 \times 10^{-3}$, the absolute error is 0.1×10^{-4}, and the relative error is $0.3\dot{3}3\dot{3} \times 10^{-1}$.

(3) $x = 0.3000 \times 10^4$ and $x^* = 0.3100 \times 10^4$, the absolute error is 0.1×10^3, and the relative error is 0.3333×10^{-1}.

This example shows that the same relative error, 0.3333×10^{-1}, occurs for widely varying absolute errors.

As a measure of accuracy, the absolute error can be misleading and the relative error is more meaningful since the relative error takes into consideration the size of the value.

Definition 1.2.2 If $|x - x^*| \leq \eta$, then η is called absolute error accuracy. If $|E_r(x)| \leq \delta$, then δ is called relative error accuracy.

In fact, $E_r(x)$ is replaced by $E_r^*(x)$:

$$E_r^*(x) = \frac{x - x^*}{x^*}, \qquad (1.2.1)$$

$$E_r(x) = \frac{x - x^*}{x} = \frac{E(x)}{x} = \frac{E(x)}{x^* + E(x)}$$

$$= \frac{E(x)}{x^*} \left(\frac{1}{1 + \frac{E(x)}{x^*}} \right)$$

$$= \frac{E(x)}{x^*} \left(1 - \frac{E(x)}{x^*} + \left(\frac{E(x)}{x^*}\right)^2 - \cdots \right)$$

$$= \frac{E(x)}{x^*} - \left(\frac{E(x)}{x^*}\right)^2 + \left(\frac{E(x)}{x^*}\right)^3 - \cdots$$

$$= E_r^*(x) - (E_r^*(x))^2 + (E_r^*(x))^3 - \cdots.$$

Hence, $E_r(x) \approx E_r^*(x)$ only if $E_r^*(x)$ is small enough.

1.2.2.2 Significant Digit

Definition 1.2.3 Let x^* be an approximation to x given by

$$x^* = \pm 0.a_1 a_2 \cdots a_k \cdots a_n \times 10^m,$$

where $0 \leq a_i (i = 1, 2, \cdots, n) \leq 9$ and $a_1 \neq 0$.

If $|x - x^*| \leq \frac{1}{2} \times 10^{m-k} \leq \frac{1}{2} \times 10^{m-i} (1 \leq i \leq k)$, then a_k is a significant digit. If $a_1, a_2, \cdots, a_n$ are significant digits, then x^* has n significant digits.

Remark 1.2.1 If x^* is got by round-off, then x^* is a significant digit.

Example 1.2.3 $x = e = 2.7182818284\cdots = 0.27182818284\cdots \times 10^1$.

x^*	2.7	2.71	2.718	2.7182
Significant digits	2	2	4	4
$\lvert E(x)\rvert$	$\frac{1}{2}\times 10^{-1}$	$\frac{1}{2}\times 10^{1-2}$	$\frac{1}{2}\times 10^{1-4}$	$\frac{1}{2}\times 10^{1-4}$

Solution a. $x^* = 2.7 = 0.27\times 10^1$,
$$|x - x^*| = 0.0018281\cdots \times 10^1$$
$$= 0.18281\cdots \times 10^{1-2}$$
$$< 0.5\times 10^{1-2}.$$

Therefore, x^* has 2 significant digits.

b. $x^* = 2.71 = 0.271\times 10^1$,
$$|x - x^*| = 0.0008281\cdots \times 10^1$$
$$= 0.8281\cdots \times 10^{1-3}$$
$$< 0.5\times 10^{1-2}.$$

Therefore, x^* has 2 significant digits.

c. $x^* = 2.718 = 0.2718\times 10^1$,
$$|x - x^*| = 0.0000281\cdots \times 10^1$$
$$= 0.281\cdots \times 10^{1-4}$$
$$< 0.5\times 10^{1-4}.$$

Therefore, x^* has 4 significant digits.

d. $x^* = 2.7182 = 0.27182\times 10^1$,
$$|x - x^*| = 0.0000081\cdots \times 10^1$$
$$= 0.81\cdots \times 10^{1-5}$$
$$< 0.5\times 10^{1-4}.$$

Therefore, x^* has 4 significant digits.

From the approximation and the significant digits, we know the accuracy.

Also, we have the following result about relative error and significant digits.

Theorem 1.2.1 Assume x^* is an approximation to x, where $x = \pm 0.a_1 a_2\cdots a_n \times 10^m$, $a_1 \neq 0$.

(1) If x^* has n significant digits, then the relative error accuracy is
$$|E_r^*(x)| \leq \frac{1}{2a_1}\times 10^{-(n-1)}.$$

(2) If the relative error accuracy satisfies

$$|E_r^*(x)| \leq \frac{1}{2(a_1+1)} \times 10^{-(n-1)},$$

then x^* has at least n significant digits.

Proof (1) $x = \pm 0.a_1 a_2 \cdots a_n \times 10^m$ has n significant digits, then

$$|E_r^*(x)| = \left|\frac{E(x)}{x^*}\right| \leq \frac{\frac{1}{2} \times 10^{m-n}}{|x^*|} \leq \frac{\frac{1}{2} \times 10^{m-n}}{a_1 \times 10^{m-1}} = \frac{1}{2a_1} \times 10^{-(n-1)}.$$

(2) If $|E_r^*(x)| \leq \frac{1}{2(a_1+1)} \times 10^{-(n-1)}$, then we have

$$|x - x^*| \leq |x^*||E_r^*(x)| \leq |x^*| \times \frac{1}{2(a_1+1)} \times 10^{-(n-1)}$$

$$\leq (a_1+1) \times 10^{m-1} \times \frac{1}{2(a_1+1)} \times 10^{-(n-1)}$$

$$= \frac{1}{2} \times 10^{m-n}.$$

So, we know that x^* has n significant digits.

Example 1.2.4 Given $\pi = 3.1415926535897932\cdots$, and π^* is an approximation to π, how many significant digits π^* has such that the relative error is less than 0.001%?

Solution Assume π^* has n significant digits, we have

$$|E_r^*(\pi)| \leq \frac{1}{2a_1} \times 10^{-(n-1)} = \frac{1}{2 \times 3} \times 10^{-(n-1)}$$

$$\leq 0.00001 = 10^{-5},$$

then, we get $n = 6$. So $\pi^* = 3.14159$.

1.2.3 Error Estimate of Numerical Computation

(1) Given the following function

$$y = f(x_1, x_2, \cdots, x_n),$$

let $x_1^*, x_2^*, \cdots, x_n^*$ be approximation to $x_1, x_2, \cdots, x_n$, respectively, and we denote the value by

$$y^* = f(x_1^*, x_2^*, \cdots, x_n^*).$$

Question: Is y^* an approximation to y?

$$E(y) = y - y^* = f(x_1, x_2, \cdots, x_n) - f(x_1^*, x_2^*, \cdots, x_n^*)$$

$$\approx \sum_{i=1}^{n} \frac{\partial}{\partial x_i} f(x_1, x_2, \cdots, x_n) \cdot (x_i - x_i^*)$$

$$= \sum_{i=1}^{n} \frac{\partial}{\partial x_i} f(x_1, x_2, \cdots, x_n) \cdot E(x_i),$$

$$E_r(y) = \frac{E(y)}{y} \approx \sum_{i=1}^{n} \frac{\partial}{\partial x_i} f(x_1, x_2, \cdots, x_n) \cdot \frac{E(x_i)}{f(x_1, x_2, \cdots, x_n)}$$

$$= \sum_{i=1}^{n} \frac{\partial}{\partial x_i} f(x_1, x_2, \cdots, x_n) \cdot \frac{x_i}{f(x_1, x_2, \cdots, x_n)} \cdot E_r(x_i).$$

(2) x_1^*, x_2^* are approximations to x_1, x_2.

a. $|E(x_1 \pm x_2)| = |x_1 \pm x_2 - (x_1^* \pm x_2^*)| \leq E(x_1) + E(x_2)$.

b. $|E(x_1 \cdot x_2)| \leq |x_2| \cdot |E(x_1)| + |x_1| \cdot |E(x_2)|$.

c. $\left| E\left(\frac{x_1}{x_2}\right) \right| \leq \dfrac{|x_2| \cdot |E(x_1)| + |x_1| \cdot |E(x_2)|}{|x_2|^2}$ (where x^* can be replaced by x).

Proof: The formula of a, b and c can be obtained by letting $f(x_1, x_2) = x_1 \pm x_2$, $x_1 \cdot x_2$ or $\dfrac{x_1}{x_2}$.

For example, $f(x_1, x_2) = \dfrac{x_1}{x_2}$,

$$\left| E\left(\frac{x_1}{x_2}\right) \right| \approx \sum_{i=1}^{n} \frac{\partial}{\partial x_i} f(x_1, x_2) \cdot E(x_i)$$

$$= \left| \frac{E(x_1)}{x_2} + \frac{-x_1 E(x_2)}{x_2^2} \right|$$

$$\leq \frac{|x_2| \cdot |E(x_1)| + |x_1| \cdot |E(x_2)|}{|x_2|^2}.$$

(3) From (2), we know that the error can be estimated. Moreover, we have the follow theorem.

Theorem 1.2.2 If $nu \leq 0.01$, then

$$f \cdot l\left(\sum_{j=1}^{n} x_j y_j\right) = \sum_{j=1}^{n} (x_j y_j)[1 + 1.01(n + 2 - j)\theta_j u],$$

where $|\theta_j| \leq 1, j = 1, 2, \cdots, n$.

§1.3 Stability Analysis of Numerical Methods

1.3.1 Algorithm and Stability

Throughout the text we will be examing approximation procedures, called algorithms, involving sequences of calculating.

We are interested in choosing methods that will produce dependably accurate results for a wide range of problems.

Definition 1.3.1 (Stable) An algorithm is called stable if small changes in the initial data produce correspondingly small changes in the final results. Otherwise, it is unstable.

If some algorithms are stable only for certain choice of initial data, the algorithms are called conditionally stable.

Definition 1.3.2 Denote E_0 by an error at some stage in the calculations, E_n by the magnitude of the error after n subsequent operations.

If $E_n \approx CE_0$, where C is a constant independent of n, then the growth of error is said to be linear; If $E_n \approx C^n E_0$, for some $C > 1$, then the growth of error is called exponential.

Remark 1.3.1 Linear growth of error is usually unavoidable, and when C and E_0 are small the results are generally acceptable.

Exponential growth of error should be avoided, since the term C^n becomes large for even relating small values of n. This leads to unacceptable in accuracies, regardless of the size of E_0.

As a consequence, an algorithm that exhibits linear growth of error is stable, whereas an algorithm exhibiting exponential error growth is unstable.

Remark 1.3.2 Error analysis methods:

(1) Probability analysis method.

(2) 1960's Wilkinson post-error analysis; Moore interval analysis.

Example 1.3.1 Compute $I_n = e^{-1} \int_0^1 x^n e^x dx, n = 1, 2, \cdots$.

Solution

$$I_n = e^{-1}\int_0^1 x^n e^x dx = \int_0^1 x^n e^{x-1} dx$$

$$= x^n e^{x-1}\Big|_0^1 - n\int_0^1 e^{x-1} x^{n-1} dx$$

$$= 1 - nI_{n-1}, \quad n = 2, 3, \cdots.$$

It is easy to calculate $I_1 = e^{-1}$ and

$$e^{-1} \approx 1 + (-1) + \frac{(-1)^2}{2!} + \cdots + \frac{(-1)^k}{k!}.$$

Taking $k = 7$, we have $e^{-1} \approx 0.3679$.

(A) $\begin{cases} \tilde{I}_1 = 0.3679, \\ \tilde{I}_n = 1 - n\tilde{I}_{n-1}, \quad n = 2, 3, \cdots. \end{cases}$

(B) $\begin{cases} I_9^* = 0.0684, \\ I_{n-1}^* = \dfrac{1}{n}(1 - I_n^*). \end{cases}$

n	$\tilde{I}_n$ (A)	I_n^* (B)
1	0.3679	0.3679
2	0.2642	0.2643
3	0.2074	0.2073
4	0.1704	0.1708
5	0.1480	0.1455
6	0.1120	0.1268
7	0.2160	0.1121
8	-0.7280	0.1035
9	7.552	0.0684

In fact, $E_1 = I_1 - \tilde{I}_1$,

$$E_n = I_n - \tilde{I}_n = 1 - nI_{n-1} - (1 - n\tilde{I}_{n-1})$$

$$= -nE_{n-1}, \quad n = 2, 3, \cdots,$$

$$E_n = -nE_{n-1} = -n \cdot [-(n-1)] \cdot E_{n-2}$$

$$= (-1)^{n-1} n!,$$

(A) is unstable.

However, $E_n^* = I_n - I_n^*$, $|E_0^*| = \dfrac{1}{n!}|E_n^*|$, (B) is stable.

1.3.2 Condition Number and Ill Problem

For function $y = f(x)$,

$$E_r(x) = \frac{E(x)}{x} = \frac{x - x^*}{x}.$$

$$E_r(y) \approx f'(x) \cdot \frac{x}{f(x)} \cdot E_r(x).$$

Definition 1.3.2 The term $\left|\dfrac{x}{f(x)} \cdot f'(x)\right|$ is called condition number of the problem, denoted by C_p.

Remark 1.3.3 Generally, $E_r(x)$ is small, so if C_p is large enough, then the problem is called ill problem. ($C_p \geqslant 10$, the problem can be regarded as an ill problem.)

Example 1.3.2 Function $f(x) = x^n$,

$$C_p = \left|\frac{x}{f(x)} \cdot f'(x)\right| = n.$$

For $n \geqslant 10$, the problem is ill.

Example 1.3.3 Solve the following linear system

$$\begin{cases} x + \alpha y = 1, \\ \alpha x + y = 0. \end{cases}$$

Solution As $\alpha = 1$, there is no solution.

For the case $\alpha \neq 1$, $x = \dfrac{1}{1 - \alpha^2}, y = -\dfrac{\alpha}{1 - \alpha^2}$.

Taking $\alpha = 0.99$, then $x \approx 50.25$; Taking $\alpha^* = 0.991$, then $x^* \approx 55.81$.

$|x - x^*| \approx 5.56$ (very large). In fact, $x = \dfrac{1}{1 - \alpha^2}$ is a function with α. So, we have

$$C_p = \left|\frac{\alpha}{\dfrac{1}{1-\alpha^2}} \cdot \frac{2\alpha}{(1-\alpha^2)^2}\right| = \left|\frac{2\alpha^2}{1-\alpha^2}\right|.$$

If $\alpha = 0.99$, $C_p \approx 100$. So, the problem is ill.

§1.4 How to Avoid Error

1.4.1 Two Almost Equal Number Minus

(1) $\sqrt{x+\varepsilon} - \sqrt{x} = \dfrac{\varepsilon}{\sqrt{x+\varepsilon}+\sqrt{x}}.$ (1.4.1)

Example 1.4.1 Find the minimum root of
$$x^2 - 16x + 1 = 0.$$

Solution The equation has two roots $x_1 = 8 + \sqrt{63}, x_2 = 8 - \sqrt{63}$.

$$x_2 = 8 - \sqrt{63} \approx 8 - 7.94 = 0.06,$$

$$x_2 = 8 - \sqrt{63} = \dfrac{1}{8+\sqrt{63}} \approx \dfrac{1}{15.94} = 0.0627.$$

We can see that x_2 has 3 significant digits.

Other cases, such as

$$\begin{cases} \ln(x+\varepsilon) - \ln(x) = \ln\left(1 + \dfrac{\varepsilon}{x}\right), \\ 1 - \cos x = 2\sin^2 \dfrac{x}{2}, \\ e^x - 1 = x\left(1 + \dfrac{1}{2}x + \dfrac{1}{6}x^2 + \cdots\right). \end{cases}$$ (1.4.2)

(2) Over flow.

(3) $x_1 + x_2: x_1 \gg x_2$.

Example 1.4.2
$$A = 52492 + \sum_{i=1}^{1000} \delta_i,$$

where $0.1 \leqslant \delta_i \leqslant 0.9$.

Solution In computing, we have
$$A = 0.52492 \times 10^5 + \sum_{i=1}^{1000} \delta_i,$$

$\delta_i = 0.9 = 0.000009 \times 10^5$.

$$A = 0.52492 \times 10^5 + 0.000009 \times 10^5 + \cdots$$

$$= 0.52492 \times 10^5.$$

So, we should caculate $\sum_{i=1}^{1000} \delta_i$, then add to 52492.

1.4.2 Qin Jiushao Algorithm

$$p(x) = a_0 x^n + a_1 x^{n-1} + \cdots + a_{n-1} x + a_n, \quad a_0 \neq 0. \quad (1.4.3)$$

(number of multiplication: $\sum_{i=0}^{n}(n-i) = 1 + 2 + \cdots + n = \frac{n(n+1)}{2} = O(n^2)$;

number of addition: n.)

On the other hand, we take

$$p(x) = (\cdots((a_0 x + a_1)x + \cdots + a_{n-1})x) + a_n, \quad (1.4.4)$$

then $b_n = p(x^*)$. (number of multiplication: $n \to O(n)$; number of addition: n.)

Qin Jiushao lived in ancient China about 1247; Hernor algorithm was produced in 1819.

Also,

$$p(x) = (x - x^*)\underbrace{(b_0 x^{n-1} + \cdots + b_{n-1})}_{q(x)} + b_n,$$

$$p(x^*) = b_n,$$

$$p'(x) = q(x) + (x - x^*)q'(x),$$

then

$$p'(x^*) = q(x^*).$$

1.4.3 Numerical Software

In the scientific computation, we should master
(1) Fortran, C, C + +.
(2) Software: Eispack, Numerical, Lapack.
(3) Matlab(Matrix Laboratory), Maple.

Excises 1

1.1 Supposed that the original data is exact, try to calculate the approximate values of $(164 + 0.913) - (143 + 21)$ and $(164 - 143) + (0.913 - 21)$ to three decimal places, and give their significant digits.

1.2 Prove that the relative error of $\sqrt{x}$ is approximately equal to the half of the relative error of x.

1.3 Supposed the t places β system number of floating point machine expression of real number a is $fl(a)$, try to prove $fl(a*b) = \dfrac{a*b}{1+\delta}, |\delta| \leq \dfrac{1}{2}\beta^{1-t}$, where the sign $*$ denotes $+/-/*/\div$.

1.4 Try to change the following representatives to make the computation more exact:

(1) $\dfrac{1}{1+2x} - \dfrac{1-x}{1+x}, |x| << 1$;

(2) $\sqrt{x+\dfrac{1}{x}} - \sqrt{x-\dfrac{1}{x}}, |x| >> 1$;

(3) $\dfrac{1-\cos x}{x}, x \neq 0, |x| << 1$.

1.5 Supposed that $a = 0.937$ has three significant digits about exact a, evaluate the relative error of a. For $f(x) = \sqrt{1-x}$, evaluate the error and relative error of $f(a)$ about $f(x)$.

1.6 Supposed A is an $n \times n$ matrix, x is a vector of n dimension, and $nu \leq 0.01$, try to prove
$$fl(Ax) = (A+E)x,$$
where the elements of $E = (e_{ij})$ satisfy
$$|e_{ij}| \leq 1.01n |a_{i1}| u, \quad i = 1,2,\cdots,n,$$
$$|e_{ij}| \leq 1.01(n-j+2) |a_{ij}| u, \quad i,j = 1,2,\cdots,n.$$

1.7 In vacuum, the distance s and time t of free fall are determined by the equation:
$$s = \dfrac{1}{2}gt^2,$$
where g is gravitational acceleration. Suppose that g is exact, but the measurement of t has error around ± 0.1s. Try to prove that when t is increasing the absolute error of distance increase and the relative error decrease.

1.8 The sequence $\{y_n\}$ satisfies the recursion formula $y_{n+1} = 100.01 y_n - y_{n-1}$. Take $y_0 = 1, y_1 = 0.01$ and $y_0 = 1 + 10^{-5}, y_1 = 0.01$, try to compute y_5, and explain that the recursion formula is unstable.

Chapter 2   Interpolation and Polynomial Approximation

§ 2.1   Introduction

Example 2.1.1   The following table lists the population in thousands of people from 1940 to 1990.

Year	1940	1950	1960	1970	1980	1990
Population (in thousands)	132165	151326	179323	203302	226542	249663

In reviewing these data, we might ask whether they could be used to provide a reasonable estimate of the population, that is to say, in 1965 or even in the year 2012.

Prediction of this type can be obtained by using a function that fits the given data. This process is called interpolation.

Taylor polynomial is written as follows

$$P_n(x) = f(x_0) + f'(x_0)(x - x_0) + \frac{f''(x_0)}{2!}(x - x_0)^2 + \cdots + \frac{f^{(n)}(x_0)}{n!}(x - x_0)^n,$$

$$(2.1.1)$$

where the error remainder is $R_n(x) = \frac{f^{(n+1)}(\xi)}{(n+1)!}(x - x_0)^{n+1}$.

When x close to x_0, it is good.

Since the Taylor polynomials have the property that all the information used in the approximation is concentrated at the single point x_0, the type of difficulty that occurs here is quite common and limits Taylor polynomial approximation to the situation in which approximations are needed only at points close to x_0.

For ordinary computational purposes it is more efficient to use methods that include information at various points.

For function $f(x) = e^x$ and point $x_0 = 0$, we obtain

$$P_1(x) = 1, \quad P_2(x) = 1 + x, \quad P_3(x) = 1 + x + \frac{x^2}{2},$$

$$P_4(x) = 1 + x + \frac{x^2}{2} + \frac{x^3}{6}, \quad \cdots.$$

For any continuous function $f(x)$, there is the conclusion as follows.

Theorem 2.1.1 (**Weierstrass approximation theorem**) Suppose that the function $f(x)$ is defined and continuous on $[a, b]$. For each $\varepsilon > 0$, there exists a polynomial $P(x)$, with the property that

$$|f(x) - P(x)| < \varepsilon \tag{2.1.2}$$

for all x in $[a, b]$.

One important reason for considering the class of polynomials in approximation functions is that the derivative and indefinite integral of a polynomial are easy to determine and also polynomials.

Theorem 2.1.2 Suppose that $f(x)$ is n-order continuous and differential in $I_\delta = (x_0 - \delta, x_0 + \delta)$, then for all $x \in I_\delta$, we have

$$f(x) = P_n(x) + R_n(x), \tag{2.1.3}$$

where $P_n(x)$ is n-th Taylor approximation polynomial, $R_n(x)$ is the remainder.

Definition 2.1.1 If $x_0, x_1, \cdots, x_n$ are $n+1$ distinct numbers and $y = f(x)$ is a function whose values $y_i = f(x_i)$ ($i = 0, 1, 2, \cdots, n$) are given at these numbers. If there exists a simply function $P(x)$, such that

$$P(x_i) = y_i, \quad i = 0, 1, \cdots, n, \tag{2.1.4}$$

then $P(x)$ is called interpolation function, $x_0, x_1, \cdots, x_n$ are called interpolation nodes.

Remark 2.1.1 If $P(x)$ is a polynomial interpolation function and

$$P(x) = a_0 + a_1 x + \cdots + a_n x^n,$$

then

$$\begin{cases} a_0 + a_1 x_0 + \cdots + a_n x_0^n = y_0, \\ a_0 + a_1 x_1 + \cdots + a_n x_1^n = y_1, \\ \quad \cdots \cdots \\ a_0 + a_1 x_n + \cdots + a_n x_n^n = y_n. \end{cases} \tag{2.1.5}$$

And its coefficient determinant is

$$D = \begin{vmatrix} 1 & x_0 & \cdots & x_0^n \\ 1 & x_1 & \cdots & x_1^n \\ \vdots & \vdots & & \vdots \\ 1 & x_n & \cdots & x_n^n \end{vmatrix},$$

which is a Vandermonde determinant.

Since $x_i \neq x_j, i \neq j$, so $D = \prod_{0 \leq i < j \leq n} (x_i - x_j) \neq 0$. Linear equations (2.1.5) has unique solution. Namely, polynomial interpolation function $P(x)$ exists and is unique. We now introduce different interpolation polynomials.

§2.2 Lagrange Interpolation Polynomial

2.2.1 Linear Lagrange Interpolation

Suppose x_k and x_{k+1} are the interpolation nodes. And the corresponding function values are $y_k = f(x_k)$ and $y_{k+1} = f(x_{k+1})$. Then we have the interpolation function

$$L_1(x) = y_k \frac{x - x_{k+1}}{x_k - x_{k+1}} + y_{k+1} \frac{x - x_k}{x_{k+1} - x_k}.$$

Letting $l_k(x) = \dfrac{x - x_{k+1}}{x_k - x_{k+1}}, l_{k+1}(x) = \dfrac{x - x_k}{x_{k+1} - x_k}$, then

$$L_1(x) = y_k l_k(x) + y_{k+1} l_{k+1}(x). \qquad (2.2.1)$$

The functions $l_k(x)$ and $l_{k+1}(x)$ are called **linear Lagrange interpolation basis functions**. The function $L_1(x)$ of (2.2.1) is called **linear Lagrange interpolation polynomial**.

And $l_k(x)$ and $l_{k+1}(x)$ satisfy

$$l_k(x_k) = 1, \quad l_k(x_{k+1}) = 0, \quad l_{k+1}(x_k) = 0, \quad l_{k+1}(x_{k+1}) = 1.$$

The graphics of the basis functions $l_k(x), l_{k+1}(x)$ are as follows (See Figure 2.2.1).

2.2.2 Parabolic Lagrange Interpolation

Suppose x_{k-1}, x_k, x_{k+1} are the interpolation nodes. And the corresponding function values are $y_{k-1} = f(x_{k-1})$, $y_k = f(x_k)$ and $y_{k+1} = f(x_{k+1})$. Seek parabolic function

$$L_2(x) = y_{k-1} l_{k-1}(x) + y_k l_k(x) + y_{k+1} l_{k+1}(x), \quad (2.2.2)$$

such that $L_2(x_j) = y_j, j = k-1, k, k+1$.
These functions $l_{k-1}(x)$, $l_k(x)$, $l_{k+1}(x)$ are called **parabolic Lagrange interpolation basis functions**.

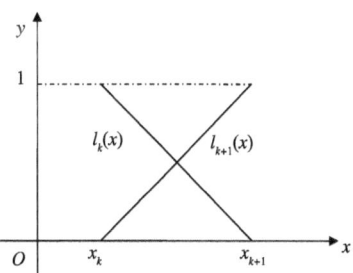

Figure 2.2.1 The graphics of the basis functions $l_k(x), l_{k+1}(x)$

They satisfy the following relations

$$l_i(x_j) = \begin{cases} 1, & i = j, \\ 0, & i \neq j, \end{cases} \quad i, j = k-1, k, k+1.$$

Since the function $l_{k-1}(x)$ has two zeros points, so we have

$$l_{k-1}(x) = A(x - x_{k+1})(x - x_k).$$

Basing on $l_{k-1}(x_{k-1}) = A(x_{k-1} - x_{k+1})(x_{k-1} - x_k) = 1$, then

$$A = \frac{1}{(x_{k-1} - x_k)(x_{k-1} - x_{k+1})},$$

so,

$$l_{k-1}(x) = \frac{(x - x_{k+1})(x - x_k)}{(x_{k-1} - x_{k+1})(x_{k-1} - x_k)}.$$

Similarly, we have

$$l_k(x) = \frac{(x - x_{k-1})(x - x_{k+1})}{(x_k - x_{k-1})(x_k - x_{k+1})},$$

$$l_{k+1}(x) = \frac{(x - x_k)(x - x_{k-1})}{(x_{k+1} - x_k)(x_{k+1} - x_{k-1})}.$$

Thus

$$L_2(x) = y_{k-1} l_{k-1}(x) + y_k l_k(x) + y_{k+1} l_{k+1}(x). \quad (2.2.3)$$

The function $L_2(x)$ of (2.2.3) is called **parabolic Lagrange interpolation polynomial**.

The graphics of the basis functions $l_{k-1}(x), l_k(x)$ and $l_{k+1}(x)$ are as follows (See Figure 2.2.2).

Remark 2.2.1 $L_2(x)$ was applied about 1000 years ago in ancient China.

2.2.3 n-th Lagrange Interpolation

Definition 2.2.1 Suppose $l_j(x)$ is n-th polynomial, satisfying

$$l_j(x_k) = \begin{cases} 1, & k = j, \\ 0, & k \neq j \end{cases}$$

$$= \delta_{j,k}, \quad j,k = 0,1,\cdots,n,$$

where $\delta_{j,k}$ is the Kronecker sign.

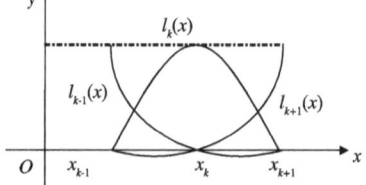

Figure 2.2.2 The graphics of the basis functions $l_{k-1}(x)$, $l_k(x)$ and $l_{k+1}(x)$

$$l_j(x) = \frac{(x-x_0)(x-x_1)\cdots(x-x_{j-1})(x-x_{j+1})\cdots(x-x_n)}{(x_j-x_0)(x_j-x_1)\cdots(x_j-x_{j-1})(x_j-x_{j+1})\cdots(x_j-x_n)},$$

$$j = 0,1,2,\cdots,n,$$

then we get

$$L_n(x) = \sum_{j=0}^{n} y_j l_j(x). \tag{2.2.4}$$

It is easy to check that

$$L_n(x_j) = y_j l_j(x_j) = y_j.$$

The function $L_n(x)$ of (2.2.4) is called **n-th Lagrange interpolation polynomial**.

Remark 2.2.2 Let $\omega_n(x) = (x-x_0)(x-x_1)\cdots(x-x_n)$, then

$$\omega_n'(x_k) = (x_k-x_0)(x_k-x_1)\cdots(x_k-x_{k-1})(x_k-x_{k+1})\cdots(x_k-x_n).$$

So, we have

$$L_n(x) = \sum_{k=0}^{n} y_k \cdot \frac{\omega_n(x)}{(x-x_k)\omega_n'(x_k)}. \tag{2.2.5}$$

Example 2.2.1 Using the number $x_0 = 100, x_1 = 121, x_2 = 144$ to find the value of $\sqrt{125}$ by linear and parabolic Lagrange interpolation, respectively.

Solution (1) Since $x_0 = 121, x_1 = 144, y_0 = 11, y_1 = 12$, then

$$L_1(x) = \frac{x-x_1}{x_0-x_1} \times 11 + \frac{x-x_0}{x_1-x_0} \times 12$$

$$= \frac{x-144}{121-144} \times 11 + \frac{x-121}{144-121} \times 12.$$

And $\sqrt{125} \approx L_1(125) = 11.17391$.

(2) Since $x_0 = 100, x_1 = 121, x_2 = 144, y_0 = 10, y_1 = 11, y_2 = 12$, then

$$L_2(x) = \frac{(x-121)(x-144)}{(100-121)(100-144)} \times 10 + \frac{(x-100)(x-144)}{(121-100)(121-144)} \times 11$$

$$+ \frac{(x-100)(x-121)}{(144-100)(144-121)} \times 12.$$

And $\sqrt{125} \approx L_2(125) = 11.18107$.

Note that $\sqrt{125} = 11.1803398\cdots$.

The next step is to calculate a remainder term or bound for the error involved in approximating function by an interpolating polynomial. This is done in the following theorem.

Theorem 2.2.1 Suppose $x_0, x_1, \cdots, x_n$ are distinct numbers in the interval $[a,b]$ and $f \in C^{n+1}[a,b]$. Then, for each x in $[a,b]$, a number $\xi(x)$ in (a,b) exists with

$$f(x) - L_n(x) = \frac{f^{(n+1)}(\xi)}{(n+1)!} \prod_{i=0}^{n} (x - x_i). \qquad (2.2.6)$$

Proof Note that if $x = x_k$ for $k = 0, 1, 2, \cdots, n$, then

$$f(x_k) = L_n(x_k),$$

and choosing x arbitrarily in (a,b).

If $x \neq x_k$ for all $k = 0, 1, 2, \cdots, n$, define the function $g(t)$ for t in $[a,b]$ by

$$g(t) = f(t) - L_n(t) - [f(x) - L_n(x)] \prod_{i=0}^{n} \frac{(t - x_i)}{(x - x_i)}.$$

Since $f(t) \in C^{n+1}[a,b]$, and $L_n(x) \in C^{\infty}[a,b]$, it follows that $g(t) \in C^{n+1}[a,b]$.

For $t = x_i$, we have

$$g(x_i) = f(x_i) - L_n(x_i) - [f(x) - L_n(x)] \prod_{k=0}^{n} \frac{(x_i - x_k)}{(x - x_k)} = 0.$$

Moreover, we have

$$g(x) = f(x) - L_n(x) - [f(x) - L_n(x)] \prod_{k=0}^{n} \frac{(x - x_k)}{(x - x_k)} = 0.$$

Thus, $g(t)$ is zero at the $n + 2$ distinct numbers $x, x_0, x_1, \cdots, x_n$.

By the generalized Rolle's theorem, there exists a number ξ in (a,b) for which $g^{(n+1)}(\xi) = 0$, so

$$0 = g^{(n+1)}(\xi)$$

$$= f^{(n+1)}(\xi) - L_n^{(n+1)}(\xi) - [f(x) - L_n(x)] \cdot \frac{d^{n+1}}{dt^{n+1}} \left[\prod_{i=0}^{n} \frac{(t-x_i)}{(x-x_i)} \right]_{t=\xi}.$$

And

$$\frac{d^{n+1}}{dt^{n+1}}\left(\prod_{i=0}^{n}\frac{t-x_i}{x-x_i}\right) = \frac{(n+1)!}{\prod_{i=0}^{n}(x-x_i)},$$

therefore, we have

$$f^{(n+1)}(\xi) = [f(x) - L_n(x)] \cdot \frac{(n+1)!}{\prod_{i=0}^{n}(x-x_i)}.$$

So,

$$f(x) - L_n(x) = \frac{f^{(n+1)}(\xi)}{(n+1)!} \cdot \prod_{i=0}^{n}(x-x_i).$$

Remark 2.2.3 The error for the Lagrange polynomial is quite similar to that for the Taylor polynomial.

The n-th Taylor polynomial about x_0 concentrates all the known information at x_0 and has an error term of the form

$$\frac{f^{(n+1)}(\xi)}{(n+1)!} \cdot (x-x_0)^{n+1}.$$

The Lagrange polynomial of degree n use information at the distinct numbers $x_0, x_1, \cdots, x_n$, and has an error term of the form

$$\frac{f^{(n+1)}(\xi)}{(n+1)!}(x-x_0)\cdots(x-x_n).$$

Example 2.2.2 Suppose a table is to be prepared for the function $f(x) = e^x$, for x in $[0,1]$. Assume that the number of decimal places to be given per entry is $d \geq 8$ and that the difference between adjacent x-values, the step size, is h. What should h be for linear interpolation (that is the Lagrange polynomial of degree of 1) to give the absolute error at most 10^{-6}?

Solution

$$L_1(x) = y_j \cdot \frac{x - x_{j+1}}{x_j - x_{j+1}} + y_{j+1} \cdot \frac{x - x_j}{x_{j+1} - x_j}.$$

Let $x_0, x_1, \cdots, x_n$ be the numbers of function f which is evaluated, x be in $[0,1]$.

The error in linear polynomial is

$$|f(x) - L_1(x)| = \left|\frac{f^{(2)}(\xi)}{2!} \cdot (x - x_j)(x - x_{j+1})\right|$$

$$= \left|\frac{f^{(2)}(\xi)}{2!}\right| \cdot |(x-jh)[x-(j+1)h]|$$

$$\leq \frac{1}{2}e^\xi \cdot \max_{x_j \leq x \leq x_{j+1}} |(x-jh)[(x-(j+1)h]|.$$

Letting $g(x) = (x-jh)[x-(j+1)h]$, then

$$g'(x) = x - jh + x - (j+1)h = 0.$$

So $x = (j+\frac{1}{2})h$. We have $g_{\min} = g\left(\left(j+\frac{1}{2}\right)h\right)$ and

$$\max_{x_j \leq x \leq x_{j+1}} |(x-jh)[x-(j+1)h]| = \left|g\left(\left(j+\frac{1}{2}\right)h\right)\right|$$

$$= \left|\left[\left(j+\frac{1}{2}\right)h - jh\right]\left[\left(j+\frac{1}{2}\right)h - (j+1)h\right]\right|$$

$$= \frac{h^2}{4},$$

$$|f(x) - L_1(x)| \leq \frac{1}{2}M \cdot \frac{h^2}{4} = M \cdot \frac{h^2}{8}.$$

By $M \cdot \frac{h^2}{8} < 10^{-6}$, we get $h < 1.72 \times 10^{-3}$, therefore $h = 0.001$. (Since $n = (1-0)/h$ must be an integer, one logical choice for step size is $h = 0.001$.)

Remark 2.2.4 The round-off error of Lagrange interpolation polynomial is

$$|R_n(x)| \leq \frac{M_{n+1}}{(n+1)!} |w_{n+1}(x)|,$$

where $M_{n+1} = \max_{a \leq x \leq b} |f^{(n+1)}(\xi)|$.

For $n = 1$, $|R_1(x)| \leq \frac{1}{2}|f''(\xi)(x-x_0)(x-x_1)|$;

For $n = 2$, $|R_2(x)| \leq \frac{1}{6}|f'''(\xi)(x-x_0)(x-x_1)(x-x_2)|$.

Example 2.2.3 For $f(x) = x^k$ ($k \leq n$), we obtain $f^{(n+1)}(x) = 0$. So, $R_n(x) = x^k - L_n(x) = 0$. Thus

$$L_n(x) = x^k = \sum_{i=0}^{n} x_i^k l_i(x), \quad k = 0, 1, 2, \cdots, n. \quad (2.2.7)$$

When $k = 0$, we have $\sum_{i=0}^{n} l_i(x) = 1$.

Example 2.2.4 Prove that

$$\sum_{i=0}^{5} (x_i - x)^2 l_i(x) = 0,$$

where $l_i(x)$ is interpolating basis function for the nodes of $x_0, x_1, \cdots, x_5$.

Proof According to (2.2.7), it can be checked that

$$\sum_{i=0}^{5}(x_i - x)^2 l_i(x) = \sum_{i=0}^{5} x_i^2 l_i(x) - \sum_{i=0}^{5} 2xx_i l_i(x) + \sum_{i=0}^{5} x^2 l_i(x) = x^2 - 2xx + x^2 = 0.$$

Example 2.2.5 If $f \in C^2[a,b]$, show that

$$\max_{a \leq x \leq b} \left| f(x) - \left[f(a) + \frac{f(b) - f(a)}{b - a}(x - a) \right] \right| \leq \frac{1}{8}(b - a)^2 M_2,$$

where $M_2 = \max_{a \leq x \leq b} |f''(x)|$.

Proof Since $L_1(x) = f(a) + \dfrac{f(b) - f(a)}{b - a}(x - a)$, so

$$\max_{a \leq x \leq b} \left| f(x) - \left[f(a) + \frac{f(b) - f(a)}{b - a}(x - a) \right] \right| = \max_{a \leq x \leq b} |f(x) - L_1(x)|$$

$$\leq \frac{|f''(\xi)|}{2} \cdot \max_{a \leq x \leq b} |(x-a)(x-b)|$$

$$= \frac{1}{8}(b - a)^2 M_2,$$

where $M_2 = \max_{a \leq x \leq b} |f''(x)|$.

§2.3 Neville's Interpolating Formula

A practical difficulty with Lagrange interpolation is that since the error term is difficult to apply, the degree of the polynomial needed for the desired accuracy is generally not known until computation are determined. The usual practice is to compute the results given from various polynomials.

However, the work done in calculating the approximation by the second polynomial does not lessen the work needed to calculate the third approximation, nor is the fourth approximation easier to obtain once the third approximation is known, and so on.

Definition 2.3.1 Let $f(x)$ be a function defined at $x_i, x_{i+1}, \cdots, x_j (i < j)$. The Lagrange polynomial that agrees with $f(x)$ at $x_i, x_{i+1}, \cdots, x_j$ is denoted $p_{i,j}(x)$. The degree of $p_{i,j}(x)$ is $j - i$.

Taking $(x_0, p_{0,1})$ and $(x_2, p_{1,2})$, from the linear interpolation we have

$$p_{0,2} = \frac{x-x_2}{x_0-x_2}p_{0,1} + \frac{x-x_0}{x_2-x_0}p_{1,2}$$

$$= \frac{x-x_2}{x_0-x_2} \cdot \left(\frac{x-x_0}{x_1-x_0}y_1 + \frac{x-x_1}{x_0-x_1}y_0\right) + \frac{x-x_0}{x_2-x_0} \cdot \left(\frac{x-x_1}{x_2-x_1}y_2 + \frac{x-x_2}{x_1-x_2}y_1\right).$$

If we have got the (n-1)-th polynomial of $p_{0,n-1}(x)$ and the (n-1)-th polynomial of $p_{1,n}(x)$, then we construct the n-th interpolation polynomial of $p_{0,n}(x)$ as follows:

$$p_{0,n} = \frac{x-x_n}{x_0-x_n}p_{0,n-1}(x) + \frac{x-x_0}{x_n-x_0}p_{1,n}(x),$$

which is called **Neville's interpolating formula** (See Table 2.3.1).

Table 2.3.1 Neville's interpolating formula

x_0	$f(x_0)$					
x_1	$f(x_1)$	$p_{0,1}$				
x_2	$f(x_2)$	$p_{1,2}$	$p_{0,2}$			
x_3	$f(x_3)$	$p_{2,3}$	$p_{1,3}$	$p_{0,3}$		
$\vdots$	$\vdots$	$\vdots$	$\vdots$	$\vdots$	$\ddots$	
x_n	$f(x_n)$	$p_{n-1,n}$	$p_{n-2,n}$	$p_{n-3,n}$	$\cdots$	$p_{0,n}$

§2.4 Newton Interpolation

2.4.1 Divided Difference

Suppose that $P_n(x)$ is n-th Lagrange polynomial that agrees with the function $f(x)$ at the distinct numbers $x_0, x_1, \cdots, x_n$.

The divided differences of $f(x)$ with respect to $x_0, x_1, \cdots, x_n$ are used to express $P_n(x)$ in the form

$$P_n(x) = a_0 + a_1(x-x_0) + a_2(x-x_0)(x-x_1) + \cdots$$
$$+ a_n(x-x_0)(x-x_1)\cdots(x-x_n)^n$$

for appropriate constants $a_0, a_1, \cdots, a_n$.

(i) By $P_n(x_0) = f(x_0)$, we have $a_0 = f(x_0)$.

(ii) By $P_n(x_1) = f(x_1)$, we have $a_1 = \dfrac{f(x_1) - f(x_0)}{x_1 - x_0}$.

(iii) By $P_n(x_2) = f(x_2)$, we have

$$a_2 = \frac{f(x_2) - f(x_0) - a_1(x_2 - x_0)}{(x_2 - x_0)(x_2 - x_1)} = \frac{\dfrac{f(x_2) - f(x_0)}{x_2 - x_0} - \dfrac{f(x_1) - f(x_0)}{x_1 - x_0}}{x_2 - x_1}.$$

Definition 2.4.1 The zero order divided difference of the function $f(x)$ with respect to x_i, denoted $f[x_i]$, is simply the value of $f(x)$ at x_i:

$$f[x_i] = f(x_i).$$

The first order divided difference of $f(x)$ with respect to x_i and x_{i+1} is denoted $f[x_i, x_{i+1}]$ and is defined as

$$f[x_i, x_{i+1}] = \frac{f[x_{i+1}] - f[x_i]}{x_{i+1} - x_i}. \tag{2.4.1}$$

The second order divided difference of $f(x)$ with respect to x_i, x_{i+1}, x_{i+2} is denoted $f[x_i, x_{i+1}, x_{i+2}]$ and is defined as

$$f[x_i, x_{i+1}, x_{i+2}] = \frac{f[x_{i+1}, x_{i+2}] - f[x_i, x_{i+1}]}{x_{i+2} - x_i}. \tag{2.4.2}$$

Similarly, after the $(k-1)$-th order divided difference

$$f[x_i, x_{i+1}, x_{i+2}, \cdots, x_{i+k-1}] \text{ and } f[x_{i+1}, x_{i+2}, \cdots, x_{i+k}]$$

have been determined, the k-th order divided difference relative to x_i, x_{i+1}, x_{i+2}, $\cdots$, x_{i+k} is given by

$$f[x_i, x_{i+1}, x_{i+2}, \cdots, x_{i+k}] = \frac{f[x_{i+1}, x_{i+2}, \cdots, x_{i+k}] - f[x_i, x_{i+1}, \cdots, x_{i+k-1}]}{x_{i+k} - x_i}.$$

$$\tag{2.4.3}$$

So

$$\begin{aligned} P_n(x) = &f[x_0] + f[x_0, x_1](x - x_0) \\ &+ f[x_0, x_1, x_2](x - x_0)(x - x_1) \\ &+ \cdots \\ &+ f[x_0, x_1, x_2, \cdots, x_k](x - x_0)(x - x_1) \cdots (x - x_{k-1}) \\ &+ \cdots \\ &+ f[x_0, x_1, x_2, \cdots, x_n](x - x_0)(x - x_1) \cdots (x - x_{n-1}), \end{aligned}$$

where $a_k = f[x_0, x_1, x_2, \cdots, x_k]$. It is easy to check that $P_n(x)$ is the interpolation polynomial, and the polynomial

$$P_n(x) = f[x_0] + \sum_{k=1}^{n} f[x_0, x_1, \cdots, x_k](x - x_0)(x - x_1) \cdots (x - x_{k-1})$$

is called **Newton's interpolation divided difference formula**.

The generation of the divided difference is outlined in the following table (See Table 2.4.1).

Table 2.4.1 Divided difference

x_i	0-th	1-st	2-nd	3-rd	...	k-th
x_0	$f[x_0]$					
x_1	$f[x_1]$	$f[x_0,x_1]$				
x_2	$f[x_2]$	$f[x_1,x_2]$	$f[x_0,x_1,x_2]$			
x_3	$f[x_3]$	$f[x_2,x_3]$	$f[x_1,x_2,x_3]$	$f[x_0,x_1,x_2,x_3]$		
$\vdots$	$\vdots$	$\vdots$	$\vdots$	$\vdots$	$\ddots$	
x_k	$f[x_k]$	$f[x_{k-1},x_k]$	$f[x_{k-2},x_{k-1},x_k]$	$f[x_{k-3},x_{k-2},x_{k-1},x_k]$	...	$f[x_0,x_1,\cdots,x_k]$

For example, $f[x_0,x_1,x_2,x_3] = \dfrac{f[x_1,x_2,x_3] - f[x_0,x_1,x_2]}{x_3 - x_0}$.

Example 2.4.1 Given $f(x) = \ln x$, and the table:

x_i	2.20	2.40	2.60	2.80	3.00
$f(x_i)$	0.78146	0.87547	0.95551	1.02962	1.09861

please give 2-th and 4-th Newton interpolation.

Solution (1) Taking divided difference:

x_i	$f(x_i)$	1-st	2-nd	3-rd	4-th
2.20	0.78146				
2.40	0.87547	0.43505			
2.60	0.95551	0.40010	0.087375		
2.80	1.02962	0.37055	−0.073875	0.02250	
3.00	1.09861	0.34495	−0.06400	0.01646	0.00755

then
$$P_2(x) = 0.78146 + 0.43505(x - 2.20) + 0.087375(x - 2.20)(x - 2.40);$$
$$P_4(x) = P_2(x) + 0.02250(x - 2.20)(x - 2.40)(x - 2.60)$$
$$+ 0.00755(x - 2.20)(x - 2.40)(x - 2.60)(x - 2.80).$$

Lemma 2.4.1 Given the function values $f(x_i)$ at nodes $x_i (i = 1, 2, \cdots, k)$, there is the following result

$$f[x_0, x_1, \cdots, x_k] = \sum_{i=0}^{k} \frac{f(x_i)}{\omega'_k(x_i)}. \qquad (2.4.4)$$

Proof By
$$P_k(x) = f[x_0] + f[x_0, x_1](x - x_0) + f[x_0, x_1, x_2](x - x_0)(x - x_1)$$
$$+ \cdots + f[x_0, x_1, x_2, \cdots, x_k](x - x_0)(x - x_1) \cdots (x - x_{k-1})$$

and the Lagrange interpolation, we have

$$P_k(x) = L_k(x) = \sum_{i=0}^{k} f(x_k) \cdot l_k(x) = \sum_{i=0}^{k} f(x_k) \cdot \frac{\omega_k(x)}{\omega'_k(x_i)}.$$

The details are as follows

$$L_k(x) = \sum_{i=0}^{k} y_i \cdot \frac{\omega_k(x)}{(x - x_i)\omega'_k(x_i)}$$

$$= y_0 \cdot \frac{(x - x_1) \cdots (x - x_k)}{(x_0 - x_1) \cdots (x_0 - x_k)} + y_1 \cdot \frac{(x - x_1) \cdots (x - x_k)}{(x_1 - x_0) \cdots (x_1 - x_k)}$$

$$+ \cdots + y_k \cdot \frac{(x - x_1) \cdots (x - x_k)}{(x_k - x_0)(x_k - x_1) \cdots (x_k - x_{k-1})}.$$

So

$$f[x_0, x_1, \cdots, x_k] = \sum_{i=0}^{k} \frac{f(x_i)}{(x_i - x_0) \cdots (x_i - x_{i-1})(x_i - x_{i+1}) \cdots (x_i - x_k)}$$

$$= \sum_{i=0}^{k} \frac{f(x_i)}{\omega'_k(x_i)}.$$

Lemma 2.4.2 Given the function $f(x)$ and nodes x_i $(i = 1, 2, \cdots, k)$, then we have the following formula

$$f[x_0, \cdots, x_i, \cdots, x_j, \cdots, x_k] = f[x_0, \cdots, x_j, \cdots, x_i, \cdots, x_k]. \qquad (2.4.5)$$

Proof Since
$$f[x_0, \cdots, x_i, \cdots, x_j, \cdots, x_k]$$

$$= \sum_{i=0}^{k} \frac{f(x_i)}{\omega'_k(x_i)}$$

$$= \frac{f(x_0)}{\omega'_k(x_0)} + \cdots + \frac{f(x_i)}{\omega'_k(x_i)} + \cdots + \frac{f(x_j)}{\omega'_k(x_j)} + \cdots + \frac{f(x_k)}{\omega'_k(x_k)}$$

$$= \frac{f(x_0)}{\omega'_k(x_0)} + \cdots + \frac{f(x_j)}{\omega'_k(x_j)} + \cdots + \frac{f(x_i)}{\omega'_k(x_i)} + \cdots + \frac{f(x_k)}{\omega'_k(x_k)}$$

$$= f[x_0, \cdots, x_j, \cdots, x_i, \cdots, x_k].$$

So lemma 2.4.2 is correct.

Lemma 2.4.3 If the degree of $f(x)$ is m, then the degree of $f[x, x_0]$ is

$m-1$.

Proof By
$$f[x,x_0] = \frac{f[x_0]-f[x]}{x_0-x} = \frac{f(x_0)-f(x)}{x_0-x},$$
because $[f(x)-f(x_0)]|_{x=x_0} = f(x_0)-f(x_0) = 0$,
then
$$f(x)-f(x_0) = (x-x_0) \cdot P_{m-1}(x).$$
Thus the conclusion is correct.

Lemma 2.4.4 Suppose that $f(x) \in C^n[a,b]$ and $x_0, x_1, \cdots, x_n$ are distinct numbers in $[a,b]$. Then a number ξ exists in (a,b) with
$$f[x_0, x_1, \cdots, x_n] = \frac{f^{(n)}(\xi)}{n!}. \tag{2.4.6}$$

Proof Let $g(x) = f(x) - P_n(x)$. Since $f(x_i) = P_n(x_i)$ for each $i = 0, 1, 2, \cdots, n$, the function $g(x)$ has $(n+1)$ distinct zero points in $[a,b]$. The generalized Rolle's theorem implies that a number ξ in (a,b) exists with
$$g^{(n)}(\xi) = f^{(n)}(\xi) - P_n^{(n)}(\xi) = 0.$$
Since $P_n^{(n)}(\xi)$ is a polynomial of degree n whose leading coefficient is $f[x_0, x_1, \cdots, x_n]$, so
$$P_n^{(n)}(\xi) = n! \, f[x_0, x_1, \cdots, x_n]$$
for all values of x.

As a consequence, $f[x_0, x_1, \cdots, x_n] = \dfrac{f^{(n)}(\xi)}{n!}$.

Lemma 2.4.5 If $f \in C^{n+1}[a,b]$, $x_0, x_1, \cdots, x_n$ are distinct numbers in $[a,b]$, then there exists $\xi \in [a,b]$, such that
$$f[x, x_0, x_1, \cdots, x_n] = \frac{f^{(n+1)}(\xi)}{(n+1)!}. \tag{2.4.7}$$

Proof For any x in $[a,b]$, we have Newton's interpolation
$$P_{n+1}(t) = f[x] + f[x,x_0](t-x) + f[x,x_0,x_1](t-x)(t-x_0)$$
$$+ \cdots + f[x,x_0,x_1,\cdots,x_n](t-x)(t-x_0)(t-x_1)\cdots(t-x_{n-1})$$
and
$$P_{n+1}(t) = P_n(t) + f[x_0, x_1, \cdots, x_n, x](t-x_0)(t-x_1)\cdots(t-x_n).$$
Then, we obtain $P_{n+1}(x) = f(x)$ and
$$P_{n+1}(x) - P_n(x) = f[x_0, x_1, \cdots, x_n, x](x-x_0)(x-x_1)\cdots(x-x_n).$$

Therefore
$$f(x) - P_n(x) = f[x_0, x_1, \cdots, x_n, x](x - x_0)(x - x_1) \cdots (x - x_n).$$
Namely
$$f[x, x_0, x_1, \cdots, x_n] = \frac{f^{(n+1)}(\xi)}{(n+1)!}.$$
Then we complete the lemma.

2.4.2 Newton's Interpolation with Equal Spacing Divided Difference Formula

Newton's interpolation divided difference formula can be expressed in a simplified form when $x_0, x_1, \cdots, x_n$ are arranged with equal spacing. In this case, we introduce the notation $h = x_{j+1} - x_j$, for each $j = 0, 1, \cdots, n-1$ and let $x = x_0 + sh$. Then the difference $x - x_i$ can be written as $x - x_i = (s - i)h$.

$$\begin{aligned}
P_n(x) &= P_n(x_0 + sh) \\
&= f[x_0] + f[x_0, x_1](x - x_0) + \cdots + f[x_0, \cdots, x_n](x - x_0) \cdots (x - x_{n-1}) \\
&= f[x_0] + f[x_0, x_1]sh + \cdots + f[x_0, \cdots, x_n]s(s-1) \cdots [s - (n-1)]h^n \\
&= \sum_{i=0}^{n} f[x_0, \cdots, x_k]s(s-1) \cdots [s - (k-1)]h^k \\
&= \sum_{i=0}^{n} f[x_0, \cdots, x_k]k!\binom{s}{k}h^k,
\end{aligned}$$

where the binomial-coefficient notating
$$\binom{s}{k} = \frac{s(s-1)(s-2) \cdots [s - (k-1)]}{k!}.$$

Definition 2.4.2 Forward differences are defined as follows
$$\Delta f_i = f_{i+1} - f_i,$$
$$\Delta^2 f_i = \Delta f_{i+1} - \Delta f_i,$$
$$\cdots \cdots$$
$$\Delta^n f_i = \Delta^{n-1} f_{i+1} - \Delta^{n-1} f_i.$$

And backward differences are

$$\nabla f_i = f_i - f_{i-1},$$
$$\nabla^2 f_i = \nabla f_i - \nabla f_{i-1},$$
$$\cdots\cdots$$
$$\nabla^n f_i = \nabla^{n-1} f_i - \nabla^{n-1} f_{i-1}.$$

Similarly, we can define the center difference

$$\delta^n f_i = \delta^{n-1} f_{i+\frac{1}{2}} - \delta^{n-1} f_{i-\frac{1}{2}}.$$

It's obvious that $\Delta^0 f_i = \nabla^0 f_i = \delta^0 f_i = f_i$.

Definition 2.4.3 Newton forward difference formula is constructed by making use of the forward difference notation introduced in Aiten's method.

With this notation, we have

$$f[x_0, x_1] = \frac{f[x_1] - f[x_0]}{x_1 - x_0} = \frac{1}{h}\Delta f(x_0),$$

$$f[x_0, x_1, x_2] = \frac{1}{2h} \frac{\Delta f(x_1) - \Delta f(x_0)}{h} = \frac{1}{2h^2}\Delta^2 f(x_0),$$

and in general,

$$f[x_0, x_1, \cdots, x_k] = \frac{1}{k! \, h^k}\Delta^k f(x_0).$$

So, we have Newton forward difference formula as

$$P_n(x) = f[x_0] + \sum_{k=1}^{n} \binom{s}{k}\Delta^k f(x_0).$$

Theorem 2.4.1

(1)
$$\Delta^n f_i = \sum_{k=0}^{n} (-1)^k C_n^k f_{n+i-k},$$

$$\nabla^n f_i = \sum_{k=0}^{n} (-1)^k C_n^k f_{i-k},$$

$$\delta^n f_i = \sum_{k=0}^{n} (-1)^k C_n^k f_{\frac{n}{2}+i-k}.$$

(2)
$$\Delta^n f_i = n! \, h^n f[x_i, x_{i+1}, \cdots, x_{i+n}],$$
$$\nabla^n f_i = n! \, h^n f[x_{i-n}, x_{i-n+1}, \cdots, x_i],$$
$$\delta^{2n} f_i = (2n)! \, h^{2n} f[x_{i-n}, x_{i-n+1}, \cdots, x_{i+n}].$$

Example 2.4.2 $f(x) = x^3, x_i = i, i = 0, 1, 2, 3, 4$. Compute 0.5^3.

Solution

x_i	f_i	Δf_i	$\Delta^2 f_i$	$\Delta^3 f_i$	$\Delta^4 f_i$
0	0				
1	1	1			
2	8	7	6		
3	27	19	12	6	
4	64	37	18	6	0

$$x = 0.5, \quad t = (0.5-0)/1 = 0.5,$$
$$P_1(0.5) = 0 + 0.5 \times 1 = 0.5,$$
$$P_2(0.5) = P_1(0.5) + \frac{0.5 \times (-0.5)}{2} \times 6 = -0.25,$$
$$P_3(0.5) = P_2(0.5) + \frac{0.5 \times (-0.5) \times (-1.5)}{6} \times 6 = -0.125,$$
$$P_4(0.5) = P_3(0.5) + \frac{0.5 \times (-0.5) \times (-1.5) \times (-2.5)}{24} \times 0 = -0.125.$$

§ 2.5 Hermite Interpolation

Definition 2.5.1 Let $x_0, x_1, \cdots, x_n$ be $n+1$ distinct numbers in $[a,b]$ and m_i be a nonnegative integer associate with x_i for $i = 0, 1, \cdots, n$. Suppose that $f \in C^m[a,b]$, where $m = \max_{0 \leq i \leq n} m_i$. The osculating polynomial approximating $f(x)$ is the polynomial $P(x)$ of last degree, such that

$$\frac{d^k P(x_i)}{dx^k} = \frac{d^k f(x_i)}{dx^k}, \quad i = 0, 1, \cdots, n, \quad k = 0, 1, \cdots, m_i.$$

Remark 2.5.1 $n = 0$, the osculating polynomial approximating $f(x)$ is the m_0-th Taylor polynomial for $f(x)$ at x_0; $m_i = 0$, Lagrange polynomial interpolating $f(x)$ at $x_0, x_1, \cdots, x_n$; $m_i = 1$, for $i = 0, 1, \cdots, n$ gives the Hermite polynomials.

Also, we think that

$$\lim_{x \to x_0} f[x_0, x] = \lim_{x \to x_0} \frac{f(x) - f(x_0)}{x - x_0} = f'(x_0),$$

denoted by $f[x_0, x_0]$. Similarly, we have

$$f[x_0,x_0,x_0] = \frac{1}{2!}f''(x_0) \text{ and } f[\underbrace{x_0,\cdots,x_0}_{n}] = \frac{1}{n!}f^{(n)}(x_0).$$

2.5.1 Two Classical Hermite Interpolation

(1) Find a polynomial $P(x)$ of degree at most 3, such that
$$\begin{cases} P(x_i) = f(x_i), & i = 0,1,2, \\ P'(x_1) = f'(x_1). \end{cases} \tag{2.5.1}$$

From (2.5.1), suppose the polynomial $P(x)$ is the form
$$\begin{aligned} P(x) &= f(x_0) + f[x_0,x_1](x-x_0) \\ &\quad + f[x_0,x_1,x_2](x-x_0)(x-x_1) \\ &\quad + A(x-x_0)(x-x_1)(x-x_2), \end{aligned}$$

we have
$$\begin{aligned} P'(x) &= f[x_0,x_1] + f[x_0,x_1,x_2](x-x_1) + f[x_0,x_1,x_2](x-x_0) \\ &\quad + A(x-x_0)(x-x_1) + A(x-x_0)(x-x_2) + A(x-x_1)(x-x_2). \end{aligned}$$

Namely,
$$\begin{aligned} P'(x)|_{x=x_1} &= f[x_0,x_1] + f[x_0,x_1,x_2](x_1-x_0) + A(x_1-x_0)(x_1-x_2) \\ &= f'(x_1). \end{aligned}$$

So,
$$A = \frac{f'(x_1) - f[x_0,x_1] - f[x_0,x_1,x_2](x_1-x_0)}{(x_1-x_0)(x_1-x_2)}.$$

Therefore, we obtain
$$\begin{aligned} P(x) &= f(x_0) + f[x_0,x_1](x-x_0) + f[x_0,x_1,x_2](x-x_0)(x-x_1) \\ &\quad + \frac{f'(x_1) - f[x_0,x_1] - f[x_0,x_1,x_2](x_1-x_0)}{(x_1-x_0)(x_1-x_2)}(x-x_0)(x-x_1)(x-x_2). \end{aligned}$$

Denote $R(x) = f(x) - P(x)$. Suppose that
$$R(x) = f(x) - P(x) = k(x)(x-x_0)(x-x_1)^2(x-x_2).$$

Construct that
$$\varphi(t) = f(t) - P(t) = k(x)(t-x_0)(t-x_1)^2(t-x_2).$$

Then $\varphi(t)$ has five zero solutions. Indeed,
$$\varphi(x_i) = 0, i=0,1,2 \text{ and } \varphi'(x_1) = 0, \varphi(x) = 0.$$

Thus, by using Rolle's theorem, we have
$$\varphi^{(4)}(\xi) = f^{(4)}(\xi) - 4!k(x) = 0,$$
$$k(x) = \frac{1}{4!}f^{(4)}(\xi).$$

Finally, we obtain
$$R(x) = \frac{1}{4!}f^{(4)}(\xi)(x-x_0)(x-x_1)^2(x-x_2).$$

(2) Find a polynomial $H_3(x)$ of degree at most 3, such that
$$\begin{aligned} H_3(x_k) &= y_k, & H_3(x_{k+1}) &= y_{k+1}, \\ H_3'(x_k) &= m_k, & H_3'(x_{k+1}) &= m_{k+1}. \end{aligned} \qquad (2.5.2)$$

From (2.5.2), suppose the polynomial $H_3(x)$ is the form
$$H_3(x) = \alpha_k(x)y_k + \alpha_{k+1}(x)y_{k+1} + \beta_k(x)m_k + \beta_{k+1}(x)m_{k+1},$$
where the basis functions $\alpha_k(x)$, $\alpha_{k+1}(x)$, $\beta_k(x)$ and $\beta_{k+1}(x)$ satisfy the following table.

Basis functions	function values for nodes		derivative values for nodes	
	x_k	x_{k+1}	x_k	x_{k+1}
$\alpha_k(x)$	1	0	0	0
$\alpha_{k+1}(x)$	0	1	0	0
$\beta_k(x)$	0	0	1	0
$\beta_{k+1}(x)$	0	0	0	1

Set $\alpha_k(x) = (ax+b)\left(\dfrac{x-x_{k+1}}{x_k-x_{k+1}}\right)^2$, then

$$1 = ax_k + b, \quad a\left(\frac{x_k-x_{k+1}}{x_k-x_{k+1}}\right)^2 + 2(ax_k+b)\cdot(x_k-x_{k+1})\cdot\frac{1}{(x_k-x_{k+1})^2} = 0.$$

Thus
$$a = -\frac{2}{x_k-x_{k+1}}, \quad b = 1 + \frac{2x_k}{x_k-x_{k+1}}.$$

Namely,
$$\alpha_k(x) = \left(1 + 2\frac{x-x_k}{x_{k+1}-x_k}\right)\left(\frac{x_{k+1}-x_k}{x_k-x_{k+1}}\right)^2.$$

Taking the same argument, we have
$$\alpha_{k+1}(x) = \left(1 + 2\frac{x-x_{k+1}}{x_k-x_{k+1}}\right)\cdot\left(\frac{x-x_k}{x_{k+1}-x_k}\right)^2.$$

Letting $\beta_k(x) = a(x-x_k)\left(\dfrac{x-x_{k+1}}{x_k-x_{k+1}}\right)^2$, then from $\beta_k'(x_k) = a = 1$, we obtain

$$\beta_k(x) = (x-x_k)\left(\frac{x-x_{k+1}}{x_k-x_{k+1}}\right)^2.$$

Similarly, we have

$$\beta_{k+1}(x) = (x - x_{k+1})\left(\frac{x - x_k}{x_{k+1} - x_k}\right)^2.$$

So

$$H_3(x) = \left(1 + 2\frac{x - x_k}{x_{k+1} - x_k}\right)\left(\frac{x - x_{k+1}}{x_k - x_{k+1}}\right)^2 y_k + \left(1 + 2\frac{x - x_{k+1}}{x_k - x_{k+1}}\right)\left(\frac{x - x_k}{x_{k+1} - x_k}\right)^2 y_{k+1}$$

$$+ (x - x_k)\left(\frac{x - x_{k+1}}{x_k - x_{k+1}}\right)^2 m_k + (x - x_{k+1})\left(\frac{x - x_k}{x_{k+1} - x_k}\right)^2 m_{k+1}.$$

$$R_3(x) = f(x) - H_3(x)$$

$$= \frac{1}{4!}f^{(n)}(\xi)(x - x_k)^2(x - x_{k+1})^2, \quad \xi \in (x_k, x_{k+1}).$$

2.5.2 General Hermite Interpolation

$$\begin{cases} f(x_0), f'(x_0), f''(x_0), \cdots, f^{(m_0)}(x_0), \\ f(x_1), f'(x_1), f''(x_1), \cdots, f^{(m_1)}(x_1), \\ \cdots\cdots \\ f(x_n), f'(x_n), f''(x_n), \cdots\cdots, f^{(m_n)}(x_n). \end{cases} \quad (2.5.3)$$

Let $N = \left(\sum_{i=0}^{n} m_i\right) + n$, $H_N^{(k_i)}(x_i) = f^{(k_i)}(x_i)$, $k_i = 0, 1, 2, \cdots, m_i$, $i = 0, 1, 2, \cdots, n$.

$$H(x) = \sum_{i=0}^{n}\sum_{k=0}^{m_i} f_i^{(k_i)} \cdot h_{i,k}(x),$$

where $h_{i,k}^l(x_j) = \begin{cases} 1, & i = j, l = k, \\ 0, & \text{others}, \end{cases}$ $l, k = 0, 1, 2, \cdots, m_i$; $i, j = 0, 1, 2, \cdots, n$.

Note $n = 0$, one node point

$$H(x) = \sum_{k=0}^{m_0} f^{(k)}(x_0) \cdot \frac{(x - x_0)^k}{k!}.$$

Theorem 2.5.1 If $f(x) \in C^3[a, b]$ and $f^{(4)}(x)$ exists, then we have

$$R_3(x) = f(x) - H_3(x) = \frac{f^{(4)}(\xi)}{4!}(x - x_0)^2(x - x_1)^2, \quad (2.5.4)$$

where $\xi \in (a, b)$.

Proof (1) For any $x \in (a, b)$, we can conclude the proof.

(2) When $x \neq x_i, i = 0, 1$, constructing the function

$$g(t) = f(t) - H_3(t) - [f(x) - H_3(x)] \frac{(t-x_0)^2 (t-x_1)^2}{(x-x_0)^2 (x-x_1)^2}.$$

It's easy to check that function $g(t)$ satisfies

$$g(x_i) = g'(x_i) = 0, \quad g(x) = 0.$$

So, using Rolle's theorem, we have

$$R_3^{(4)}(\xi) = 0.$$

Namely,

$$f^{(4)}(\xi) - [f(x) - H_3(x)] \frac{4!}{(x-x_0)^2 (x-x_1)^2} = 0.$$

Then we complete the theorem.

Example 2.5.1 Given $f(x) = \sqrt{x}, f'(x) = \dfrac{1}{2\sqrt{x}}$.

x	121	144
$f(x)$	11	12
$f'(x)$	1/22	1/24

Please give $H_3(x)$ and calculate $H_3(125)$.

Solution

$$H_3(x) = \left(1 + 2\frac{x-121}{144-121}\right)\left(\frac{x-144}{121-144}\right)^2 \times 11 + \left(1 + 2\frac{x-144}{121-144}\right)\left(\frac{x-121}{144-121}\right)^2 \times 12$$

$$+ (x-121)\left(\frac{x-144}{121-144}\right)^2 \times \frac{1}{22} + (x-144)\left(\frac{x-121}{144-121}\right)^2 \times \frac{1}{24},$$

$$\sqrt{125} \approx H_3(125) = 11.18035.$$

$$|R_3(x)| \le \frac{M}{4!} \cdot \left(\frac{h}{2}\right)^4$$

$$= \frac{Mh^4}{24 \times 16} = \frac{M}{384} h^4, \quad h = x_1 - x_0.$$

§2.6 Piecewise Polynomial Approximation

The precious section concerned the approximation use of polynomials. However, the oscillatory nature of high-degree polynomials and the property that a fluctuation over a small portion of the interval can induce large fluctuation over the entire range restricts their use.

Definition an alternative approach is to divide the interval into a collection of subintervals and construct a different approximating polynomial on each subinterval.

Approximation by functions of this type is called piecewise polynomial approximation.

a) Numerical Convergence

Example 2.6.1 (Runge phenomena, 1901)

$$f(x) = \frac{1}{1 + 25x^2} = \frac{1}{1 + (5x)^2}, \quad -1 \leqslant x \leqslant 1.$$

$$L_n(x) = \sum_{i=0}^{n} \frac{1}{1 + 25x_i^2} \cdot l_i(x), \quad x_i = -1 + \frac{2i}{n}, \quad i = 0, 1, 2, \cdots, n.$$

From Figure 2.6.1, we see that $L_n(x)$ does not convergent to $f(x)$.

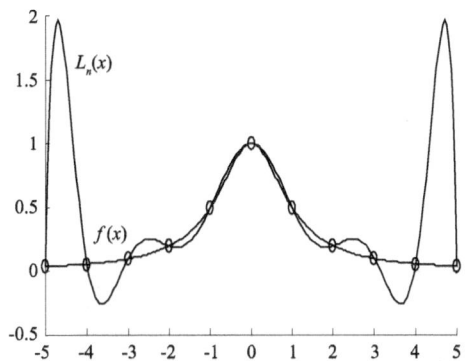

Figure 2.6.1 The graphics of the different functions

b) Numerical Stability

Newton interpolation or Lagrange interpolation needed higher order difference, for example, forward difference: Δ.

Suppose that $f(x_k) = 0, k = 0, 1, 2, \cdots, n$. An error occurs at x_i.

x_k	f	Δ	Δ^2	Δ^3	Δ^4
	0				
	0		ε		
	0		ε		
	0	ε	-3ε		

Continued

x_k	f	Δ	Δ^2	Δ^3	Δ^4
i	ε		-2ε	6ε	
	0	ε	3ε		
	0		ε		
	$\vdots$		$-\varepsilon$		
	0				

If $f(x)$ has an error ε at x_i, then the error will become greater with the order of the forward difference.

Piecewise Linear Lagrange Interpolation

Given $[a,b]$; $\Delta: a = x_0 < x_1 < x_2 < \cdots < x_{n-1} < x_n = b$. x_i are nodes, $x_1, x_2, \cdots, x_{n-1}$ are inner nodes, $e_j = [x_{j-1}, x_j]$ is the j-th cell.

$$L_1^{(j)}(x) = y_{j-1} \cdot \frac{x - x_j}{x_{j-1} - x_j} + y_j \cdot \frac{x - x_{j-1}}{x_j - x_{j-1}}, \text{ for all } x \in e_j, \quad j = 0, 1, \cdots, n.$$

```
         e_j           e_{j+1}
   |————————|————————|
   x_{j-1}   x_j      x_{j+1}
```

So, we can construct the basis functions

$$l_0(x) = \begin{cases} \dfrac{x - x_1}{x_0 - x_1}, & x_0 \leqslant x \leqslant x_1, \\ 0, & x_1 \leqslant x \leqslant x_n, \end{cases}$$

$$l_j(x) = \begin{cases} \dfrac{x - x_{j-1}}{x_j - x_{j-1}}, & x_{j-1} \leqslant x \leqslant x_j, \\ \dfrac{x - x_{j+1}}{x_j - x_{j+1}}, & x_j \leqslant x \leqslant x_{j+1}, \\ 0, & [a,b] \setminus [x_{j-1}, x_{j+1}], \end{cases}$$

$$l_n(x) = \begin{cases} \dfrac{x - x_{n-1}}{x_n - x_{n-1}}, & x_{n-1} \leqslant x \leqslant x_n, \\ 0, & x_0 \leqslant x \leqslant x_{n-1}. \end{cases}$$

Then,

$$f(x) = \sum_{j=0}^{n} y_j \cdot l_j(x). \tag{2.6.1}$$

The graphics of the basis functions are as follows (See Figure 2.6.2).

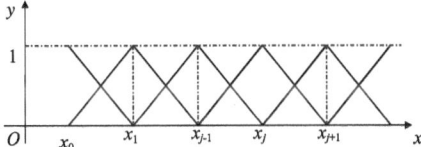

Figure 2.6.2 The graphics of the basis functions

Error Estimation

As $x \in e_i = [x_{i-1}, x_i]$, $i = 0, 1, \cdots, n$, we have

$$f(x) - L_1^{(i)}(x) = \frac{f''(\xi_i)}{2!}(x - x_{i-1})(x - x_i), \quad x_{i-1} \leq \xi_i \leq x_i,$$

which implies that

$$|f(x) - L_1^{(i)}(x)| \leq \frac{1}{2}|(x - x_{i-1})(x - x_i)| \cdot \max_{x_{i-1} \leq x \leq x_i} |f''(x)|.$$

Since $\max_{x_{i-1} \leq x \leq x_i} |(x - x_{i-1})(x - x_i)| \leq \frac{h_i^2}{4}$, $h_i = x_i - x_{i-1}$, $h = \max_{1 \leq i \leq h} \{h_i\}$, so we have

$$|f(x) - L_1^{(i)}(x)| \leq \frac{h^2}{8} \cdot \max_{a \leq x \leq b} |f''(x)|. \qquad (2.6.2)$$

Piecewise 2-nd Lagrange Interpolation

$$L_2^{(k)}(x) = y_{k-1} \frac{(x - x_k)(x - x_{k+1})}{(x_{k-1} - x_k)(x_{k-1} - x_{k+1})} + y_k \frac{(x - x_{k-1})(x - x_{k+1})}{(x_k - x_{k-1})(x_k - x_{k+1})}$$

$$+ y_{k+1} \frac{(x - x_{k-1})(x - x_k)}{(x_{k+1} - x_{k-1})(x_{k+1} - x_k)}, \quad x \in [x_{k-1}, x_{k+1}].$$

Error Estimation

Since $R_n(x) = f(x) - L_n(x) = \frac{f^{(n+1)}(\xi)}{(n+1)!} \omega_n(x)$. So the remainder of $L_2^{(k)}(x)$ is

$$R_2(x) = f(x) - L_2^{(k)}(x) = \frac{f'''(\xi)}{6}(x - x_{k-1})(x - x_k)(x - x_{k+1}).$$

$$|R_2(x)| \leq \frac{1}{6} \max_{a \leq x \leq b} |f'''(\xi)| \cdot \max_{x_{k-1} \leq x \leq x_{k+1}} |(x - x_{k-1})(x - x_k)(x - x_{k+1})|$$

$$\leq \frac{1}{6} M_3 \frac{2\sqrt{3}}{9} h^3 = \frac{\sqrt{3}}{27} M_3 h^3.$$

Piecewise 3-rd Polynomial Interpolation

The piecewise Hermite interpolation satisfies

$$H(x_i) = f_i, \quad H'(x_i) = f_i', \quad i = 0, 1, \cdots, n.$$

$$H(x) = f_{i-1} \cdot h_{i-1,0}(x) + f_i \cdot h_{i,0}(x) + f'_{i-1} \cdot h_{i-1,1}(x) + f'_i \cdot h_{i,1}(x)$$
$$= f_{i-1} \cdot \alpha_{i-1}(x) + f_i \cdot \alpha_i(x) + f'_{i-1} \cdot \beta_{i-1}(x) + f'_i \cdot \beta_i(x)$$
$$= f_{i-1} \cdot \left(1 + 2\frac{x - x_{i-1}}{x_i - x_{i-1}}\right)\left(\frac{x - x_i}{x_{i-1} - x_i}\right)^2 + f_i \cdot \left(1 + 2\frac{x - x_i}{x_{i-1} - x_i}\right)\left(\frac{x - x_{i-1}}{x_i - x_{i-1}}\right)^2$$
$$+ f'_{i-1} \cdot (x - x_{i-1})\left(\frac{x - x_i}{x_{i-1} - x_i}\right)^2 + f'_i \cdot (x - x_i)\left(\frac{x - x_{i-1}}{x_i - x_{i-1}}\right)^2$$
$$= f_{i-1} \cdot (1 + 2l_i(x))l_{i-1}^2(x) + f_i \cdot (1 + 2l_{i-1}(x))l_i^2(x)$$
$$+ f'_{i-1} \cdot (x - x_{i-1})l_{i-1}^2(x) + f'_i \cdot (x - x_i)l_i^2(x).$$

Theorem 2.6.1 Suppose $f \in C^4[a,b]$, $H_{3,k}$ is piecewise 3-rd Hermite interpolation, then

$$\max_{a \leq x \leq b} |f(x) - H(x)| \leq \frac{h^4}{384} \max_{a \leq x \leq b} |f^{(4)}(x)|, \qquad (2.6.3)$$

where $h = \max\{x_{k+1} - x_k\}$.

Proof See the proof of theorem 2.5.1.

§2.7 Cubic Spline Interpolation

The word "spline" comes from Engineering. (1946, Schoenberg)

2.7.1 Cubic Spline Function

Definition 2.7.1 If $S(x) \in C^2[a,b]$, and $S(x)|_{I_j = [x_{j-1}, x_j]} \in P_3$.

$$\Delta: a = x_0 < x_1 < x_2 < \cdots < x_n = b.$$

Then $S(x)$ is called cubic spline function.

If $S(x_i) = f(x_i)$, then $S(x)$ is called cubic spline interpolation function.

For $I_j = [x_{j-1}, x_j]$, we need calculate 4 parameters. So, $4n$ parameters satisfy

$$\begin{cases} S(x_i - 0) = S(x_i + 0), \\ S(x_i) = f(x_i), \\ S'(x_i - 0) = f'(x_i + 0), \quad i = 1, 2, \cdots, n-1, \\ S''(x_i - 0) = f''(x_i - 0), \\ S(x_i) = f(x_i). \end{cases}$$

So we need two boundary conditions.

Pose one $x_0 = a$ and $x_n = b$.

(1) I type boundary conditions:
$$S'(x_0) = f'_0, \quad S'(x_n) = f'_n.$$

(2) II type boundary conditions:
$$S''(x_0) = f''_0, \quad S''(x_n) = f''_n.$$

(3) III type boundary conditions:
$$S'(x_0) = S'(x_n), \quad S''(x_n) = f''_n.$$

2.7.2 Construct Cubic Spline Interpolation Function

Letting
$$S(x) = \sum_{j=0}^{n} (y_j \alpha_j(x) + m_j \beta_j(x)),$$

then
$$S'(x) = \sum_{j=0}^{n} (y_j \alpha'_j(x) + m_j \beta'_j(x)), \quad S''(x) = \sum_{j=0}^{n} (y_j \alpha''_j(x) + m_j \beta''_j(x)).$$

Theorem 2.7.1 I type is well posed.

Proof Let $M_i = S''_I(x_i), i = 1, \cdots, n$.

Since $S_I(x)|_{e_i} \in P_3$, so we know that $S''_I(x)$ is linear on e_i.

$$S''_I(x) = M_{i-1} \frac{x - x_i}{x_{i-1} - x_i} + M_i \frac{x - x_{i-1}}{x_i - x_{i-1}}$$

$$= M_{i-1} \frac{x_i - x}{h_i} + M_i \frac{x - x_{i-1}}{h_i}, \quad i = 1, \cdots, n.$$

$$S_I(x) = \frac{1}{6h_i}[(x_i - x)^3 M_{i-1} + (x - x_{i-1})^3 M_i]$$

$$+ \frac{1}{h_i}[(x_i - x)f_{i-1} + (x - x_{i-1})f_i]$$

$$- \frac{h_i}{6}[(x_i - x)M_{i-1} + (x - x_{i-1})M_i], \quad x \in e_i, i = 1, \cdots, n.$$

So, M_i need to be decided.

$$S'_I(x_j + 0) = S'_I(x_j - 0), \quad j = 1, \cdots, n-1.$$

$$S'_I(x) = -M_{i-1} \frac{(x_i - x)^2}{2h_i} + M_i \frac{(x - x_{i-1})^2}{2h_i}$$

$$+\frac{f_i - f_{i-1}}{h_i} - \frac{(M_i - M_{i-1})h_i}{6}, \quad x \in e_i, i = 1, \cdots, n.$$

$$S_I'(x_j - 0) = -M_{j-1}\frac{(x_j - x_{j-1})^2}{2h_j} + \frac{M_j(x_j - x_{j-1})^2}{2h_j}$$

$$+\frac{f_j - f_{j-1}}{h_j} - \frac{(M_j - M_{j-1})h_j}{6}$$

$$= \frac{1}{6}M_{j-1}h_j + \frac{h_j}{3}M_j + \frac{f_j - f_{j-1}}{h_j}, \quad j = 1, \cdots, n.$$

$$S_I'(x_{j-1} + 0) = -\frac{h_j}{3}M_{j-1} - \frac{h_j}{6}M_j + \frac{f_j - f_{j-1}}{h_j}.$$

So, we have

$$-\frac{h_{j+1}}{3}M_j - \frac{h_{j+1}}{6}M_{j+1} + \frac{f_{j+1} - f_j}{h_{j+1}} = \frac{h_j}{6}M_{j-1} + \frac{h_j}{3}M_j + \frac{f_j - f_{j-1}}{h_j},$$

$$\frac{h_j}{6}M_{j-1} + \frac{h_j + h_{j+1}}{3}M_j + \frac{h_{j+1}}{6}M_{j+1} = \frac{f_{j+1} - f_j}{h_{j+1}} - \frac{f_j - f_{j-1}}{h_j}, \quad j = 1, \cdots, n-1.$$

$$\frac{h_j}{h_j + h_{j+1}}M_{j-1} + 2M_j + \frac{h_{j+1}}{h_j + h_{j+1}}M_{j+1} = \frac{f_{j+1} - f_j}{h_{j+1}} \cdot \frac{6}{h_j + h_{j+1}} - \frac{6(f_j - f_{j-1})}{h_j(h_j + h_{j+1})}.$$

Letting $\lambda_j = \frac{h_{j+1}}{h_j + h_{j+1}}$, $\mu_j = 1 - \lambda_j = \frac{h_j}{h_j + h_{j+1}}$.

$\mu_j M_{j-1} + 2M_j + \lambda_j M_{j+1} = d_j$ with $d_j = 6f[x_{j-1}, x_j, x_{j+1}], j = 1, \cdots, n-1.$

$$\begin{cases} -\frac{h_1}{3}M_0 - \frac{h_1}{6}M_1 + \frac{f_1 - f_0}{h_1} = f_0', \\ \frac{h_n}{6}M_{n-1} + \frac{h_n}{3}M_n + \frac{f_n - f_{n-1}}{h_n} = f_n', \end{cases}$$

so

$$\begin{cases} 2M_0 + M_1 = \frac{6}{h_1}\left(\frac{f_1 - f_0}{h_1} - f_0'\right) := d_0, \\ M_{n-1} + 2M_n = \frac{6}{h_n}\left(f_n' - \frac{f_n - f_{n-1}}{h_n}\right) := d_n. \end{cases}$$

So, we have

$$\begin{pmatrix} 2 & 1 & & & & \\ \mu_1 & 2 & \lambda_1 & & 0 & \\ & \mu_2 & 2 & \lambda_2 & & \\ & & \ddots & \ddots & \ddots & \\ & 0 & & \ddots & \ddots & \ddots \\ & & & & 1 & 2 \end{pmatrix} \begin{pmatrix} M_0 \\ M_1 \\ M_2 \\ \vdots \\ M_n \end{pmatrix} = \begin{pmatrix} d_0 \\ d_1 \\ d_2 \\ \vdots \\ d_n \end{pmatrix},$$

the coefficient matrix, denoting A, is strictly diagonally dominant, so M_i is unique.

Example 2.7.1 $S(x)$ is a cubic spline function, and satisfies
$$S'(x_0) = f'_0 = 1, \quad S'(x_3) = f'_3 = 0.$$

x_i	0	1	2	3
f_i	0	0	0	0

Solution $M_i = S''(x_i)$, $i = 0, 1, 2, 3$. For $i = 1, 2$,
$$\mu_i M_{i-1} + 2M_i + \lambda_i M_{i+1} = d_i,$$
$$\lambda_i = \frac{h_{i+1}}{h_i + h_{i+1}} = \frac{1}{2}, \quad \mu_i = 1 - \lambda_i = \frac{1}{2},$$
$$d_i = 6f[x_{i-1}, x_i, x_{i+1}] = 0.$$
$$2M_0 + M_1 = -6, \quad M_2 + 2M_3 = 0.$$

So
$$\begin{pmatrix} 2 & 1 & & \\ \frac{1}{2} & 2 & \frac{1}{2} & \\ & \frac{1}{2} & 2 & \frac{1}{2} \\ & & 1 & 2 \end{pmatrix} \begin{pmatrix} M_0 \\ M_1 \\ M_2 \\ M_3 \end{pmatrix} = \begin{pmatrix} -6 \\ 0 \\ 0 \\ 0 \end{pmatrix},$$

$$M_0 = -\frac{52}{15}, \quad M_1 = \frac{14}{15}, \quad M_2 = -\frac{4}{15}, \quad M_3 = \frac{2}{15}.$$

So, we have
$$S(x) = \begin{cases} \frac{1}{15}x(1-x)(15-11x), & x \in [0,1], \\ \frac{1}{15}(x-1)(x-2)(7-3x), & x \in [1,2], \\ \frac{1}{15}(x-2)(x-3)^2, & x \in [2,3]. \end{cases}$$

2.7.3 Error Estimation

Lemma 2.7.1 If $f \in C^2[a,b]$, $S_I(x)$ is a cubic spline of I type. Then
$$\int_a^b [f''(x) - S_I''(x)] g''(x) dx = 0,$$
where $g(x)$ is a cubic spline function.

Proof Letting $\omega(x) = f(x) - S_I(x)$, then $\omega(x) \in C^2[a,b]$ and satisfies
$$\omega(x_i) = 0, i = 0,1,2,\cdots,n; \quad \omega'(a) = \omega'(b) = 0.$$

$$\int_a^b [f''(x) - S_I''(x)] g''(x) dx = \int_a^b \omega''(x) g''(x) dx$$

$$= \omega'(x) g''(x) \Big|_a^b - \int_a^b \omega'(x) g'''(x) dx$$

$$= -g'''(x) \int_a^b \omega'(x) dx$$

$$= -\sum_{i=1}^n g'''(x_{i+\frac{1}{2}}) \cdot \int_{e_i} \omega'(x) dx$$

$$= -\sum_{i=1}^n g'''(x_{i+\frac{1}{2}}) \cdot [\omega(x_{i+1}) - \omega(x_i)]$$

$$= 0.$$

Theorem 2.7.2 If $f \in C^2[a,b]$, $S_I(x)$ is a spline of I type, then we have
$$\int_a^b [f''(x) - S_I''(x)]^2 dx \leq \int_a^b [f''(x) - g''(x)]^2 dx.$$

Proof By lemma 2.7.1, we have
$$\int_a^b [f''(x) - S_I''(x)]^2 dx$$

$$= \int_a^b [f''(x) - S_I''(x)] \cdot [f''(x) - S_I''(x)] dx$$

$$= \int_a^b [f''(x) - S_I''(x)] \cdot [f''(x) - g''(x) + g''(x) - S_I''(x)] dx$$

$$= \int_a^b [f''(x) - S_I''(x)] \cdot [f''(x) - g''(x)] dx$$

$$\leq \left(\int_a^b |f''(x) - S_I''(x)|^2 dx \right)^{\frac{1}{2}} \cdot \left(\int_a^b |f''(x) - g''(x)|^2 dx \right)^{\frac{1}{2}}.$$

$$\Rightarrow \int_a^b [f''(x) - S_I''(x)]^2 dx \leq \int_a^b [f''(x) - g''(x)]^2 dx.$$

Theorem 2.7.3 Let $e(x) = f(x) - S_I(x)$, then

(1) $\|e''\|_0 \leq CMh^2$;

(2) $\|e'\|_\infty \leq CMh^{\frac{5}{2}}$;

(3) $\|e\|_\infty \leq CMh^{\frac{7}{2}}$, $C = \dfrac{\sqrt{b-a}}{2}$.

Proof (1) From theorem 2.7.2, we have

$$\int_a^b |e''(x)|^2 dx = \min \int_a^b [f''(x) - g''(x)]^2 dx,$$

$g''(x)$ is a linear function.

Taking $g''(x) = V_I(x)$. We have

$$\int_a^b |e''(x)|^2 dx \leq \min \int_a^b [f''(x) - V_I(x)]^2 dx$$

$$= \sum_{i=1}^n \int_{e_i} \left[\frac{f^{(4)}(\xi)}{2!}(x - x_{i-1})(x - x_i)\right]^2 dx$$

$$\leq \left(\frac{M}{2}\right)^2 \cdot \frac{h^4}{4^2} \sum_{i=1}^n \int_{e_i} dx$$

$$= \frac{M^2}{64} h^4 (b - a).$$

Namely, $\|e''\|_0 \leq \dfrac{M}{8} h^2 \sqrt{b-a}$.

(2) $e(x_{i-1}) = e(x_i) = 0$. $\exists \xi \in e_i$, s.t. $e'(\xi) = 0$.

$$e'(x) = \int_\xi^x e''(t) dt \leq \left(\int_\xi^x 1^2 dt\right)^{\frac{1}{2}} \cdot \left(\int_\xi^x e''^2(t) dt\right)^{\frac{1}{2}} \leq h^{\frac{1}{2}} \|e''\|_0 \leq CMh^{\frac{5}{2}}.$$

So, $\|e'\|_\infty \leq CMh^{\frac{5}{2}}$.

(3) $e(x_{i-1}) = 0$, $\forall x \in e_i$, we have

$$|e(x)| = \left|\int_{x_{i-1}}^x e'(t) dt\right| \leq \int_{x_{i-1}}^x |e'(t)| dt \leq h \|e'\|_\infty \leq CMh^{\frac{7}{2}}.$$

(1978, Atkinson)

Theorem 2.7.4 Suppose $f \in C^4[a,b]$, $S(x)$ ($= S_I(x)$ 或 $S_{II}(x)$), then

$$\|(f-S)^{(l)}\|_\infty \leq C_l M h^{4-l}, \quad l = 0,1,2,3.$$

$C_0 = \dfrac{5}{384}$, $C_1 = \dfrac{1}{24}$, $C_2 = \dfrac{3}{8}$, $C_3 = \dfrac{\beta + \beta^{-1}}{2}$, $\beta = \dfrac{\max\{h_i\}}{\min\{h_i\}}$.

Excises 2

2.1 Make use of the Lagrange interpolation formula solve the interpolation formula of following discrete function (the results should simplify):

(1)

x_i	-1	0	1/2	1
f_i	-3	-1/2	0	1

(2)

x_i	-1	0	1/2	1
f_i	-3/2	0	0	1/2

2.2 Supposed that $l_0(x), l_1(x), \cdots, l_n(x)$ are basis functions of Lagrange interpolation problems of n degrees with $x_0, x_1, \cdots, x_n$ as the nodes. Try to prove:

(1) $\sum_{i=0}^{n} x_i^k l_i(x) = x^k, k = 0, 1, 2, \cdots, n.$

(2) $l_0 = 1 + \dfrac{x - x_0}{x_0 - x_1} + \dfrac{(x - x_0)(x - x_1)}{(x_0 - x_1)(x_0 - x_2)} + \cdots + \dfrac{(x - x_0)(x - x_1)\cdots(x - x_{n-1})}{(x_0 - x_1)(x_0 - x_2)\cdots(x_0 - x_n)}.$

2.3 Supposed that $f(x) \in C^2[a, b], 0 < \varepsilon < b - a$. Consider the Lagrange interpolation formula with $a, a+\varepsilon, b$ as the nodes, what's the limit of the formula when $\varepsilon \to 0$ and prove

$$f(x) = p(x) + R(x)$$

where

$$p(x) = \dfrac{(b-x)(x+b-2a)}{(b-a)^2} f(a) + \dfrac{(x-a)(b-x)}{b-a} f'(a) + \dfrac{(x-a)^2}{(b-a)^2} f(b),$$

$$R(x) = \dfrac{1}{6}(x-a)^2(x-b) f'''(\xi), \quad \xi \in (a, b).$$

And compute $p(a), p(b), p'(a)$.

2.4 The polynomial $p(x)$ of degrees no more than n value as $f_0, \cdots, f_n$ at the nodes $x_0, x_1, \cdots, x_n$ can be written as

$$p(x) = C \begin{vmatrix} 0 & 1 & \cdots & x^n \\ f_0 & 1 & \cdots & x_0^n \\ \vdots & \vdots & & \vdots \\ f_n & 1 & \cdots & x_n^n \end{vmatrix}$$

where C is a constant. Determine the value of C and prove the above formula.

2.5 Give the numerical results of $f(x) = e^{x^2-1}$ as follows:

x_i	1.0	1.1	1.2	1.3	1.4
f_i	1.00000	1.23368	1.55271	1.99372	2.61170

Try to solve the value of $f(1.25)$ by using Neville method.

2.6 Supposed $f(x) = x^7 + x^3 + 1$, try to solve:

(1) $f[3^0, 3^1, \cdots, 3^7]$;

(2) $f[2^0, 2^1, \cdots, 2^8]$.

2.7 Supposed $f(x) = 1/(a-x)$, try to prove

$$f[x_0, x_1, \cdots, x_n] = \frac{1}{(a-x_0)(a-x_1)\cdots(a-x_n)}$$

and

$$\frac{1}{a-x} = \frac{1}{a-x_0} + \frac{x-x_0}{(a-x_0)(a-x_1)} + \cdots + \frac{(x-x_0)\cdots(x-x_n)}{(a-x_0)(a-x_n)\cdots(a-x)}.$$

2.8 Try to prove the following relational expression:

(1) $\Delta(f_i \cdot g_i) = f_i \Delta g_i + g_{i+1} \Delta f_i$;

(2) $\Delta(f_i/g_i) = (g_i \Delta f_i - f_i \Delta g_i)/(g_i g_{i+1})$;

(3) $\Delta^n(1/x) = (-1)^n n! \, h^n/x(x+h)\cdots(x+nh)$.

2.9 Try to prove the following relational expression:

(1) $\Delta^n f_i = \sum_{k=0}^{n} (-1)^k C_n^k f_{n+i-k}$;

(2) $\Delta^n f_i = n! h^n f[x_i, x_{i+1}, \cdots, x_{i+n}]$.

2.10 Try to prove the following equation by using the difference property:

$$g(n) = 1^3 + 2^3 + \cdots + n^3 = \left[\frac{n(n+1)}{2}\right]^2.$$

2.11 Use the Newton forward and backward interpolation formula and the following data respectively:

x_i	0.0	0.2	0.4	0.6	0.8
f_i	1.00000	1.22140	1.49182	1.82212	2.22554

Compute the approximate values of $f(0.05)$ and $f(0.65)$.

2.12 Give the values of natural logarithm $\ln x$ and its derivatives $1/x$ as follows:

x	0.50	0.70
$\ln x$	-0.693147	-0.356675
$1/x$	2.00	1.43

Solve $\ln 0.06$ using Hermite interpolation formula.

2.13 Try to find a polynomial $p_{2n-1}(x)$ of $2n-1$ degrees which satisfies the following interpolation conditions:

$$p_{2n-1}(a) = f(a),$$
$$p'_{2n-1}(a) = f'(a),$$
$$\cdots\cdots$$
$$p_{2n-1}^{(n-1)}(a) = f^{(n-1)}(a),$$
$$p_{2n-1}(b) = f(b),$$
$$p'_{2n-1}(b) = f'(b),$$
$$\cdots\cdots$$
$$p_{2n-1}^{(n-1)}(b) = f^{(n-1)}(b).$$

2.14 Supposed $x_0 = 0, x_2 = 1, x_1 \in (0,1)$, and we know
$$f(x_0) = f_0, \quad f'(x) = f'_1, \quad p(x_2) = f_2.$$
Try to solve an interpolation polynomial $p \in P_2$ which satisfies
$$p(x_0) = f_0, \quad p'(x_1) = f'_1, \quad p(x_2) = f_2.$$

(1) What condition does the x_1 satisfy when above interpolation problem is well-posed?

(2) When the interpolation problem is well-posed, try to solve $p(x)$;

(3) Try to analyze the error for $p(x)$ of (2).

2.15 Supposed $f(x) \in C^4[a,b]$, x_{i_1} and x_{i_2} are two equal points of subdivision e_i, try to give the error estimation of the piecewise cubic Lagrange interpolation polynomial within the section $[a,b]$.

2.16 Supposed $f(x) = x^4$, solve the piecewise cubic Hermite interpolation polynomial $f_h(x)$ within the section $[0, 1]$ of $f(x)$ and estimate the error, taking equidistant nodes and $h = 1/10$.

2.17 Supposed $f(x) \in C^2[0,1]$ and $f(0) = 0$, $f(1/2) = f(1) = 1$, try to prove
$$\int_0^1 [f''(x)]^2 dx \geq 12.$$

2.18 Let us define piecewise cubic Lagrange polynomial interpolation problem as follows: try to solve $u \in Sp(3;0;\Delta)$ and satisfies the interpolation conditions
$$u(x_i) = f_i, \quad i = 0,1,\cdots,n,$$
$$u(x_{k_j}) = f_{k_j}, \quad j = 1,2; \quad k = 1,2,\cdots,n,$$
where $x_{k_j}(j = 1,2)$ are two different points in the element of section k. Try to give out the piecewise expression of $u(x)$.

2.19 For arbitrary nonnegative integer k, try to prove that
$$x_+^k + (-1)^k (-x)_+^k = x^k.$$

2.20 Supposed that $x_1 < x_2 < \cdots < x_n$, the following spline function
$$s(x) = a_0 + a_1 x + \sum_{j=1}^n c_j (x - x_j)_+^3$$
is called cubic natural spline when the function becomes a linear polynomial at $(-\infty, x_1)$ and $(x_n, +\infty)$. Try to prove that $s(x)$ is a cubic natural spline if and only if the coefficients $c_j(j = 1,2,\cdots,n)$ satisfy the relationships $\sum_{j=1}^n c_j = 0$, $\sum_{j=1}^n c_j x_j = 0$.

2.21 Known the interpolation conditions as follows:

x	1	2	3
$f(x)$	2	4	12
$f'(x)$	1		-1

Solve the corresponding cubic spline interpolation function.

2.22 Try to prove that isometrical B-spline $B_k(x)$ could be defined as
$$B_0(x) = \begin{cases} 1, & |x| < 1/2, \\ 1/2, & |x| = 1/2, \\ 0, & |x| > 1/2, \end{cases} \quad B_{k+1}(x) = \int_{-\infty}^{+\infty} B_0(t) B_k(x - t) dt.$$

2.23 Try to prove the positivity of B-spline:
$$B_k(x) > 0, \quad |x| < \frac{k+1}{2}.$$

2.24 Try to prove:
$$B_4(0) = \frac{115}{192}, \quad B_4(\pm 1) = \frac{19}{96}, \quad B_4(\pm 2) = \frac{1}{384}.$$

Chapter 3 Approximation Theory

The study of approximation theory involves two general types of problems.

One problem arises when a function is given explicitly, but we wish to find a "simpler" type of function, such as polynomial, that can be used to determine approximate values of the given function.

The other problem in approximation theory is concerned with fitting functions to given data and finding the "best" function in a certain class to represent data.

Example:

(1) Taylor polynomial: neighborhood of x_0;

(2) Lagrange interpolation polynomial: fit given data;

(3) Cubic splines.

§ 3.1 Optimal Approximation

Definition 3.1.1 Suppose $f(x) \in C[a,b]$, say
$$E_n(f;p_n) = \inf_{p_n \in P_n} \max_{a \leq x \leq b} |f(x) - p_n(x)|$$
is an optimal uniform approximation to $f(x)$ in P_n, also called optimal approximation or Chebyshev approximation, denoted by $E_n(f)$. If $p_n^* \in P_n$ satisfies
$$E_n(f) = \max_{a \leq x \leq b} |f(x) - p_n^*(x)|,$$
then $p_n^*(x)$ is called an n-th optimal uniform approximation polynomial to $f(x)$.

Example 3.1.1 Suppose $f(x) = e^x$, $x \in [-1, 1]$, find the optimal approximation polynomial $p_1^*(x)$ of $f(x)$.

Solution Letting $p_1^*(x) = a_0 + a_1 x$. Denote $\varepsilon(x) = e^x - p_1^*(x)$, $\rho_1 = \max_{-1 \leq x \leq 1} |\varepsilon(x)|$.

$$\varepsilon(-1) = \rho_1, \quad \varepsilon(x_3) = -\rho_1, \quad \varepsilon(1) = \rho_1, \quad \varepsilon'(x_3) = 0,$$
$$e^{-1} - (a_0 - a_1) = \rho_1,$$
$$e^1 - (a_0 + a_1) = \rho_1,$$
$$e^{x_3} - (a_0 + a_1 x_3) = -\rho_1,$$
$$e^{x_3} - a_1 = 0,$$
$$\Rightarrow a_1 = \frac{e - e^{-1}}{2} \approx 1.1752, \quad x_3 = \ln(a_1) \approx 0.1614,$$
$$\rho_1 = \frac{1}{2}(e^{-1} + a_1 x_3) \approx 0.2788,$$
$$a_0 = \rho_1 + (1 - x_3) a_1 \approx 1.2643,$$

so

$$p_1^*(x) \approx 1.2643 + 1.1752x.$$

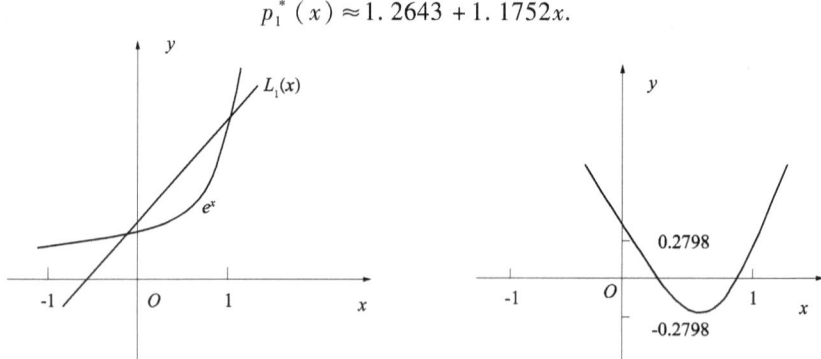

Figure 3.1.1 The optimal approximation of e^x

Figure 3.1.2 The optimal approximation error of e^x

Remark 3.1.1 From the above figures (See Figure 3.1.1 and Figure 3.1.2), we can see that the linear Lagrange interpolation $L_1(x)$ is not optimal uniform approximation to e^x. So, it is difficult to find the optimal uniform approximation. So we also study other optimal approximation such as optimal square approximation.

§3.2 Optimal Approximation of Normed Linear Space

Definition 3.2.1 Say $\|f\|$ is a norm if $\|\cdot\|$ satisfying
(1) $\|f\| \geq 0, \forall f \in E, \|f\| = 0 \Leftrightarrow f = 0;$

(2) $\|cf\| = |c| \cdot \|f\|$, $\forall c \in \mathbf{R}$, $\forall f \in E$;

(3) $\|f_1 + f_2\| \leq \|f_1\| + \|f_2\|$, $\forall f_1, f_2 \in E$.

If E with $\|\cdot\|$, we say E is a normal linear space, denoted by $(E, \|\cdot\|)$.

Remark 3.2.1 From the condition of (3), we have

$$\|\|f_1\| - \|f_2\|\| \leq \|f_1 - f_2\| \leq \|f_1\| + \|f_2\|, \quad \forall f_1, f_2 \in E.$$

Proof To prove the above result, one only see

$$\|f_1\| = \|f_1 - f_2 + f_2\| \leq \|f_1 - f_2\| + \|f_2\| \Leftrightarrow \|\|f_1\| - \|f_2\|\| \leq \|f_1 - f_2\|.$$

Example 3.2.1

$$\|f\| = \max_{a \leq x \leq b} |f(x)|, \quad \forall f \in C[a,b].$$

The above norm is called by uniform norm or Chebyshev norm.

Example 3.2.2

$$\|x\|_2 = \left(\sum_{i=1}^{n} |x_i|^2\right)^{\frac{1}{2}}, \quad \forall x = (x_1, x_2, \cdots, x_n)^T \in \mathbf{R}^n.$$

Definition 3.2.2 Let $(E, \|\cdot\|)$, $H_m \subseteq E$ is m-dimension linear subspace, $\forall f \in E$, say

$$E_n(f; H_m) = \inf_{\varphi \in H_m} \|f(x) - \varphi(x)\|$$

is the optimal approximation to f in H_m. And φ^* is called by an optimal approximation element, if φ^* satisfies $E_n(f; H_m) = \|f - \varphi^*\|$.

Remark 3.2.2 Say

$$f(x) \in C[a,b], \quad E_n(f; p_n) = \inf_{p_n \in P_n} \max_{a \leq x \leq b} |f(x) - p_n(x)|$$

is optimal uniform approximation or Chebyshev approximation. So, we see that definition 3.2.2 is an abstract definition.

Next, we have the following questions:

(1) Whether $\varphi^*(x)$ exists;

(2) Whether $\varphi^*(x)$ is unique or not;

(3) what is $\varphi^*(x)$, and how to construct.

Denote $H_m = \text{span}\{\varphi_1, \varphi_2, \cdots, \varphi_m\}$, where $\varphi_i \in E$, $i = 1, 2, \cdots, m$, and $\varphi_1, \varphi_2, \cdots, \varphi_m$ are linear independent on $[a,b]$.

Hence, $\forall \varphi \in H_m$, we have

$$\varphi = \sum_{i=1}^{m} \alpha_i \varphi_i(x), \quad \alpha_i \in \mathbf{R}, \quad i = 1, 2, \cdots, m,$$

i.e. $\varphi \leftrightarrow \boldsymbol{\alpha} = (\alpha_1, \cdots, \alpha_m)^T \in \mathbf{R}^m.$

Definition 3.2.2' Say $\varphi^* = \sum_{i=1}^{m} \alpha_i^* \varphi_i(x) \in H_m$ is an optimal approximation element, if φ^* satisfies

$$\| f - \sum_{i=1}^{m} \alpha_i^* \varphi_i \| = \inf_{(\alpha_1, \cdots, \alpha_m)^T \in \mathbf{R}^m} \| f - \sum_{k=1}^{m} \alpha_k \varphi_k \|.$$

Letting $\boldsymbol{\alpha} = (\alpha_1, \cdots, \alpha_m)^T \in \mathbf{R}^m$, define

$$g(\boldsymbol{\alpha}) := g(\alpha_1, \cdots, \alpha_m) = \|\varphi\| = \| \sum_{i=1}^{m} \alpha_i \varphi_i \|, \quad (3.2.1)$$

$$h(\boldsymbol{\alpha}) := h(\alpha_1, \cdots, \alpha_m) = \| f - \varphi \| = \| f - \sum_{i=1}^{m} \alpha_i \varphi_i \|. \quad (3.2.2)$$

Lemma 3.2.1 The functions $g(\boldsymbol{\alpha})$, $h(\boldsymbol{\alpha})$ are continuous functions.

Proof One can only prove

$$\lim_{\boldsymbol{\alpha} \to \boldsymbol{\alpha}_0} g(\boldsymbol{\alpha}) = \lim_{\boldsymbol{\alpha} \to \boldsymbol{\alpha}_0} \| \sum_{i=1}^{m} \alpha_i \varphi_i \| = \| \sum_{i=1}^{m} \alpha_i^0 \varphi_i \|.$$

So we have

$$|g(\boldsymbol{\alpha}) - g(\boldsymbol{\alpha}_0)| = \left| \| \sum_{i=1}^{m} \alpha_i \varphi_i \| - \| \sum_{i=1}^{m} \alpha_i^0 \varphi_i \| \right| \leq \| \sum_{i=1}^{m} (\alpha_i - \alpha_i^0) \varphi_i \|$$

$$\leq \sum_{i=1}^{m} |(\alpha_i - \alpha_i^0)| \|\varphi_i\|$$

$$\to 0$$

as $\boldsymbol{\alpha} \to \boldsymbol{\alpha}_0$.

Lemma 3.2.2 $\forall f \in E, \boldsymbol{\alpha} = (\alpha_1, \cdots, \alpha_m)^T \in \mathbf{R}^m$, we have

$$h(\boldsymbol{\alpha}) \to \infty \quad \text{as} \quad \sum_{i=1}^{m} \alpha_i^2 \to \infty.$$

Proof Since $g(\boldsymbol{\alpha})$ is continuous, so $g(\boldsymbol{\alpha})$ can reach its minmum value μ in the set of $\{\boldsymbol{\alpha} \mid \sum_{i=1}^{m} \alpha_i^2 = 1\}$ at $\boldsymbol{\alpha}^*$, i.e. $g(\boldsymbol{\alpha}^*) = \mu > 0$ (using the definition of the above set and the basis is independent),

$$h(\boldsymbol{\alpha}) = \| f - \sum_{i=1}^{m} \alpha_i \varphi_i \| \geq \left| \| \sum_{i=1}^{m} \alpha_i \varphi_i \| - \| f \| \right|$$

$$\geq \beta \cdot \| \sum_{i=1}^{m} \frac{\alpha_i}{\beta} \varphi_i \| - \| f \|$$

$$\geq \beta \cdot \mu - \| f \|.$$

As $\sum_{i=1}^{m} \alpha_i^2 \to \infty$, $\beta \to \infty$, then $h(\boldsymbol{\alpha}) \to \infty$.

Theorem 3.2.1 $\forall f \in E$, there exists optimal approximation element $\varphi^* \in H_m$.

Proof Using lemma 3.2.2, $\exists r > 0$ s.t. $K_r = \{\boldsymbol{\alpha} \mid \sum_{i=1}^{m} \alpha_i^2 \leq r^2\}$, we have $h(\boldsymbol{\alpha}) = h(\alpha_1, \cdots, \alpha_n) \geq \|f\|$, outside of K_r.

In K_r, $\exists \boldsymbol{\alpha}^* \in \mathbf{R}^n$, $\boldsymbol{\alpha}^* = (\alpha_1^*, \cdots, \alpha_n^*)^T$ s.t.
$$h_{\min}(\boldsymbol{\alpha}^*) = h(\alpha_1^*, \cdots, \alpha_n^*) = \min_{\boldsymbol{\alpha} \in K_r} h(\alpha_1, \cdots, \alpha_n) \leq h(0, \cdots, 0) = \|f\|.$$

So, $(\alpha_1^*, \cdots, \alpha_n^*)$ is min point of $h(\boldsymbol{\alpha})$.

§3.3 Optimal Uniform Approximation Polynomial

Definition 3.3.1 If $f \in C[a, b]$,
$$a \leq x_0 < x_1 < \cdots < x_K \leq b : \{x_i\}_{i=0}^{K}$$
are called interleaving points. If
$$f(x_i) = (-1)^i \sigma \|f\|, \quad i = 0, 1, \cdots, K, \quad \sigma = 1 \text{ or } -1,$$
x_i are called interleaving poins, denoted by (e).

Example 3.3.1 Letting $f(x) = \cos 5\pi x, 0 \leq x \leq 1$, then $x_i = \dfrac{i}{5}$ ($i = 0, 1, \cdots, 5$) are interleaving points,
$$f(x_i) = \cos(5\pi \cdot \dfrac{i}{5}) = \cos(\pi i).$$

Theorem 3.3.1 (Vallee-Poussin) If $f \in C[a, b]$, suppose $\exists p \in P_n$, s.t. $f(x) - p(x)$ is at least $(n+2)$ points in $[a, b]$: $x_0, x_1, \cdots, x_{n+1}$ interleaving of the value, then
$$E_n(f) \geq \lambda = \min_{1 \leq i \leq n+1} |f(x_i) - p(x_i)|.$$

Proof Let $p_n^* \in P_n$ be the optimal approximation, and assume that $E_n(f) < \lambda$, then
$$p_n^*(x) - p(x) = f(x) - p(x) - (f(x) - p_n^*(x)).$$
Since $|f(x_i) - p(x_i)| > E_n(f) \geq |f(x_i) - p_n^*(x_i)|$, so we see that the sign of $p_n^*(x_i) - p(x_i)$ is determined by $f(x_i) - p(x_i)$. Hence, $p_n^* - p$ has at least $(n+1)$ zeroes. So $p_n^* \equiv p$.

Theorem 3.3.2 (Chebyshev) $\forall f \in C[a,b], f \notin P_n, p$ is n-th optimal uniform approximation polynomial to $f \Leftrightarrow f - p$ has at least $(n+2)$ interleaving points.

Proof $\Rightarrow$): Omitting.

$\Leftarrow$): Suppose $f - p$ has at least $(n+2)$ interleaving points: $\{x_i\}_{i=0}^{n+1}$, by theorem 3.3.1, we have

$$E_n(f) \geq \min_{0 \leq i \leq n+1} |f(x_i) - p(x_i)| = \|f - p\|.$$

Since $E_n(f) \leq \|f - p\|$, so we have $E_n(f) = \|f - p\|$.

Theorem 3.3.3 (Unique) If $f \in C[a,b]$, then $p_n^* \in P_n$ is unique.

Proof Suppose p_1, p_2 are two optimal uniform approximation polynomials.

Denote $p_0 = \dfrac{p_1 + p_2}{2} \in P_n$, then

$$\|f - p_0\| \leq \frac{1}{2}(\|f - p_1\| + \|f - p_2\|) = E_n(f).$$

$\Rightarrow p_0$ is also optimal uniform approximation polynomial.

From theorem 3.3.2, we know that there exist $(n+2)$ interleaving points $\{x_i\}_{i=0}^{n+1}$ such that

$$E_n(f) = |f(x_i) - p_0(x_i)| = \left|\frac{f(x_i) - p_1(x_i)}{2} + \frac{f(x_i) - p_2(x_i)}{2}\right|.$$

In fact, from the above equality we know that the sign of $f(x_i) - p_1(x_i)$ is same as one of $f(x_i) - p_2(x_i)$, and

$$|f(x_i) - p_1(x_i)| \leq \|f - p_1\| = E_n(f), \quad |f(x_i) - p_2(x_i)| \leq \|f - p_2\| = E_n(f).$$

So, we have

$$f(x_i) - p_1(x_i) = f(x_i) - p_2(x_i) = \sigma E_n(f),$$

$\sigma = 1$ or $\sigma = -1$, then $p_1(x_i) = p_2(x_i)$, $i = 0, 1, \cdots n+1 \Rightarrow p_1 - p_2$ have $(n+2)$ roots $\Rightarrow p_1 \equiv p_2$.

Corollary 3.3.1 $p(x)$ is n-th optimal uniform approximation to $f(x)$, if $f^{(n+1)}(x)$ exists and the sign of $f^{(n+1)}(x)$ never changes in $[a,b]$, then $f - p$ has $(n+2)$ interleaving points of and $a, b \in (e)$.

Proof Assume that the number of interleaving points $\geq (n+2)$, or a or b $\notin (e)$. $(n+1)$ interleaving points are min/max point in (a,b).

$$f'(x_i) - p'(x_i) = 0, \quad i = 0, 1, \cdots, n,$$

$\exists q \in (a,b)$, s.t. $f^{n+1}(q) - p^{n+1}(q) = f^{(n+1)}(q) = 0$.

Contradiction to the condition of the sign of $f^{(n+1)}(x)$ remains the same.

Example 3.3.2 Suppose that $f(x) = \sqrt{x}$, $\frac{1}{4} \leqslant x \leqslant 1$. Find 1-th optimal uniform approximation to $f(x)$.

Solution Let $p_1^*(x) = a + bx$ is the optimal uniform approximation to $f(x)$. Since $f''(x) = -x^{-3/2}/4$, so the same sign in $[\frac{1}{4}, 1]$. From the corollary 3.3.1, we see that $f(x) - p_1^*(x)$ has 3 points (interleaving): $x_0 = \frac{1}{4}, x_2 = 1 \in (e), x_1 \in (\frac{1}{4}, 1)$, and satisfying

$$\begin{cases} R'(x_1) = \dfrac{1}{2\sqrt{x_1}} - b = 0, \\ f(\dfrac{1}{4}) - (a + \dfrac{b}{4}) = f(1) - (a+b), \end{cases} \Rightarrow b = 2/3, x_1 = 9/16.$$

$$f(1) - (a+b) = -[f(x_1) - (a+bx_1)] \Rightarrow a = 17/48.$$

So, the 1-th optimal uniform approximation to $f(x)$ is $p_1^* = \dfrac{2}{3}x + \dfrac{17}{48}$.

Remes Algorithm

Letting $p_n^*(x) = \sum_{i=0}^{n} a_i^* x^i$, optimal uniform approximation to $f - p_1^*$ has $(n+2)$ (e) points $\{x_i\}_{i=0}^{n+1}$, s.t.

$$p_n^*(x_i) - f(x_i) = (-1)^i \mu, \quad i = 0, 1, \cdots, n+1,$$
$$\mu = \sigma E_n(f), \quad \sigma = 1 \text{ or } \sigma = -1.$$

So, we can obtain $a_0^*, \cdots, a_n^*$ and $E_n(f)$.

Remes algorithm:

Step 1: given

$$\varepsilon > 0, \quad a \leqslant x_0^0 < x_1^0 \cdots < x_{n+1}^0 \leqslant b,$$

we obtain $p_0(x) = \sum a_i^0 x^i, \mu^0$.

Step 2: assume that get μ^l at step1, $x^l = \{x_i^l\}_{i=0}^{n+1}$ and $p_l(x) = \sum_{i=0}^{n} a_i^l x^i$.

Letting $v^l := \max_{a \leqslant x \leqslant b} |f(x) - p_l(x)| = |f(\hat{x}^l) - p_l(\hat{x}^l)|$.

Case 1 $\hat{x}^l \in (x_j^l, x_{j+1}^l), 0 \leqslant j \leqslant n$. If $f(x_j^l) - p_l(x_j^l)$ and $f(\hat{x}^l) - p_l(\hat{x}^l)$ are the same sign, then x_j^l is replaced by $\hat{x}^l$, otherwise x_{j+1}^l is replaced by $\hat{x}^l$.

Case 2 $\{x_0^l, \cdots, x_{n+1}^l\}$, $\hat{x}^l < x_0^l$, if $f(\hat{x}^l) - p_l(\hat{x}^l)$ and $f(x_0^l) - p_l(x_0^l)$ are the same sign, the x_0^l is replaced by $\hat{x}^l$; else $\{\hat{x}^l, x_0^l, \cdots, x_n^l\}$ is replaced with $\{x_0^l, \cdots, x_{n+1}^l\}$.

Case 3 $\hat{x}^l > x_{n+1}^l$, if $f(\hat{x}^l) - p_l(\hat{x}^l)$ and $f(x_{n+1}^l) - p_l(x_{n+1}^l)$ are the same sign, then x_{n+1}^l is replaced by $\hat{x}^l$; else $\{\hat{x}_1^l, \cdots, x_{n+1}^l, \hat{x}^l\}$ is replaced with $\{x_0^l, \cdots, x_{n+1}^l\}$.

Remark 3.3.1 Remes algorithm need large algorithms, so we need some new algorithms.

§3.4 Minimum Error to Zero-Chebyshev Polynomial

3.4.1 Minimum Error to Zero

Find $p_{n-1}^*(x) \in P_{n-1}$, s. t. $x \in [-1, 1]$,

$$E_{n-1}(x^n) = \min_{p_{n-1} \in P_{n-1}} \|x^n - p_{n-1}\| = \|x^n - p_{n-1}^*\|, \quad (3.4.1)$$

where the norm is defined by

$$\|f\| = \max_{-1 \leq x \leq 1} |f(x)|.$$

The above problem is equivalent to the following problem: find $p_n^*(x) \in P_n^1$ s. t.

$$\|p_n^*(x) - 0\| = \min_{p_n(x) \in P_n^1} \|p_n(x) - 0\|,$$

$$(\because x^n - p_{n-1}(x) \in P_n^1)$$

where $P_n^1 := \{p \in P_n : p(x) = a_n x^n + \cdots + a_0, a_n = 1\}$.

The problem is solved by the new tool-Chebyshev polynomial.

3.4.2 Chebyshev Polynomial

Define

$$x = \cos\theta : [0, \pi] \to [-1, 1],$$

then

$$\theta = \arccos x,$$

$$T_n(x) = \cos(n \arccos x). \quad (3.4.2)$$

Since $\cos n\theta + \cos(n-2)\theta = 2\cos\theta\cos(n-1)\theta$, we have
$$T_{n-1}(x) = \cos((n-1)\arccos x), \quad T_{n-2}(x) = \cos((n-2)\arccos x).$$

Lemma 3.4.1
$$\begin{cases} T_n(x) = 2xT_{n-1}(x) - T_{n-2}(x), n = 2,3,\cdots, \\ T_0(x) = 1, T_1(x) = x. \end{cases} \quad (3.4.3)$$

Proof $T_0(x) = \cos 0 = 1$, $T_1(x) = \cos(\arccos x) = x$.
$$\begin{aligned} T_n(x) + T_{n-2}(x) &= \cos(n\arccos x) + \cos((n-2)\arccos x) \\ &= 2\cos(\arccos x) \cdot \cos((n-1)\arccos x) \\ &= 2xT_{n-1}(x). \end{aligned}$$

Lemma 3.4.2 The coefficient of highest degree term is 2^{n-1}, and $T_n(x)$ is an n-th polynomial. $T_{2k}(x)$: the power of x is even. $T_{2k+1}(x)$: the power of x is odd.

Proof
$$\begin{aligned} T_n(x) &= 2xT_{n-1}(x) - T_{n-2}(x) \\ &= 2x(2xT_{n-2}(x) - T_{n-3}(x)) - T_{n-2}(x) \\ &= 2^2 x^2 T_{n-2}(x) - 2xT_{n-3}(x) - 2xT_{n-3}(x) + T_{n-4}(x) \\ &= 2^2 x^2 T_{n-2}(x) - 2^2 x T_{n-3}(x) + T_{n-4}(x) \\ &= 2^{n-1} x^{n-1} T(x) \cdots T_0(x). \end{aligned}$$

Table of Chebyshev polynomial:
$$T_0(x) = 1,$$
$$T_1(x) = x,$$
$$T_2(x) = 2x^2 - 1,$$
$$T_3(x) = 4x^3 - 3x,$$
$$T_4(x) = 8x^4 - 8x^2 + 1,$$
$$T_5(x) = 16x^5 - 20x^3 + 5x,$$
$$T_6(x) = 32x^6 - 48x^2 + 18x^2 - 1,$$
······

Theorem 3.4.1
$$\tilde{T}_0(x) = 1, \quad \tilde{T}_n(x) = \frac{1}{2^{n-1}} T_n(x), \quad n = 1,2,\cdots.$$

Then $\tilde{T}_n(x)$ is Chebyshev polynomial.

Example 3.4.1 Given $f(x) = 2x^3 + x^2 + 2x - 1, x \in [-1, 1]$. Find 2-th optimal uniform approximation polynomial.

Solution To prove $\|f(x) - P_2^*(x)\| = \min$, only show that
$$f(x) - P_2^*(x) = 2 \times 2^{1-3} T_3(x)$$
$$= 2 \times 2^{-2}(4x^3 - 3x),$$
$$\Rightarrow P_2^*(x) = f(x) - \frac{1}{2}(4x^3 - 3x)$$
$$= x^2 + \frac{7}{2}x - 1.$$

Also, we can get
$$f(x) = 2 \cdot \frac{3T_1 + T_3}{4} + \frac{T_0 + T_2}{2} + 2T_1 + T_0$$
$$= \frac{3}{2}T_0 + \frac{7}{2}T_1 + \frac{1}{2}T_2 + \frac{1}{2}T_3.$$

Lemma 3.4.3 Chebyshev polynomials $\{T_k(x)\}_0^n, x \in [-1, 1]$ are orthogonal about the weight function $\dfrac{1}{\sqrt{1-x^2}}$.

Proof Letting $x = \cos\theta, dx = -\sin\theta d\theta$,
$$\int_{-1}^{1} \frac{1 \cdot T_m(x) T_n(x)}{\sqrt{1-x^2}} dx \stackrel{x=\cos\theta}{=\!=\!=} \int_{\pi}^{0} \frac{\cos(m \arccos\cos\theta) \cdot \cos(n \arccos\cos\theta)}{\sin\theta} \cdot (-\sin\theta) d\theta$$
$$= \int_0^{\pi} \cos m\theta \cdot \cos n\theta d\theta = \begin{cases} 0, & m \neq n, \\ \dfrac{\pi}{2}, & m = n \neq 0, \\ \pi, & m = n = 0. \end{cases}$$

Lemma 3.4.4 $T_n(x)$ has n zeroes at $[-1, 1]$, given by
$$x_k = \cos\frac{2k-1}{2n}\pi, \quad k = 1, 2, \cdots, n.$$

Proof It is easy to check that
$$T_n(x) = \cos(n \arccos x)$$
$$= \cos\left(n \arccos\left(\cos\frac{2k-1}{2n}\pi\right)\right)$$
$$= \cos\left(n \frac{2k-1}{2n}\pi\right) (k = 1, \cdots, n)$$
$$= 0.$$

So, we see that $T_n(x)$ has $n+1$ interleaving points. Using Rolle's theorem, we know that $T_n(x)$ has n zeroes.

3.4.3 Application of Chebyshev Polynomial

a) Estimation of the Remainder $R_n(x)$

$$\|f(x) - p_n(x)\| \leq \frac{\|f^{(n+1)}\|}{(n+1)!} \max_{|x| \leq 1} |(x - x_0) \cdots (x - x_n)|,$$

for $f(x)$ is defined in $[-1, 1]$.

Interpolation points:

$$x_k = \frac{1}{2}\left[a + b + (b - a)\cos\frac{(2k-1)\pi}{2(n+1)}\right], \quad k = 1, 2, \cdots, n+1,$$

$$x_k = \cos\frac{2k-1}{2n}\pi,$$

$$x_k = \cos\frac{k}{n}\pi.$$

$(n+1)$-th Chebyshev polynomial zeroes:

$$x_k = \cos\frac{2k-1}{2(n+1)}\pi, \quad k = 1, 2, \cdots, n+1.$$

$$|f(x) - p_n(x)| \leq \frac{\|f^{(n+1)}\|}{(n+1)!} \cdot 2^{[1-(n+1)]} \|T_{n+1}\|$$

$$= \frac{\|f^{(n+1)}\|}{(n+1)!} \cdot 2^{-n}.$$

Remark 3.4.1

(1) $p_n(x)$ is optimal uniform approximation to $f(x)$, where $f^{(n+1)}(x)$ does not change sign in $[-1, 1]$.

(2) $x_k = \frac{a+b}{2} + \frac{b-a}{2}\cos\frac{2k-1}{2(n+1)}\pi.$ \hfill (3.4.4)

b) Taylor of e^{-x}

$$e^{-x} \approx p_{12}(x) = 1 - x + \frac{x^2}{2!} + \cdots + \frac{x^{12}}{12!}$$

$$\approx 1.2661 T_0 - 1.1301 T_1 + 0.2715 T_2 + \cdots + 0.0000001 T_{12}. \quad (3.4.5)$$

§3.5 Optimal Approximation of the Inner Product Space

Definition 3.5.1 Let X be a real linear space, if $(.\,,\,.)$ satisfies
(1) $(x,y) = (y,x)$;
(2) $(\lambda x, y) = \lambda(x,y)$;
(3) $(x+y, z) = (x,z) + (y,z)$;
(4) $(x,x) \geqslant 0$, if $(x,x) = 0 \Leftrightarrow x = 0$,

X is called inner product space.

Example 3.5.1 The simplest inner product space is $\mathbf{R}^n$, define $(x,y) = x^T y = \sum_{i=1}^{n} x_i y_i$, $x = (x_1, \cdots, x_n)^T$, $y = (y_1, \cdots, y_n)^T$.

Example 3.5.2 $L_\rho^2[a,b]: \{\int_a^b \rho f^2 \, dx < +\infty\}$. Say $\rho(x)$ is weight function on $[a,b]$, if $\rho(x)$ satisfies:

(1) $\int_a^b |x|^n \rho(x) \, dx < +\infty$, $\forall n$.

(2) If $\int_a^b \rho(x) g(x) = 0$ $(g(x) \geqslant 0) \Rightarrow g(x) \equiv 0$ on $[a,b]$.

Define the inner product of $L_\rho^2[a,b]$ by

$$(f,g) = \int_a^b \rho(x) f(x) g(x) \, dx, \quad \forall f, g \in L_\rho^2[a,b].$$

Lemma 3.5.1 (Cauchy-Schwarz inequality) Letting X is inner product space,

$$|(x,y)| \leqslant (x,x)^{\frac{1}{2}} (y,y)^{\frac{1}{2}}, \quad \forall x, y \in X. \tag{3.5.1}$$

Proof For any λ, we have
$$0 \leqslant (x + \lambda y, x + \lambda y) = (x,x) + 2\lambda(x,y) + \lambda^2(y,y),$$
$$\Delta = 4(x,y)^2 - 4(y,y)(x,x) < 0$$
$$\Rightarrow (x,y)^2 \leqslant (y,y)(x,x).$$

Lemma 3.5.2 The parallelogram equation $2(\|x\|^2 + \|y\|^2) = (\|x+y\|^2 + \|x-y\|^2)$. The geometric interpretation of this equation is shown in figure 3.5.1. If $\|x+y\|^2 = \|x\|^2 + \|y\|^2$, $(x,y) = 0$, then x, y of the inner product space are orthogonal. It's analogous to the Pythagorean theorem, as shown in the figure 3.5.2.

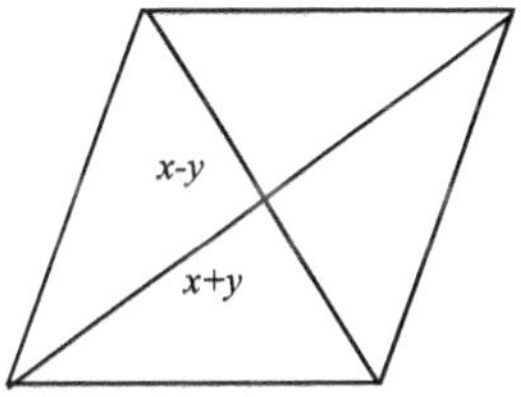

Remark 3.5.1 If $(x, y) = 0$, then x is orthogonal to y.

Lemma 3.5.3 $\|x\| = (x,x)^{\frac{1}{2}}$ is a norm. Hence, X is also normal linear space.

Figure 3.5.1 The geometric interpretation of parallelogram equation

Proof Only check the condition of norm, and the following condition is very important:

$$\|x+y\|^2 = (x+y, x+y) = (x,x) + (y,y) + 2(x,y)$$
$$\leq (x,x) + (y,y) + 2(x,x)^{\frac{1}{2}}(y,y)^{\frac{1}{2}}$$
$$\leq (\|x\|^2 + \|y\|^2).$$

Lemma 3.5.4 $(\|x+y\|^2 + \|x-y\|^2) = 2(\|x\|^2 + \|y\|^2).$ (3.5.2)

Definition 3.5.2 X: the inner product space. The finite dim space $M \subseteq X$, $\forall f \in X$. Say $E(f; M) = \inf_{\phi \in M} \|f - \phi\|$ is optimal approximation to f for M, denoted by $E(f)$. $\phi^* \in M$ satisfies $E(f) = \|f - \phi^*\|$.

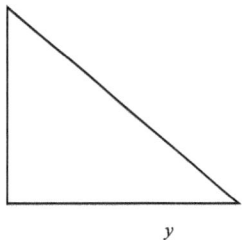

Figure 3.5.2 Pythagorean theorem

Theorem 3.5.1 $\forall f \in X$, $\exists$ optimal approximation element $\phi^* \in M$: $= \text{span}\{\phi_1, \cdots, \phi_m\}$.

Proof ϕ^* exists. Assume that there exist two different ϕ_1^*, ϕ_2^*, let $\phi_0^* = \dfrac{\phi_1^* + \phi_2^*}{2}$, and $\mu = \|f - \phi_1^*\| = \|f - \phi_2^*\|$, then

$$\mu \leq \|f - \frac{1}{2}(\phi_1^* + \phi_2^*)\| \leq \frac{1}{2}\|f - \phi_1^*\| + \frac{1}{2}\|f - \phi_2^*\| = \mu.$$

$\Rightarrow \phi_0^*$ is also an optimal approximation element.

$$\mu^2 = \|f - \varphi_0^*\|^2 = \left\|\frac{f - \varphi_1^*}{2} + \frac{f - \varphi_2^*}{2}\right\|^2$$
$$= 2\left(\left\|\frac{f - \phi_1^*}{2}\right\|^2 + \left\|\frac{f - \phi_2^*}{2}\right\|^2\right) - \left\|\frac{f - \phi_1^*}{2} - \frac{f - \phi_2^*}{2}\right\|^2$$
$$= \mu^2 - \frac{1}{4}\|\phi_2^* - \phi_1^*\|^2.$$

$\Rightarrow \phi_1^* \equiv \phi_2^*.$

Theorem 3.5.2 $\forall f \in X$, $M \subseteq X$ is a finite dimension space. $\phi^* \in M$ is an optimal approximation element to $f \Leftrightarrow (f-\phi^*, \phi) = 0$, $\forall \phi \in M$.

Proof $\Rightarrow)$: $\exists \phi \in M$, s.t. $(f-\phi^*, \phi) \neq 0$.

Letting $\varphi = \dfrac{\phi}{\|\phi\|}$, $\alpha = (f-\phi^*, \varphi) \neq 0$, then we obtain

$$\|f-\phi^* - \alpha\varphi\|^2 = (f-\phi^* - \alpha\varphi, f-\phi^* - \alpha\varphi)$$
$$= \|f-\phi^*\|^2 - 2\alpha(f-\phi^*, \varphi) + \alpha^2$$
$$= \|f-\phi^*\|^2 - \alpha^2 < \|f-\phi^*\|^2.$$

$\Rightarrow \phi^*$ is not an optimal approximation.

$\Leftarrow)$: $\forall \phi \in M$, $(f-\phi^*, \phi) = 0$, then

$$\|f-\phi\|^2 - \|f-\phi^*\|^2 = \|\phi\|^2 - \|\phi^*\|^2 - 2(f,\phi) + 2(f,\phi^*)$$
$$= \|\phi-\phi^*\|^2 + 2(f-\phi^*, \phi^* - \phi)$$
$$= \|\phi-\phi^*\|^2 \geq 0.$$

$\Rightarrow \phi^*$ is an optimal approximation. The geometric meaning of the theorem 3.5.2 is shown in figure 3.5.3.

$E(f;M)^2 = \|f-\phi^*\|^2$ (error estimation)
$= (f-\phi^*, f-\phi^*)$
$= (f,f) - (f,\phi^*) - (\phi^*, f-\phi^*)$,

$M \subseteq X$, $M = \text{span}\{\phi_1, \cdots, \phi_n\}$ and $\phi_1, \cdots, \phi_n$ are linearly independently.

$$\phi^* = \sum_{i=1}^{n} c_i^* \phi_i,$$

$(f - \sum_{i=1}^{n} c_i^* \phi_i, \phi_j) = 0$, $j = 1, 2, \cdots, n$.

$\Rightarrow$ (normal equations)

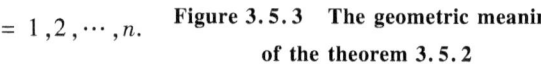

Figure 3.5.3 The geometric meaning of the theorem 3.5.2

$$\sum_{i=1}^{n} (\phi_i, \phi_j) c_i^* = (f, \phi_j), \quad j = 1, 2, \cdots, n.$$

Normal equations:

$$G = \begin{bmatrix} (\phi_1, \phi_1) & \cdots & (\phi_1, \phi_n) \\ \vdots & & \vdots \\ (\phi_n, \phi_1) & \cdots & (\phi_n, \phi_n) \end{bmatrix},$$

$$G\begin{pmatrix} c_1^* \\ \vdots \\ c_n^* \end{pmatrix} = \begin{pmatrix} (f,\phi_1) \\ \vdots \\ (f,\phi_n) \end{pmatrix},$$

G is called by Gram matrix.

If $\phi_1,\cdots,\phi_n$ are orthogonal basis, G is diagonal, then

$$c_j^* = \frac{(f,\phi_j)}{(\phi_j,\phi_j)}, \quad \phi^* = \sum_{j=1}^n \frac{(f,\phi_j)}{(\phi_j,\phi_j)}\phi_j,$$

$$\|f - \phi^*\|^2 = \|f\|^2 - (f, \sum_{j=1}^n \frac{(f,\phi_j)}{(\phi_j,\phi_j)}\phi_j)$$

$$= \|f\|^2 - \sum_{j=1}^n c_j^*(f,\phi_j) = \|f\|^2 - \sum_{j=1}^n c_j^* c_j^* \|\phi_j\|^2$$

$$= \|f\|^2 - \sum_{i=1}^n (c_i^*)^2 \|\phi_i\|^2.$$

Letting $n\to\infty$, then Bessel inequality:

$$\sum_{i=1}^n (c_i^*)^2 \|\phi_i\|^2 \leq \|f\|^2, \quad c_i^* = \frac{(f,\phi_i)}{(\phi_i,\phi_i)}.$$

Theorem 3.5.3 Finite dimension space M has orthogonal basis.

Proof Letting $\phi_1,\cdots,\phi_n$ by Gram-Schmit orthogonal method.

Letting $e_1 = \phi_1$, find $e_2 = \phi_2 + \alpha e_1$ s.t. $(e_1,e_2) = 0$, we get

$$(\phi_1,\phi_2 + \alpha\phi_1) = 0 \Leftrightarrow (\phi_1,\phi_2) + \alpha(\phi_1,\phi_1) = 0.$$

$$\Rightarrow \alpha = -\frac{(\phi_2,\phi_1)}{(\phi_1,\phi_1)} = -\frac{(\phi_2,e_1)}{(e_1,e_1)},$$

$$\Rightarrow e_2 = \phi_2 - \frac{(\phi_2,e_1)}{(e_1,e_1)}e_1.$$

Suppose that $(k-1)$ basis functions are constructed: $e_1,e_2,\cdots,e_{k-1}$.

$$e_k = \phi_k + \lambda_{k-1}e_{k-1} + \cdots \lambda_1 e_1, \quad (e_k,e_j) = 0, \quad j=1,2,\cdots,k-1,$$

$$\Rightarrow \lambda_j = -\frac{(\phi_k,e_j)}{(e_j,e_j)}, \quad j=1,2,\cdots,k-1.$$

So, $e_1,e_2,\cdots,e_n$ is a group of orthogonal basis.

Definition 3.5.3 If $f(x) \in L_\rho^2[a,b]$, $H_m = \text{span}\{\phi_1,\cdots,\phi_m\} = P_{m-1}$, then

$$\|f-\phi^*\|^2_{L_\rho^2[a,b]} = \inf_{\phi\in P_n} \|f-\phi\|^2_{L_\rho^2[a,b]} \quad (3.5.3)$$

is called optimal square approximation.

§3.6 Optimal Square Approximation and Orthogonal Polynomials

3.6.1 Optimal Square Approximation

Consider $L_\rho^2[a,b]$ ($\rho(x) \equiv 1, L^2[a,b]$), the inner product and norm are as follows:

$$(f,g) = \int_a^b \rho(x)f(x)g(x)\,dx, \quad \forall f,g \in L_\rho^2[a,b], \quad (3.6.1)$$

$$\|f\|^2 = (f,f), \quad \forall f \in L_\rho^2[a,b].$$

$\forall f \in L_\rho^2[a,b]$, $\exists 1$ optimal square approximation polynomial

$$p_n^*(x) = \sum_{j=0}^n a_j^* x^j \in P_n = \text{span}\{1, x, x^2, \cdots, x^n\}, \quad (3.6.2)$$

where a_j^* satisfying

$$\sum_{j=0}^n (x^i, x^j) a_j^* = (f, x^i), \quad i = 0, 1, \cdots, n, \quad (3.6.3)$$

and $(x^i, x^j) = \int_a^b \rho(x) x^{i+j}\,dx$, $(f, x^i) = \int_a^b \rho(x) f(x) x^i\,dx$.

Example 3.6.1 Let $f(x) = \sqrt{x} \in L^2[\frac{1}{4}, 1]$ i.e. $\rho(x) \equiv 1$, find the optimal square approximation polynomial to $f(x)$ in $[\frac{1}{4}, 1]$.

Solution Letting the optimal square approximation polynomial be

$$p_1^*(x) = a_0^* + a_1^* x, \quad x \in [\frac{1}{4}, 1].$$

$\{1, x\}$, $(1,1), (1,x), (x,1), (x,x)$,

$$\begin{pmatrix} (1,1) & (x,1) \\ (1,x) & (x,x) \end{pmatrix} \begin{pmatrix} a_0^* \\ a_1^* \end{pmatrix} = \begin{pmatrix} (f,1) \\ (f,x) \end{pmatrix}.$$

Calculate: $(1,1) = \int_{\frac{1}{4}}^1 1\,dx = \frac{3}{4}$,

$(1,x) = \int_{\frac{1}{4}}^1 x\,dx = \frac{15}{32} = (x,1)$,

$$(x,x) = \int_{\frac{1}{4}}^{1} x^2 dx = \frac{21}{64},$$

$$(f,1) = \frac{7}{12}, \quad (f,x) = \int_{\frac{1}{4}}^{1} x^{\frac{1}{2}} \cdot x dx = \frac{31}{80},$$

$$\begin{pmatrix} \frac{3}{4} & \frac{15}{32} \\ \frac{15}{32} & \frac{21}{64} \end{pmatrix} \begin{pmatrix} a_0^* \\ a_1^* \end{pmatrix} = \begin{pmatrix} \frac{7}{12} \\ \frac{31}{80} \end{pmatrix}.$$

$$\Rightarrow a_0^* = \frac{10}{27}, \quad a_1^* = \frac{88}{135}.$$

So, we can get $p_1^*(x) = \frac{88}{135}x + \frac{10}{27}$.

Remark 3.6.1 The optimal uniform approximation is

$$p_1^*(x) = \frac{2}{3}x + \frac{17}{48}.$$

Remark 3.6.2 The error of optimal approximation is the value of $E_n(f;P_n)$ or $E(f;H_m)$.

Remark 3.6.3

$$\|f - \phi^*\|_2^2 = \min_{\phi \in H_m} \|f - \phi\|_2^2$$

$$= \inf_{\phi \in H_m} \int_a^b \rho(x)(f - \phi)^2 dx$$

$$\Leftrightarrow \min I(a) = \inf_{\phi \in H_m} \int_a^b \rho(x)(f(x) - \sum_{j=0}^{n} a_j \varphi_j(x))^2 dx.$$

In fact, we have

$$\frac{\partial I(a)}{\partial a_k} = 0, \quad k = 0, 1, \cdots, n,$$

$$\frac{\partial I(a)}{\partial a_k} = 2 \int_a^b \rho(x)(f(x) - \sum_{j=0}^{n} a_j \varphi_j(x))^2 dx = 0$$

$$\Leftrightarrow (f - \phi, \varphi_k) = 0, \quad k = 0, 1, \cdots, n$$

$$\Leftrightarrow (\sum_{j=0}^{n} a_j \varphi_j(x), \varphi_k(x)) = (f(x), \varphi_k(x))$$

$$\Leftrightarrow \sum_{j=0}^{n} (\varphi_j(x), \varphi_k(x)) a_j = (f(x), \varphi_k(x)), \quad k = 0, 1, \cdots, n.$$

Remark 3.6.4 If $\varphi_k(x) = x^k, \rho(x) \equiv 1, f(x) \in C[0,1]$,

$$S^*(x) = a_0^* + a_1^* x + \cdots + a_n^* x^n, \quad x \in [0,1].$$

$$(\varphi_j(x), \varphi_k(x)) = \int_0^1 x^{j+k} dx = \frac{1}{k+j+1},$$

$$(f(x), \varphi_k(x)) = \int_0^1 f(x) x^k dx \equiv dk.$$

$$H = \begin{pmatrix} 1 & \frac{1}{2} & \cdots & \frac{1}{n+1} \\ \frac{1}{2} & \frac{1}{3} & \cdots & \frac{1}{n+2} \\ \vdots & \vdots & & \vdots \\ \frac{1}{n+1} & \frac{1}{n+2} & \cdots & \frac{1}{2n+1} \end{pmatrix},$$

H is called by Hilbert matrix.

3.6.2 Orthogonal Function

Definition 3.6.1 If $f(x), g(x) \in C[a,b]$, $\rho(x)$ is a weight function, and satisfy $(f(x), g(x)) = \int_a^b \rho(x) f(x) g(x) dx = 0$, then $f(x)$ is orthogonal to $g(x)$ with $\rho(x)$, i.e.

$$(\varphi_j, \varphi_k) = \int_a^b \rho(x) \varphi_j(x) \varphi_k(x) dx = \begin{cases} 0, & j \neq k, \\ A_j > 0, & j = k. \end{cases} \quad (3.6.4)$$

If $A_k \equiv 1$, $\{\varphi_i\}_{i=1}^n$ is normal orthogonal sequence.

Example 3.6.2

(1) $\cos x$, $\sin x$, $\cos 2x$, $\sin 2x$, $\cdots$, $x \in [-\pi, \pi]$ are a group of orthogonal functions.

(2) Given $[a,b]$ and the weight function $\rho(x) \equiv 1$, $\{1, x, x^2, \cdots, x^n, \cdots\}$ are linear independent functions.

Orthogonal Polynomial Sequences

Gram-Schmit orthogonal method: $\{\varphi_0(x), \cdots, \varphi_j(x), \cdots, \varphi_n(x)\}$,

$$\varphi_0(x) = 1,$$

$$\varphi_n(x) = x^n - \sum_{j=0}^{n-1} \frac{(x^n, \varphi_j(x))}{(\varphi_j(x), \varphi_j(x))} \varphi_j(x), \quad n = 1, 2, \cdots. \quad (3.6.5)$$

Remark 3.6.5 $\varphi_n(x), p(x) \in P_{n-1}$, then

$$(\varphi_n, p(x)) = \int_a^b \rho(x) \varphi_n(x) p(x) dx = 0.$$

Theorem 3.6.1 Letting $g_l^*(x) = g_l(x)/\alpha_l, l = 0, 1, \cdots, n,$

$$g_{k+1}^*(x) = (x - \beta_k)g_k^*(x) - \alpha_k g_{k-1}^*(x), \quad k = 1, 2, \cdots, n-1,$$

$$g_0^*(x) = 1, \quad g_1^*(x) = x - \frac{(xg_0^*, g_0^*)}{(g_0^*, g_0^*)},$$

where $\beta_k = \dfrac{(xg_k^*, g_k^*)}{(g_k^*, g_k^*)}, \alpha_k = \dfrac{(g_k^*, g_k^*)}{(g_{k-1}^*, g_{k-1}^*)}.$

Theorem 3.6.2 $g_l^*(x)$ ($l \geq 1$) has l different zeroes solutions in (a, b).

Proof Assume that $g_l^*(x)$ has zeroes solution with odd order $\varphi_n(x)$, then we have

$$(\varphi_n(x), \varphi_0) = \int_a^b \rho(x)\varphi_n(x)\varphi_0(x)\,dx \neq 0.$$

So, we assume that x_i ($i = 1, 2, \cdots, l_1$) are zeroes with odd order, such that $a < x_1 < x_2 < \cdots < x_l < b$, then

$$\varphi_n(x)q(x) > 0 \text{ or } < 0,$$

where $q(x) = (x - x_1) \cdots (x - x_{l_1})$.

If $l_1 < l$, then

$$(\varphi_n, q) = \int_a^b \rho(x)\varphi_n(x)q(x)\,dx = 0.$$

So, $l \geq l_1$.

Hence, $g_l^*(x)$ has only l different zeroes.

3.6.3 Orthogonal Polynomial

Several important orthogonal polynomials are given below.

a) Legendre Polynomial

Let $\rho(x) \equiv 1$, $\{1, x, \cdots, x^n, \cdots\}$, we can though Gram-Schmit orthogonal method to obtain Legendre polynomial $\{l_i(x)\}_0^n$, $x \in [-1, 1]$.

$$l_k(x) = \frac{1}{2^k k!}\sqrt{\frac{2k+1}{2}} \cdot \frac{d^k}{dx^k}[(x^2 - 1)^k], \quad k = 0, 1, \cdots, n.$$

1785, Legendre gave the above polynomial.

1814, Rodrigul gave a simple

$$(P_1(x), P_2(x)) = \int_{-1}^1 x \cdot \frac{3x^2 - 1}{2}\,dx$$

$$= \frac{1}{2}\int_{-1}^1 (3x^3 - x)\,dx$$

$$= 0,$$

$$(P_1(x), P_3(x)) = \int_{-1}^{1} x \cdot \frac{5x^3 - 3x}{2} dx$$

$$= \frac{1}{2} \int_{-1}^{1} (5x^4 - 3x^2) dx$$

$$= \frac{1}{2} \left(5 \cdot \frac{1}{5} x^5 \Big|_{-1}^{1} - 3 \cdot \frac{1}{3} x^3 \Big|_{-1}^{1} \right)$$

$$= 0,$$

$$P_n(x) = \frac{1}{2^n n!} \frac{d^n}{dx^n} [(x^2 - 1)^n].$$

$$x^{2n} \to 2n \cdot \cdots \cdot (n+1) \cdot x^n = \frac{(2n)!}{n!} x^n.$$

$P_n(x)$: the coefficient of x^n is $\frac{1}{2^n n!} \cdot \frac{(2n)!}{n!}$.

$$\tilde{P}_n(x) = \frac{2^n \cdot (n!)^2}{(2n)!} P_n(x)$$

$$= \frac{2^n \cdot (n!)^2}{(2n)!} \cdot \frac{1}{2^n n!} \frac{d^n}{dx^n} [(x^2 - 1)^n]$$

$$= \frac{n!}{(2n)!} \frac{d^n}{dx^n} [(x^2 - 1)^n].$$

$$P_0(x) = 1, \quad P_n(x) = \frac{1}{2^n n!} \frac{d^n}{dx^n} [(x^2 - 1)^n], \quad n = 1, 2, \cdots.$$

$$\int_{-1}^{1} P_n(x) P_m(x) dx = \begin{cases} 0, & m \neq n, \\ \frac{2}{2n+1}, & m = n. \end{cases} \tag{3.6.6}$$

$$P_n(-x) = (-1)^n P_n(x). \tag{3.6.7}$$

$$(n+1) P_{n+1}(x) = (2n+1) x P_n(x) - n P_{n-1}(x), \quad n = 1, 2, \cdots.$$

$$\tag{3.6.8}$$

$$P_0(x) = 1,$$
$$P_1(x) = x,$$
$$P_2(x) = (3x^2 - 1)/2,$$
$$P_3(x) = (5x^3 - 3x)/2,$$
$$P_4(x) = (35x^4 - 30x^2 + 3)/8,$$
$$P_5(x) = (63x^5 - 70x^3 + 15x)/8,$$

$$P_6(x) = (231x^6 - 315x^4 + 105x^2 - 5)/16,$$

......

b) Chebyshev Polynomial I

$$(T_i, T_j) = \int_{-1}^{1} \frac{1}{\sqrt{1-x^2}} T_i \cdot T_j \mathrm{d}x,$$

$$T_n(x) = \cos(n\arccos x), \quad x \in [-1, 1].$$

$$\rho = \frac{1}{\sqrt{1-x^2}}.$$

c) Chebyshev Polynomial II

$$U_n(x) = \frac{\sin((1+n)\arccos x)}{\sqrt{1-x^2}}, \quad n = 0, 1, \cdots. \tag{3.6.9}$$

$$x \in [-1, 1], \quad \rho(x) = \sqrt{1-x^2}.$$

$$\int_{-1}^{1} \sqrt{1-x^2} U_n(x) U_m(x) \mathrm{d}x \stackrel{x=\cos\theta}{=} \int_0^{\pi} \sin(n+1)\theta \sin(m+1)\theta \mathrm{d}\theta$$

$$= \begin{cases} 0, & m \neq n, \\ \dfrac{\pi}{2}, & m = n. \end{cases} \tag{3.6.10}$$

$$\begin{cases} U_0(x) = 1, U_1(x) = 2x, \\ U_{n+1}(x) = 2xU_n(x) - U_{n-1}(x), \quad n = 1, 2, \cdots. \end{cases} \tag{3.6.11}$$

d) Laguerre Polynomial

$$[a, b] = [0, +\infty),$$

$$\rho(x) = e^{-x},$$

$$L_n(x) = e^x \frac{\mathrm{d}^n}{\mathrm{d}x^n}(x^n e^{-x}),$$

$$\int_0^{+\infty} e^{-x} L_n(x) L_m(x) \mathrm{d}x = \begin{cases} 0, & m \neq n, \\ (n!)^2, & m = n. \end{cases} \tag{3.6.12}$$

$$\begin{cases} L_0(x) = 1, L_1(x) = 1 - x, \\ L_{n+1}(x) = (1 + 2n - x)L_n(x) - n^2 L_{n-1}(x), \quad n = 1, 2, \cdots. \end{cases} \tag{3.6.13}$$

e) Hermite Polynomial

$$[a, b] = (-\infty, +\infty), \quad \rho(x) = e^{-x^2},$$

$$H_n(x) = (-1)^n e^{x^2} \frac{\mathrm{d}^n}{\mathrm{d}x^n}(e^{-x^2}).$$

$$\int_{-\infty}^{+\infty} e^{-x^2} H_m(x) H_n(x) \, dx = \begin{cases} 0, & m \neq n, \\ 2^n n! \sqrt{n}, & m = n. \end{cases} \quad (3.6.14)$$

$$\begin{cases} H_0(x) = 1, H_1(x) = 2x, \\ H_{n+1}(x) = 2xH_n(x) - 2nH_{n-1}(x), \quad n = 1, 2, \cdots. \end{cases} \quad (3.6.15)$$

Example 3.6.3 Find 3-th optimal square approximation to $f(x) = e^x$, $x \in [-1, 1]$.

Solution $\rho(x) \equiv 1$, $x \in [-1, 1]$. We can choose Legendre polynomial.

$$(f(x), P_0(x)) = \int_{-1}^{1} e^x \cdot 1 \, dx = e - \frac{1}{e} \approx 2.3504,$$

$$(f(x), P_1(x)) = \int_{-1}^{1} e^x \cdot x \, dx = 2e^{-1} \approx 0.7358,$$

$$(f(x), P_2(x)) = \int_{-1}^{1} e^x \cdot \left(\frac{3}{2}x^2 - \frac{1}{2}\right) dx = e - \frac{7}{e} \approx 0.1431,$$

$$(f(x), P_3(x)) = \int_{-1}^{1} e^x \cdot \left(\frac{5}{2}x^3 - \frac{3}{2}x\right) e^x \, dx = 37\frac{1}{e} - 5e \approx 0.02013,$$

$$C_j^* = \frac{(f, P_j(x))}{(P_j(x), P_j(x))} = \frac{2j+1}{2}(f, P_j(x)),$$

$$C_0^* = \frac{1}{2}(f, P_0(x)) \approx 1.1752,$$

$$C_1^* = \frac{3}{2}(f, P_1(x)) \approx 1.1036,$$

$$C_2^* = \frac{5}{2}(f, P_2(x)) \approx 0.3578,$$

$$C_3^* = \frac{7}{2}(f, P_3(x)) \approx 0.07046,$$

$$S_3^*(x) = 1.1752 + 1.1036x + 0.3578x^2 + 0.07046x^3.$$

$$\|\delta(x)\|_2 = \left(\int_{-1}^{1} e^{2x} dx - \sum_{k=0}^{2} \frac{2}{2k+1} C_k^{*2}\right)^{\frac{1}{2}} \leq 0.0084,$$

$$\|\delta(x)\|_\infty = \|e^x - S_3^*(x)\|_\infty \leq 0.0112.$$

Remark 3.6.6 Legendre polynomial can simply problem, and does not need to solve a linear algebraic system.

3.6.4 Approximating Chebyshev Approximation

The weight function $\rho(x) = (1 - x^2)^{-\frac{1}{2}}$, $x \in [-1, 1]$. $\forall f(x) \in L_\rho^2[-1, 1]$, the n-th optimal square approximation to $f(x)$ is

$$S_n(x) = \sum_{j=0}^{n} C_j^* T_j(x), \qquad (3.6.16)$$

$$M = \text{span}\{T_0(x), T_1(x), \cdots, T_n(x)\},$$

$$C_0^* = \frac{(f(x), T_0(x))}{(T_0(x), T_0(x))} = \frac{1}{\pi} \int_{-1}^{1} \frac{1}{\sqrt{1-x^2}} \cdot f(x)\,dx,$$

$$C_j^* = \frac{(f(x), T_j(x))}{(T_j(x), T_j(x))} = \frac{2}{\pi} \int_{-1}^{1} \frac{1}{\sqrt{1-x^2}} \cdot f(x) \cdot T_j(x)\,dx, \quad j = 0,1,2,\cdots,$$

$$S_n(x) = C_0^* \frac{T_0(x)}{2} + \sum_{j=1}^{n} C_j^* \cdot T_j(x).$$

1978, Atkinson proved that

$$S_n(x) \to f(x), n \to \infty \text{ for } f \in C^1[-1,1].$$

Also, $n \to \infty$ (large enough),

$$f(x) - S_n(x) \approx C_{n+1} T_{n+1}(x),$$

$T_{n+1}(x)$ has $(n+1)$ zeroes and $(n+2)$ interleaving points, using Chebyshev theorem, we see that $S_n(x)$ can be regarded as an n-th Chebyshev approximation polynomial.

Example 3.6.4 Letting $f(x) = e^x, x \in [-1,1]$, find the 3-th Chebyshev optimal square approximation.

Solution $$S_3(x) = \frac{a_0}{2} + \sum_{j=1}^{3} a_j T_j(x),$$

$$a_j = \frac{2}{\pi} \int_{-1}^{1} \frac{e^x T_j(x)}{\sqrt{1-x^2}} dx = \frac{2}{\pi} \int_{0}^{\pi} e^{\cos\theta} \cdot \cos(j\theta)\,d\theta,$$

$a_0 \approx 2.5321318, \quad a_1 \approx 1.1303182, \quad a_2 \approx 0.2714953, \quad a_3 \approx 0.0443369,$

$$S_3(x) = 0.994571 + 0.997308x + 0.542991x^2 + 0.177347x^3,$$

$$\|e^x - S_3(x)\|_\infty \approx 0.00607.$$

Better than Legendre polynomial.

§3.7 Discrete Optimal Square Approximation and Least Square Method (L-S)

In this chapter, we will condider the optimal approximation in $\mathbf{R}^n$, which is also called by discrete optimal square approximation, and its application——fitting data by least square method.

3.7.1 The Best Squared Approximation of the Discrete Case

Discrete optimal square approximation:
$$X = (x_1, \cdots, x_n)^T, Y = (y_1, \cdots, y_n)^T \in \mathbf{R}^n.$$
Denote $w_i > 0$ by the weight coefficient, then the weighted inner product is
$$(X, Y) = \sum_{i=1}^{n} w_i x_i y_i, \quad \|X\| = \sqrt{(X, X)}.$$
Letting $X_i = (x_{1i}, \cdots, x_{ni})^T$ be linearly independent in $\mathbf{R}^n$.
$$X = \sum_{k=1}^{l} c_k X_k, l\text{-dimension subspace } \mathbf{R}^l \subset \mathbf{R}^n, \quad \forall Y = (y_1, \cdots, y_n)^T, \text{ find } X^*$$
$$= \sum_{k=1}^{l} c_k^* X_k \in \mathbf{R}^l,$$
$$\|Y - X^*\| = \inf_{X \in \mathbf{R}^l} \|Y - X\|, \quad \|Y - X\| = \left(\sum_{i=1}^{n} w_i (y_i - x_i)^2\right)^{\frac{1}{2}}.$$
X^* is called the optimal square approximation vector quantity.

Normal equations:
$$\sum_{j=1}^{l} (X_i, X_j) c_j^* = (Y, X_i), \quad i = 1, \cdots, l. \tag{3.7.1}$$

For an over-determined equations: $A_{l \times n} x = b$, $l \gg n$. So, the linear system has no solution, but we can find the solution——LS solution. One can do the following steps:

As the weight coefficient is $(1, 1, 1, \cdots, 1)^T$, for the over-determined equations $X_j = (a_{1j}, \cdots, a_{nj})^T \in \mathbf{R}^n, j = 1, 2, \cdots, l$ and $A = (a_{ij})_{l \times n}$, then we have
$$(X_i, X_j) = \sum_{k=1}^{n} a_{ki} \cdot a_{kj} = A^T A,$$
$$(Y, x_i) = A^T Y,$$
$$A^T A x = A^T Y.$$

3.7.2 Applications

Fitting data and least square method.
Given $f(x_i)$, x_i, $i = 0, 1, \cdots, m$. Find a function $y = S^*(x)$

$(= \sum_{j=0}^{n} a_j^* \varphi_j(x))$. The error $\delta_i = S^*(x_i) - y_i = \sum_{j=0}^{n} a_j^* \varphi_j(x_i) - y_i, i = 0, 1, \cdots, m$, $\boldsymbol{\delta} = (\delta_0, \delta_1, \cdots, \delta_m)^T$.

Question: $H_m = \text{span}\{\varphi_0, \varphi_1, \cdots, \varphi_m\}$ is given, how to find $S^*(x)$ in H_m satisfying

$$\|\boldsymbol{\delta}\|_2^2 = \sum_{i=0}^{m} \delta_i^2 = \sum_{i=0}^{m} (S^*(x_i) - y_i)^2 = \inf \sum_{i=0}^{m} (S(x_i) - y_i)^2, S(x) \in H_m.$$

Generally,

$$\|\boldsymbol{\delta}\|_2^2 = \sum_{i=0}^{m} w_i (S^*(x_i) - y_i)^2 = \inf_{S(x) \in H_m} \sum_{i=0}^{m} w_i (S(x_i) - y_i)^2$$

$$= \sum_{i=0}^{m} w_i (\sum_{i=0}^{n} a_j^* \varphi_j(x_i) - y_i)^2 = \sum_{i=1}^{m} w_i (y_j - \varphi^*(x_i))^2$$

$$= \sum_{i=0}^{n} w_i (y_i - (\alpha_1 \varphi_1(x_i) + \alpha_2 \varphi_2(x_i) + \cdots + \alpha_l \varphi_l(x_i)))^2,$$

$$Y = (y_1, y_2, \cdots, y_n)^T \in \mathbf{R}^n,$$

$$\boldsymbol{\Phi}_j = (\varphi_j(x_1), \varphi_j(x_2), \cdots, \varphi_j(x_n))^T \in \mathbf{R}^n, \quad j = 1, 2, \cdots, l,$$

l-dimension of $\mathbf{R}^n$: $H_l = \text{span}\{\varphi_1, \varphi_2, \cdots, \varphi_l\}$.

$$\sum_{j=0}^{l} (\boldsymbol{\Phi}_j, \boldsymbol{\Phi}_i) a_j = (Y, \boldsymbol{\Phi}_i), \quad i = 1, 2, \cdots, l.$$

$$(\boldsymbol{\Phi}_j, \boldsymbol{\Phi}_i) = \sum_{k=1}^{n} w_k \boldsymbol{\Phi}_j(x_k) \boldsymbol{\Phi}_i(x_k),$$

$$(Y, \boldsymbol{\Phi}_i) = \sum_{k=1}^{n} w_k y_k \cdot \boldsymbol{\Phi}_i(x_k),$$

$$\begin{pmatrix} (\boldsymbol{\Phi}_1, \boldsymbol{\Phi}_1) & \cdots & (\boldsymbol{\Phi}_l, \boldsymbol{\Phi}_1) \\ (\boldsymbol{\Phi}_1, \boldsymbol{\Phi}_2) & \cdots & (\boldsymbol{\Phi}_l, \boldsymbol{\Phi}_2) \\ \vdots & & \vdots \\ (\boldsymbol{\Phi}_1, \boldsymbol{\Phi}_l) & \cdots & (\boldsymbol{\Phi}_l, \boldsymbol{\Phi}_l) \end{pmatrix} \begin{pmatrix} a_1 \\ a_2 \\ \vdots \\ a_l \end{pmatrix} = \begin{pmatrix} \sum_{i=1}^{n} y_i \varphi_1(x_i) \\ \sum_{i=1}^{n} y_i \varphi_2(x_i) \\ \vdots \\ \sum_{i=1}^{n} y_i \varphi_l(x_i) \end{pmatrix}.$$

As, we can obtain

$$I(a_0, a_1, \cdots, a_m) = \sum_{i=0}^{m} w_i (\sum_{i=0}^{n} a_j \varphi_j(x_i) - y_j)^2,$$

$$\frac{\partial I}{\partial a_k} = \sum_{i=0}^{m} w_i 2 \left(\sum_{j=0}^{m} a_j \varphi_j(x_j) - y_j \right) \cdot \varphi_k(x_i) = 0,$$

$$\Rightarrow \sum_{i=0}^{m} w_i \left(\sum_{j=0}^{n} (a_j \varphi_j(x_i) - y_i \varphi_k(x_i)) \right) = 0, \quad k = 0, 1, \cdots, n.$$

Denote

$$(\varphi_j, \varphi_k) = \sum_{i=0}^{m} w(x_i) \varphi_j(x_i) \varphi_k(x_i),$$

$$(f, \varphi_k) = \sum_{i=0}^{m} w(x_i) f(x_i) \varphi_k(x_i) \equiv d_k, \quad k = 0, 1, \cdots, n,$$

then we get the normal equations as follows:

$$\sum_{j=0}^{n} (\varphi_j, \varphi_k) a_j - (f, \varphi_k) = 0, \quad k = 0, 1, \cdots, n,$$

i. e. **Ga = d**,

$$G = \begin{pmatrix} (\varphi_0, \varphi_0) & (\varphi_0, \varphi_1) & \cdots & (\varphi_0, \varphi_m) \\ \vdots & \vdots & & \vdots \\ (\varphi_m, \varphi_0) & (\varphi_m, \varphi_1) & \cdots & (\varphi_m, \varphi_m) \end{pmatrix}.$$

$H_m = \text{span}\{1, x, x^2, \cdots, x^m\}$. Then, the normal equations is

$$\begin{pmatrix} \sum_{i=1}^{m} 1 & \sum_{i=1}^{m} x_i & \cdots & \sum_{i=1}^{m} x_i^n \\ \sum_{i=1}^{m} x_i & \sum_{i=1}^{m} x_i^2 & \cdots & \sum_{i=1}^{m} x_i^{n+1} \\ \vdots & \vdots & & \vdots \\ \sum_{i=1}^{m} x_i^n & \sum_{i=1}^{m} x_i^{n+1} & \cdots & \sum_{i=1}^{m} x_i^{2n} \end{pmatrix} \begin{pmatrix} a_0 \\ a_1 \\ \vdots \\ a_n \end{pmatrix} = \begin{pmatrix} \sum_{k=1}^{m} y_k \cdot 1 \\ \sum_{k=1}^{m} y_k \cdot x_k \\ \vdots \\ \sum_{k=1}^{m} y_k \cdot x_k^n \end{pmatrix}. \quad (3.7.2)$$

Example 3.7.1 Given data as follows:

x_i	1	2	3	4	5
f_i	4	4.5	6	8	8.5
w_i	2	1	3	1	1

Solution From the data, we find out that the law closes to line. So, we find

$$S_1(x) = a_0 + a_1 x,$$

$$(\varphi_0, \varphi_0) = \sum_{i=0}^{4} w_i = 8,$$

$$(\varphi_0, \varphi_1) = (\varphi_1, \varphi_0) = \sum_{i=0}^{4} x_i \cdot w_i = 22,$$

$$(\varphi_1, \varphi_1) = \sum_{i=0}^{4} w_i x_i^2 = 74,$$

$$(\varphi_0, f) = \sum_{i=0}^{4} w_i y_i = 47,$$

$$(\varphi_1, f) = \sum_{i=0}^{4} w_i y_i x_i = 145.5,$$

$$\begin{pmatrix} 8 & 22 \\ 22 & 74 \end{pmatrix} \begin{pmatrix} a_0 \\ a_1 \end{pmatrix} = \begin{pmatrix} 47 \\ 145.5 \end{pmatrix},$$

$$\Rightarrow a_0 = 2.5648, \quad a_1 = 1.2037.$$

So, $S_1^*(x) = 2.5648 + 1.2037x$.

Example 3.7.2 The data are given:

i	0	1	2	3	4
x_i	1.00	1.25	1.5	1.75	2.00
y_i	5.10	5.79	6.53	7.45	8.46
$\bar{y}_i = \ln y_i$	1.629	1.756	1.876	2.008	2.135

Solve a and b by least square method.

Solution From the above table, we see that

$$y = a e^{bx}.$$

It is easy to check that

$$y = a e^{bx} \Rightarrow \ln y = bx + \ln a.$$

Denote $\bar{y} = \ln y$, $A = \ln a$, then we obtain

$$\bar{y} = A + bx, \quad \varphi = \{1, x\}.$$

Taking $\varphi_0(x) = 1, \varphi_1(x) = x, w(x) \equiv 1$, we get

$$(\varphi_0, \varphi_0) = \sum_{i=0}^{4} 1 = 5,$$

$$(\varphi_1,\varphi_0) = (\varphi_0,\varphi_1) = \sum_{i=0}^{4} x_i = 7.5,$$

$$(\varphi_1,\varphi_1) = \sum_{i=0}^{4} x_i^2 = 11.875,$$

$$(\varphi_0,\bar{y}) = \sum_{i=0}^{4} \bar{y}_i = 9.404,$$

$$(\varphi_1,\bar{y}) = \sum_{i=0}^{4} x_i \bar{y}_i = 14.422,$$

$$\begin{pmatrix} 5 & 7.5 \\ 7.5 & 11.875 \end{pmatrix} \begin{pmatrix} A \\ b \end{pmatrix} = \begin{pmatrix} 9.404 \\ 14.422 \end{pmatrix},$$

$$\Rightarrow A = 1.122, \quad b = 0.505, \quad a = e^A = 3.071,$$

$$y = 3.071 e^{0.505x}.$$

3.7.3 Least Square Method by Orthogonal Polynomial

Definition 3.7.1 $\{\varphi_0(x), \varphi_1(x), \cdots, \varphi_n(x)\}$ are orthogonal functions with weight function $w(x_i)$:

$$(\varphi_j,\varphi_k) = \sum_{i=0}^{m} w(x_i)\varphi_j(x_i)\varphi_k(x_i) = \begin{cases} 0, & j \neq k, \\ A_j > 0, & j = k. \end{cases} \quad (3.7.3)$$

From the normal equations, we have

$$a_j = \frac{(f,\varphi_j)}{(\varphi_j,\varphi_j)} = \frac{\sum_{i=0}^{m} w(x_i)f(x_i)\varphi_j(x_i)}{\sum_{i=0}^{m} w(x_i)\varphi_j^2(x)}, \quad j = 0,1,\cdots,n. \quad (3.7.4)$$

Excises 3

3.1 Prove that the functions $1, x, \cdots, x^n$ are linear independence.

3.2 Calculate the norms $\|f\|_\infty$, $\|f\|_1$ and $\|f\|_2$ of the following functions $f(x)$ on $C[0,1]$.

(1) $f(x) = (x-1)^3$;

(2) $f(x) = \left| x - \frac{1}{2} \right|$;

(3) $f(x) = x^m (1-x)^n$, m and n are positive integers.

3.3 Prove that $\|f-g\| \geq \|f\| - \|g\|$.

3.4 For $f(x), g(x) \in C^1[a,b]$, define

(1) $(f,g) = \int_a^b f'(x)g'(x)\,dx$;

(2) $(f,g) = \int_a^b f'(x)g'(x)\,dx + f(a)g(a)$,

ask whether they constitute inner product.

3.5 Let $T_m^*(x) = T_n(2x-1), x \in [0,1]$, trying to prove that $\{T_n^*(x)\}$ is an orthogonal polynomial with weighted $\rho = \dfrac{1}{\sqrt{x-x^2}}$ on the interval $[0,1]$.

3.6 For the weight function $\rho(x) = 1 + x^2$, interval $[-1,1]$, try to seek for the orthogonal polynomials $\varphi_n(x)$ with first coefficient of 1, for $n = 0,1,2,3$.

3.7 Please try to prove that the second kinds of Chebyshev polynomials $\{U_n(x)\}$, which is given by $U_n(x) = \dfrac{\sin[(n+1)\arccos x]}{\sqrt{1-x^2}}$ is orthogonal polynomial with weighted $\rho = \sqrt{1-x^2}$ on the interval $[-1,1]$.

3.8 Please try to prove that, for each Chebyshev polynomial $T_n(x)$, the equality $\int_{-1}^{1} \dfrac{[T_n(x)]^2}{\sqrt{1-x^2}} dx = \dfrac{\pi}{2}$ is established.

3.9 With the $T_3(x)$ of the zero point to do the interpolation point, find the quadratic interpolation polynomial of $f(x) = e^x$ on interval $[-1,1]$ and estimate its maximum error bound.

3.10 Let $f(x) = x^2 + 3x + 2$ for $x \in [0,1]$, please try to find the optimal square approximation polynomial of $f(x)$ about $\rho(x) = 1$ and $\Phi = \text{span}\{1, x\}$ on interval $[0,1]$. If so $\Phi = \text{span}\{1, x, x^2\}$, what is the best square approximation polynomial?

3.11 Find the optimal square approximation to the function of $f(x) = x^3$ about $\rho(x) = 1$ on interval $[-1,1]$.

3.12 Please try to find the best square approximation polynomial of $f(x)$ about $\Phi = \text{span}\{1, x\}$ on the specified interval.

(1) $f(x) = \dfrac{1}{x}, [1,3]$;

(2) $f(x) = e^x, [0,1]$;

(3) $f(x) = \cos\pi x$, $[0,1]$;

(4) $f(x) = \ln x$, $[1,2]$.

3.13 Let $f(x) = \sin\dfrac{\pi}{2}x$, please try to find the third best square approximation polynomial is obtained by the Legendre polynomial on the interval $[-1,1]$.

3.14 Observe the linear motion of the object, the following data:

Time t/s	0	0.9	1.9	3.0	3.9	5.0
Distance s/m	0	10	30	50	80	110

Find the equation of motion.

3.15 Known experimental data are as follows:

x_i	19	25	31	38	44
y_i	19.0	32.3	49.0	73.3	97.8

Using the least square method to find the empirical formula such that $y = a + bx^2$, and calculate the mean square error.

3.16 In a chemical reaction, the concentration of the analyte is determined by the following:

Time $t(\text{s})$	0	5	10	15	20	25	35	40	45	50	55
Concentration ($\times 10^{-4}$)	0	1.27	2.16	2.85	3.44	3.87	4.15	4.58	4.58	4.62	4.64

Please try to find $y = f(t)$ with the least square method.

3.17 Using the method of successive division to $R_{22}(x) = \dfrac{3x^2 + 6x}{x^2 + 6x + 6}$ into continued fraction.

3.18 Given $f(x) = \cos 2x$, $m = 4$, $n = 2$, try to find the discrete least square polynomial $S_2(x)$ on interval $[-\pi, \pi]$.

Chapter 4 Numerical Integration and Differentiation

§4.1 Introduction

4.1.1 Numerical Integration

For the integral $I(f) = \int_a^b f(x)\,dx$, by Newton-Leibniz formula we have

$$\int_a^b f(x)\,dx = F(x)\Big|_a^b = F(b) - F(a).$$

However, when $f(x) = \sin(x^2)$, $\dfrac{\sin x}{x}$ or some discrete data, we can not use the Newton-Leibniz formula.

Example 4.1.1 Calculate the length of sine wave

$$f(x) = \sin x, \quad x \in [0, 48].$$

Solution The length of sine wave is

$$s = \int_0^{48} \sqrt{1 + [f'(x)]^2}\,dx = \int_0^{48} \sqrt{1 + (\cos x)^2}\,dx.$$

Although the sine function is out of the most common on mathematical functions, the calculation of its length involves an elliptic integral of the second kind, which can not be evaluated by the ordinary method.

The basic method involved in approximating $\int_a^b f(x)\,dx$ is called numerical quadrature:

$$\int_a^b f(x)\,dx \approx \sum_{k=0}^n A_k f(x_k), \quad a \leqslant x_0 \leqslant x_1 \leqslant \cdots \leqslant x_n \leqslant b.$$

Example 4.1.2 $I = \int_a^b f(x)\,dx = f(\xi) \cdot (b - a)$, how to calculate $f(\xi)$?

Figure 4.1.1 illustrates geometric meaning of the definite integral.

Trapezoidal rule:

$$\int_a^b f(x)\,dx \approx \frac{b-a}{2}(f(a)+f(b)).$$

Middle rectangle rule:

$$\int_a^b f(x)\,dx \approx (b-a)f\left(\frac{a+b}{2}\right).$$

Simpson's rule:

$$\int_a^b f(x)\,dx \approx (b-a)\frac{1}{6}\left(f(a) + 4f\left(\frac{a+b}{2}\right) + f(b)\right).$$

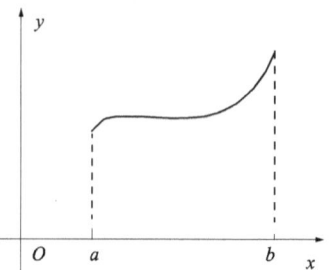

Figure 4.1.1 The graphics of curve trapezoid

4.1.2 Degree of Accuracy

Definition 4.1.1 The degree of accuracy of a quadrature formula is the largest positive integer n, such that the formula is exact for x^k ($k=0,1,\cdots,n$).

For example:

(1) Trapezoidal rule: $\int_a^b f(x)\,dx \approx \frac{b-a}{2}(f(a)+f(b)).$

For $f(x) = 1$, then $\int_a^b dx = b-a = (b-a)\frac{1+1}{2}$;

For $f(x) = x$, then $\int_a^b x\,dx = \frac{b^2-a^2}{2} = (b-a)\frac{b+a}{2}$;

For $f(x) = x^2$, then $\int_a^b x^2\,dx = \frac{b^3-a^3}{3} \neq (b-a)\frac{b^2+a^2}{2}.$

So the degree of accuracy of trapezoidal rule is 1.

(2) Middle rectangle rule: $\int_a^b f(x)\,dx \approx (b-a)f\left(\frac{a+b}{2}\right).$

For $f(x) = 1$, then $\int_a^b dx = b-a = (b-a)\cdot 1$;

For $f(x) = x$, then $\int_a^b x\,dx = \frac{b^2-a^2}{2} = (b-a)\frac{b+a}{2}$;

For $f(x) = x^2$, then $\int_a^b x^2\,dx = \frac{b^3-a^3}{3} \neq (b-a)\frac{(b+a)^2}{4}.$

So the degree of accuracy of middle rectangle rule is 1.

(3) Simpson's rule: $\int_a^b f(x)\,dx \approx (b-a)\dfrac{1}{6}(f(a)+4f(c)+f(b))$.

For $f(x)=1$, then $\int_a^b dx = b-a = (b-a)\cdot\dfrac{1+4+1}{6}$;

For $f(x)=x$, then $\int_a^b x\,dx = \dfrac{b^2-a^2}{2} = (b-a)\dfrac{b+4\times\dfrac{a+b}{2}+a}{6}$;

For $f(x)=x^2$, then $\int_a^b x^2\,dx = \dfrac{b^3-a^3}{3} = (b-a)\dfrac{a^2+4\left(\dfrac{a+b}{2}\right)^2+b^2}{6}$;

For $f(x)=x^3$, then $\int_a^b x^3\,dx = \dfrac{b^4-a^4}{4} = (b-a)\dfrac{a^3+4\cdot\dfrac{(a+b)^3}{8}+b^3}{6}$;

For $f(x)=x^4$, it does not hold.

So the degree of accuracy of Simpson's rule is 3.

Generally, x_k and A_k are calculated. In fact, $\{x_k\}_{k=0}^n$ can be given, then one can easily calculate $A_k, k=0,1,2,\cdots,n$.

Theorem 4.1.1 Given $n+1$ distinct points $a\leqslant x_0\leqslant x_1\leqslant\cdots\leqslant x_n\leqslant b$, then $\{A_k\}_{k=0}^n$ existing such that the degree of $\sum_{k=0}^n A_k f(x_k)$ is at least n.

Proof Assume that $\int_a^b f(x)\,dx \approx \sum_{k=0}^n A_k f(x_k)$. Taking

$$f(x) = x^i\ (i=0,1,\cdots,n),$$

we have

$$\sum_{k=0}^n A_k x_k^i = \int_a^b x^i\,dx = \dfrac{1}{i+1}(b^{i+1}-a^{i+1}),\quad i=0,1,\cdots,n.$$

And its coefficient determinant is

$$\begin{vmatrix} 1 & 1 & \cdots & 1 \\ x_0 & x_1 & \cdots & x_n \\ \vdots & \vdots & & \vdots \\ x_0^n & x_1^n & \cdots & x_n^n \end{vmatrix} = \prod_{0\leqslant i<j\leqslant n}(x_j - x_i) \neq 0.$$

The proof is completed.

4.1.3 Interpolating Quadrature Formula

Given $n+1$ points $a\leqslant x_0\leqslant x_1\leqslant\cdots\leqslant x_n\leqslant b$. Denote

$$l_k(x) = \prod_{\substack{j=0 \\ j \neq k}}^{n} \frac{x - x_j}{x_k - x_j}, \quad k = 0, 1, \cdots, n,$$

then $\{l_k(x)\}_{k=0}^{n}$ is interpolating basis function of n-th Lagrange interpolation.

We have a formula of the form

$$\int_a^b f(x) \, dx \approx \int_a^b L_n(x) \, dx = \int_a^b \sum_{k=0}^{n} f(x_k) l_k(x) \, dx = \sum_{k=0}^{n} f(x_k) \int_a^b l_k(x) \, dx.$$

Accordingly,

$$\int_a^b f(x) \, dx \approx \sum_{k=0}^{n} A_k f(x_k), \tag{4.1.1}$$

where

$$A_k = \int_a^b l_k(x) \, dx = \int_a^b \prod_{\substack{j=0 \\ j \neq k}}^{n} \frac{x - x_j}{x_k - x_j} dx, \quad k = 0, 1, \cdots, n.$$

Definition 4.1.2 (4.1.1) is called **interpolating quadrature formula**.

Remark 4.1.1 The remainder of formula (4.1.1) is

$$R(f) = \int_a^b [f(x) - L_n(x)] \, dx = \int_a^b \frac{f^{(n+1)}(\xi)}{(n+1)!} \prod_{j=0}^{n} (x - x_j) \, dx.$$

Theorem 4.1.2 The quadrature formula $\int_a^b f(x) \, dx \approx \sum_{k=0}^{n} A_k f(x_k)$ has at least n-th degree of accuracy if and only if it is an interpolating quadrature formula.

Proof If the formula $\int_a^b f(x) \, dx \approx \sum_{k=0}^{n} A_k f(x_k)$ has at least n-th degree of accuracy, then we have

$$\int_a^b l_k(x) \, dx = \sum_{i=0}^{n} A_i l_k(x_i),$$

where $l_k(x_i) = \delta_{ki} = \begin{cases} 0, & k \neq i, \\ 1, & k = i. \end{cases}$

Therefore, we get

$$\int_a^b l_k(x) \, dx = \sum_{i=0}^{n} A_i l_k(x_i) = \sum_{i=0}^{n} A_i \delta_{ki} = A_k.$$

Suppose that $f(x) = x^k$ for $0 \leq k \leq n$, then n-th Lagrange interpolation is

$$\sum_{i=0}^{n} f(x_i) l_i(x) = f(x).$$

And
$$\int_a^b f(x)\,dx = \int_a^b \sum_{i=0}^n f(x_i) l_i(x)\,dx = \sum_{i=0}^n f(x_i) \int_a^b l_i(x)\,dx.$$

So the degree of accuracy is at least n.

Remark 4.1.2 If $\{A_k\}_{k=0}^n$ are quadrature coefficients of interpolating quadrature formula, then $\sum_{k=0}^n A_k = b - a$.

Example 4.1.3 Given
$$\int_0^1 f(x)\,dx = A_0 f(0) + A_1 f(1) + B_0 f'(0).$$

Try to determine A_0, A_1, B_0, such that the degree of accuracy is highest.

Solution Letting $f(x) = x^0, x^1, x^2$, then
$$A_0 + A_1 = \int_0^1 dx = 1,$$
$$A_1 + B_0 = \int_0^1 x\,dx = \frac{1}{2},$$
$$A_1 = \int_0^1 x^2\,dx = \frac{1}{3},$$

whose solution is
$$A_0 = \frac{2}{3}, \quad A_1 = \frac{1}{3}, \quad B_0 = \frac{1}{6}.$$

Since $\int_0^1 f(x)\,dx = \frac{1}{4}$ and $A_0 f(0) + A_1 f(1) + B_0 f'(0) = \frac{1}{3}$ for $f(x) = x^3$, so the quadrature formula is 2-order degree.

Example 4.1.4 Given
$$\int_{-1}^1 f(x)\,dx \approx \omega_0 f(-1) + \omega_1 f(0) + \omega_2 f(1).$$

Try to determine $\omega_0, \omega_1, \omega_2$, such that the degree of accuracy is highest.

Solution Choose $f(x) = 1, x, x^2$ for
$$\int_{-1}^1 f(x)\,dx \approx \omega_0 f(-1) + \omega_1 f(0) + \omega_2 f(1),$$

then

$$\begin{cases} \omega_0 + \omega_1 + \omega_2 = \int_{-1}^{1} 1 \, dx = 2, \\ -\omega_0 + \omega_2 = \int_{-1}^{1} x \, dx = 0, \\ \omega_0 + \omega_2 = \int_{-1}^{1} x^2 \, dx = \frac{2}{3}. \end{cases}$$

Thus

$$\omega_0 = \frac{1}{3}, \quad \omega_1 = \frac{4}{3}, \quad \omega_2 = \frac{1}{3}.$$

Therefore

$$\int_{-1}^{1} f(x) \, dx \approx \frac{1}{3} f(-1) + \frac{4}{3} f(0) + \frac{1}{3} f(1).$$

Indeed, $\int_{-1}^{1} f(x) \, dx = 0$ and $\frac{1}{3} f(-1) + \frac{4}{3} f(0) + \frac{1}{3} f(1) = 0$ for $f(x) = x^3$.

On the other hand, $\int_{-1}^{1} f(x) \, dx = \frac{2}{5}$ and $\frac{1}{3} f(-1) + \frac{4}{3} f(0) + \frac{1}{3} f(1) = \frac{2}{3}$ for $f(x) = x^4$. So the degree of accuracy is 3.

§4.2 Newton-Cotes Quadrature Formula

4.2.1 Newton-Cotes Formula

Definition 4.2.1 Divide the interval $[a, b]$ into n parts. Then the mesh step size is $h = \dfrac{b-a}{n}$ and the mesh points are $x_k = a + kh$ for $k = 0, 1, \cdots, n$. The interpolating quadrature

$$\int_a^b f(x) \, dx = (b-a) \sum_{k=0}^{n} C_k^{(n)} f(x_k) \qquad (4.2.1)$$

is called **n-order Newton-Cotes formula**, where $C_k^{(n)}$ is called **Cotes coefficient**.

Remark 4.2.1 Since

$$\int_a^b f(x) \, dx \approx \sum_{k=0}^{n} A_k f(x_k),$$

where $A_k = \int_a^b l_k(x) \, dx = \int_a^b \prod_{\substack{j=0 \\ j \neq k}}^{n} \frac{(x - x_j)}{(x_k - x_j)} \, dx$, $x = a + th$. Then

$$C_k^{(n)} = \frac{1}{b-a}\int_a^b \prod_{\substack{j=0 \\ j \neq k}}^{n} \frac{(x-x_j)}{(x_k-x_j)}dx$$

$$= \frac{h}{b-a}\int_0^n \prod_{\substack{j=0 \\ j \neq k}}^{n} \frac{t-j}{k-j}dt$$

$$= \frac{(-1)^{n-k}}{n \cdot k!(n-k)!}\int_0^n \prod_{\substack{j=0 \\ j \neq k}}^{n}(t-j)\,dt.$$

For $n=1$, then $x_0 = a, x_1 = b, h = b-a$,

$$C_0^{(1)} = -\int_0^1 (t-1)\,dt = \frac{1}{2}, \quad C_1^{(1)} = \int_0^1 t\,dt = \frac{1}{2}.$$

For $n=2$, then $x_0 = a, x_1 = \frac{b+a}{2}, x_2 = b, h = \frac{b-a}{2}$,

$$C_0^{(2)} = \frac{1}{4}\int_0^2 (t-1)(t-2)\,dt = \frac{1}{6}, \quad C_1^{(2)} = \frac{-1}{2}\int_0^2 t(t-2)\,dt = \frac{4}{6},$$

$$C_2^{(2)} = \frac{1}{4}\int_0^2 (t-1)t\,dt = \frac{1}{6}.$$

4.2.2 Error Analysis

a) Interpolating Quadrature Formula

$$R(f) = \int_a^b f(x)\,dx - \sum_{k=0}^{n} A_k f(x_k) = K \cdot f^{(n+1)}(\eta),$$

where K is a parameter but independent of $f(x)$.

If $\int_a^b f(x)\,dx \approx \sum_{k=0}^{n} A_k f(x_k)$ has n-th degree of accuracy, then we have $R(f) = 0$ for $f(x) = x^k, k \leq n$.

Taking $f(x) = x^{n+1}, R(f) \neq 0$, namely

$$\int_a^b x^{n+1}\,dx - \sum_{k=0}^{n} A_k f(x_k) = K \cdot (n+1)!,$$

then

$$K = \frac{1}{(n+1)!}\left[\frac{1}{n+2}(b^{n+2} - a^{n+2}) - \sum_{k=0}^{n} A_k x_k^{n+1}\right].$$

So the remainder is

$$R(f) = K \cdot f^{(n+1)}(\eta) = \frac{1}{(n+1)!}\left[\frac{1}{n+2}(b^{n+2} - a^{n+2}) - \sum_{k=0}^{n} A_k x_k^{n+1}\right] \cdot f^{(n+1)}(\eta).$$

(4.2.2)

Remark 4.2.2 (4.2.2) shows that the relation between the degree of accuracy and the remainder.

For example, the degree of accuracy is 1 and the remainder is

$$R(f) = \frac{1}{2}[\frac{1}{3}(b^3 - a^3) - \sum_{k=0}^{n} A_k x_k^2] \cdot f''(\eta)$$

$$= -\frac{(b-a)^3}{12} f''(\eta)$$

for trapezoidal rule.

The degree of accuracy is 3 and the remainder is

$$R(f) = \frac{1}{(n+1)!}[\frac{1}{n+2}(b^{n+2} - a^{n+2}) - \sum_{k=0}^{n} A_k x_k^{n+1}] \cdot f^{(n+1)}(\eta)$$

$$= -\frac{b-a}{180}(\frac{b-a}{2})^4 f^{(4)}(\eta)$$

for Simpson's rule.

b) Convergence and Stability of Quadrature Formula

Definition 4.2.2 If

$$\lim_{\substack{h \to 0 \\ n \to \infty}} \sum_{k=0}^{n} A_k f(x_k) = \int_a^b f(x) \, dx, \qquad (4.2.3)$$

where $h = \max_{1 \leq i \leq n} |x_i - x_{i-1}|$, the formula $\int_a^b f(x) \, dx \approx \sum_{k=0}^{n} A_k \tilde{f}(x_k)$ is **convergent**.

For simplicity, we denote that

$$I_n(f) = \sum_{k=0}^{n} A_k f(x_k), \quad I_n(\tilde{f}) = \sum_{k=1}^{n} A_k \tilde{f}(x_k),$$

$$f(x_k) = \tilde{f} + \delta_k, \quad \delta = \max_{0 \leq k \leq n} |\delta_k|.$$

If $\forall \varepsilon > 0$, $|f(x_k) - \tilde{f}| \leq \delta$ for $k = 0, 1, \cdots, n$, such that

$$|I_n(f) - I_n(\tilde{f})| = \left|\sum_{k=0}^{n} A_k (f(x_k) - \tilde{f}(x_k))\right| < \varepsilon,$$

then we say that the quadrature formula is **stable**.

Theorem 4.2.1 If $A_k > 0$, then the quadrature formula

$$\int_a^b f(x) \, dx \approx \sum_{k=0}^{n} A_k f(x_k) \qquad (4.2.4)$$

is stable.

Proof For any $\varepsilon > 0$, taking $\delta = \frac{\varepsilon}{b-a}$ for $k = 0, 1, \cdots, n$, then

$$|I_n(f) - I_n(\tilde{f})| = \left|\sum_{k=0}^{n} A_k(f(x_k) - \tilde{f}(x_k))\right|$$

$$\leq \sum_{k=0}^{n} |A_k||f(x_k) - \tilde{f}(x_k)|$$

$$\leq \delta \sum_{k=0}^{n} |A_k| \leq \varepsilon.$$

c) n-order Newton-Cotes Formula

$$I(f) = \int_a^b f(x)\,dx, \quad I_n(f) = (b-a)\sum_{k=0}^{n} C_k^{(n)} f(x_k),$$

$$E_n(f) = I(f) - I_n(f),$$

where

$$p_1(x) = f(a) + (x-a)f'(a),$$

$$R_1(x) = \int_a^x (x-t)f''(t)\,dt = \int_a^b (x-t)_+ f''(t)\,dt,$$

$$x_+^m = \begin{cases} x^m, & x \geq 0, \\ 0, & x < 0. \end{cases}$$

Note

$$\int_a^b (x-t)_+ f''(t)\,dt = \int_a^x (x-t)f''(t)\,dt + \int_x^b 0 \cdot f''(t)\,dt,$$

$$E(p_1) = 0,$$

$$E(f) = E(R_1) + E(p_1) = E(R_1),$$

$$E(R_1) = \int_a^b R_1(x)\,dx - \frac{b-a}{2}[R_1(a) + R_1(b)]$$

$$= \int_a^b \int_a^b (x-t)_+ f''(t)\,dt\,dx - \frac{b-a}{2}\int_a^b (b-t)f''(t)\,dt$$

$$= \int_a^b f''(t)\int_a^b (x-t)_+ \,dx\,dt - \frac{b-a}{2}\int_a^b (b-t)f''(t)\,dt$$

$$= \int_a^b \frac{(b-t)^2}{2} f''(t) - \frac{b-a}{2}\int_a^b (b-t)f''(t)\,dt$$

$$= \int_a^b \frac{b-t}{2} f''(t)(b-t-b+a)\,dt$$

$$= \int_a^b \frac{(b-t)(a-t)}{2} f''(t)\,dt.$$

$K_1(t) = \dfrac{(t-a)(t-b)}{2}$ is **Peano kernal of trapezoidal rule.**

$n = 1$ (Simpson's rule),

$$f(x) = p_2(x) + R_2(x), \quad R_3(x) = \frac{1}{6}\int_a^x (x-t)^3 f^{(4)}(t)\,dt,$$

$$E_2(f) = E(R_3(x)) = \int_a^b K_2(t) f^{(4)}(t)\,dt,$$

$$K_2(t) = \begin{cases} \dfrac{1}{72}(t-a)^3(3t-a-2b), & a \leqslant t \leqslant \dfrac{a+b}{2}, \\ \dfrac{1}{72}(b-t)^3(b+2a-3t), & \dfrac{a+b}{2} \leqslant t \leqslant b \end{cases}$$

is called **Simpson's Peano kernal**.

$$E_1(f) = f''(\xi)\int_a^b K_1(t)\,dt, \quad E_2(f) = f^{(4)}(\xi)\int_a^b K_2(t)\,dt.$$

Denote $h = \dfrac{b-a}{n}$, then the error of n-order Newton-Cotes formula as follows:

$$E_n(f) = \begin{cases} -\dfrac{1}{12}h^3 f^{(2)}(\xi), & n = 1, \\[4pt] -\dfrac{1}{90}h^5 f^{(4)}(\xi), & n = 2, \\[4pt] -\dfrac{3}{80}h^5 f^{(4)}(\xi), & n = 3, \\[4pt] -\dfrac{8}{945}h^7 f^{(6)}(\xi), & n = 4, \\[4pt] -\dfrac{1}{90}h^7 f^{(6)}(\xi), & n = 5. \end{cases}$$

Theorem 4.2.2 If n is odd, then the degree of accuracy of Newton-Cotes formula is n. If n is even, then the degree of accuracy is $n+1$.

Proof If n is even for $f(x) = x^{n+1}$, we have

$$R(f) = \int_a^b R_n(0)\,dx = \int_a^b \frac{(n+1)!}{(n+1)!}\prod_{j=0}^n (x - x_j)\,dx.$$

Letting $x = a + th$, $x_j = a + jh$, then

$$R(f) = h^{n+2}\int_0^n \prod_{j=0}^n (t - j)\,dt.$$

If n is even, then $\dfrac{n}{2}$ is an integer, $t = n + \dfrac{n}{2}$, then we have

$$R(f) = h^{n+2}\int_{-\frac{n}{2}}^{\frac{n}{2}} \prod_{j=0}^n \left(n + \frac{n}{2} - j\right)\,dt,$$

$$H(u) = \prod_{j=0}^{n}(u + \frac{n}{2} - j) = \prod_{j=-\frac{n}{2}}^{\frac{n}{2}}(u - j),$$

$$-H(-u) = -\prod_{j=-\frac{n}{2}}^{\frac{n}{2}}(-u - j) = \prod_{j=-\frac{n}{2}}^{\frac{n}{2}}(u + j) = \prod_{j=-\frac{n}{2}}^{\frac{n}{2}}(u - j) = H(u).$$

d) Convergence

$n = 8$, we have

$$\int_a^b f(x)\,dx \approx I_8(f) = \frac{4(b-a)}{14175}[989(f_0 + f_8) + 5888(f_1 + f_7) - 928(f_2 + f_8)$$
$$+ 10496(f_3 + f_5) + 4540 f_4].$$

Lemma 4.2.1 If $\sigma_n = \sum_{k=0}^{n} |C_k^{(n)}|$, then $\sup_n \{\sigma_n\} = +\infty$, so the sign of $C_k^{(n)}$ must be changed. When $n \leq 7$, it is stable.

§4.3 Composite Numerical Integration

4.3.1 Newton-Cotes Formula

The Newton-Cotes formula is generally unsuitable for over large integration intervals. High-degree formulas would be required.

Idea: Divide the interval $[a, b]$ into equal subintervals and take $h = \frac{b-a}{n}$, then the nodes are $x_k = a + kh$, $k = 0, 1, 2, \cdots, n$.

Take the low order numerical integration on each mesh $I_k = [x_k, x_{k+1}]$ ($k = 0, 1, 2, \cdots, n-1$), we have

$$\int_a^b f(x)\,dx = \sum_{k=0}^{n-1} \int_{x_k}^{x_{k+1}} f(x)\,dx.$$

Composite trapezoidal rule is

$$\int_a^b f(x)\,dx = \sum_{k=0}^{n-1} \int_{x_k}^{x_{k+1}} f(x)\,dx$$
$$\approx \sum_{k=0}^{n-1} \frac{x_{k+1} - x_k}{2}[f(x_k) + f(x_{k+1})]$$

$$= \frac{h}{2} \sum_{k=0}^{n-1} [f(x_k) + f(x_{k+1})]$$

$$= \frac{h}{2} [f(a) + 2\sum_{k=1}^{n-1} f(x_k) + f(b)]. \qquad (4.3.1)$$

Composite Simpson's rule is

$$\int_a^b f(x)\,dx = \sum_{k=0}^{n-1} \int_{x_k}^{x_{k+1}} f(x)\,dx$$

$$\approx \sum_{k=0}^{n-1} \frac{x_{k+1} - x_k}{6} [f(x_k) + 4f(x_{k+\frac{1}{2}}) + f(x_{k+1})]$$

$$= \frac{h}{6} \sum_{k=0}^{n-1} [f(x_k) + 4f(x_{k+\frac{1}{2}}) + f(x_{k+1})]$$

$$= \frac{h}{6} [f(a) + 2\sum_{k=1}^{n-1} f(x_k) + 4\sum_{k=0}^{n-1} f(x_{k+\frac{1}{2}}) + f(b)]. \qquad (4.3.2)$$

4.3.2 Error of Composite Numerical Integration

Denote

$$T_n = \frac{h}{2} [f(a) + 2\sum_{k=1}^{n-1} f(x_k) + f(b)],$$

$$S_n = \frac{h}{6} [f(a) + 2\sum_{k=1}^{n-1} f(x_k) + 4\sum_{k=0}^{n-1} f(x_{k+\frac{1}{2}}) + f(b)].$$

Then

$$\int_a^b f(x)\,dx - T_n = \sum_{k=0}^{n-1} \left\{ \int_{x_k}^{x_{k+1}} f(x)\,dx - \frac{h}{2}[f(x_k) + f(x_{k+1})] \right\}$$

$$= \sum_{k=0}^{n-1} [-\frac{h^3}{12} f''(\xi_k)]$$

$$= -\frac{(b-a)}{12} h^2 \cdot \frac{1}{n} \sum_{k=0}^{n-1} f''(\xi_k).$$

If $f''(x) \in C[a,b]$, then

$$\min_{a \leq x \leq b} f''(x) \leq \sum_{k=0}^{n-1} \frac{f''(\xi_k)}{n} \leq \max_{a \leq x \leq b} f''(x).$$

There exists $\xi \in [a,b]$, such that $\sum_{k=0}^{n-1} \frac{f''(\xi_k)}{n} = f''(\xi)$.

Therefore,

$$\int_a^b f(x)\,dx - T_n = -\frac{(b-a)}{12}h^2 f''(\xi).$$

Similarly, we get

$$\int_a^b f(x)\,dx - S_n = -\frac{(b-a)}{180}\left(\frac{h}{2}\right)^4 f^{(4)}(\eta), \quad \eta \in [a,b].$$

Theorem 4.3.1 If $f(x) \in C^2[a,b]$, then

$$\left|\int_a^b f(x)\,dx - T_n\right| \le \frac{(b-a)}{12}h^2 \max_{a \le x \le b}|f''(x)|. \qquad (4.3.3)$$

If $f(x) \in C^4[a,b]$, then

$$\left|\int_a^b f(x)\,dx - S_n\right| \le \frac{(b-a)}{2880}h^4 \max_{a \le x \le b}|f^{(4)}(x)|. \qquad (4.3.4)$$

4.3.3 Adaptive Composite Quadrature Formula

Step: $h \to \dfrac{h}{2} \to \dfrac{h}{2^2} \to \dfrac{h}{2^3} \to \cdots$.

So: composite Simpson's rule

$$S_n = \frac{h}{6}\sum_{k=0}^{n-1}[f(x_k) + 4f(x_{k+\frac{1}{2}}) + f(x_{k+1})], \quad I_k = [x_k, x_{k+1}].$$

$$S_{2n} = \frac{h}{12}\sum_{k=0}^{n-1}[f(x_k) + 4f(x_{k+\frac{1}{4}}) + 2f(x_{k+\frac{1}{2}}) + 4f(x_{k+\frac{3}{4}}) + f(x_{k+1})]$$

$$= \frac{S_n}{2} + \frac{h}{6}\sum_{k=0}^{n-1}[2f(x_{k+\frac{1}{4}}) - f(x_{k+\frac{1}{2}}) + 2f(x_{k+\frac{3}{4}})].$$

$$I - S_n = -\frac{1}{180}\left(\frac{h}{2}\right)^4 f^{(4)}(\eta_n) \cdot (b-a), \quad \eta_n \in [a,b],$$

$$I - S_{2n} = -\frac{1}{180}\left(\frac{h}{2}\right)^4 \cdot \frac{(b-a)}{2^4} f^{(4)}(\eta_{2n}),$$

$$S_{2n} - S_n = -\frac{1}{180}\left(\frac{h}{2}\right)^4 (b-a)[f^{(4)}(\eta_n) - \frac{1}{16}f^{(4)}(\eta_{2n})],$$

$$f^{(4)}(\eta_n) \approx f^{(4)}(\eta_{2n}).$$

So

$$I - S_{2n} \approx \frac{1}{15}(S_{2n} - S_n) < \varepsilon'.$$

Test condition: $\quad S_{2n} - S_n < \varepsilon = 15\varepsilon'$.

Step 1: $h := b - a, \; S_1 := \dfrac{h}{6}\left[f(a) + 4f\left(\dfrac{a+b}{2}\right) + f(b)\right].$

Step 2: $S := \sum_{k=0}^{n-1} \left[2f\left(a + \left(k + \frac{1}{4}\right)h\right) - f\left(a + \left(k + \frac{1}{2}\right)h\right) + 2f\left(a + \left(k + \frac{3}{4}\right)h\right) \right]$,

$S_2 := \frac{1}{2} S_1 + \frac{h}{6} S$.

Step 3: check $S_2 - S_1 < \varepsilon$.

Step 4: $h := \frac{h}{2}$, $S_2 := S_1$.

Step 5: output S_2.

§4.4 Richardson Extrapolation and Romberg Integration

4.4.1 Extrapolation of Composite Trapezoidal Rule

$$T_n = \frac{h}{2}[f(a) + 2\sum_{k=1}^{n-1} f(x_k) + f(b)], \quad h = (b-a)/n, \; x_k = a + kh.$$

Theorem 4.4.1 Assume that $f(x) \in C^\infty[a,b]$, then

$$T_n = \int_a^b f(x)\,dx + \tau_1 h^2 + \tau_2 h^4 + \cdots + \tau_m h^{2m} + \cdots, \qquad (4.4.1)$$

where $\tau_i \, (i = 1, 2, \cdots)$ is independent of h.

Proof Using Taylor formula, we have

$$f(x) = f_{k+\frac{1}{2}} + (x - x_{k+\frac{1}{2}}) f'_{k+\frac{1}{2}} + \frac{(x - x_{k+\frac{1}{2}})^2}{2!} f''_{k+\frac{1}{2}} + \frac{(x - x_{k+\frac{1}{2}})^3}{3!} f'''_{k+\frac{1}{2}} + \cdots,$$

$$f(x_k) = f_{k+\frac{1}{2}} + (x_k - x_{k+\frac{1}{2}}) f'_{k+\frac{1}{2}} + \frac{(x_k - x_{k+\frac{1}{2}})^2}{2!} f''_{k+\frac{1}{2}} + \frac{(x_k - x_{k+\frac{1}{2}})^3}{3!} f'''_{k+\frac{1}{2}} + \cdots,$$

$$f(x_{k+1}) = f_{k+\frac{1}{2}} + (x_{k+1} - x_{k+\frac{1}{2}}) f'_{k+\frac{1}{2}} + \frac{(x_{k+1} - x_{k+\frac{1}{2}})^2}{2!} f''_{k+\frac{1}{2}}$$
$$+ \frac{(x_{k+1} - x_{k+\frac{1}{2}})^3}{3!} f'''_{k+\frac{1}{2}} + \cdots,$$

then

$$\int_{x_k}^{x_{k+1}} f(x)\,dx = h f_{k+\frac{1}{2}} + \frac{2}{3!}\left(\frac{h}{2}\right)^3 f''_{k+\frac{1}{2}} + \frac{2}{5!}\left(\frac{h}{2}\right)^5 f^{(4)}_{k+\frac{1}{2}} + \frac{2}{7!}\left(\frac{h}{2}\right)^7 f^{(6)}_{k+\frac{1}{2}} + \cdots,$$

$$\frac{h}{2}[f(x_k) + f(x_{k+1})] = hf_{k+\frac{1}{2}} + \frac{h}{2!}\left(\frac{h}{2}\right)^2 f''_{k+\frac{1}{2}} + \frac{h}{4!}\left(\frac{h}{2}\right)^4 f^{(4)}_{k+\frac{1}{2}} + \cdots.$$

So

$$T_n = \frac{h}{2} \sum_{k=0}^{n-1} [f(x_k) + f(x_{k+1})]$$

$$= h \sum_{k=0}^{n-1} f_{k+\frac{1}{2}} + \frac{h^3}{2! \times 2^2} \sum_{k=0}^{n-1} f''_{k+\frac{1}{2}} + \frac{h^5}{4! \times 2^4} \sum_{k=0}^{n-1} f^{(4)}_{k+\frac{1}{2}} + \cdots,$$

$$I = \int_a^b f(x)\,dx = h \sum_{k=0}^{n-1} f_{k+\frac{1}{2}} + \frac{h^3}{3! \times 2^2} \sum_{k=0}^{n-1} f''_{k+\frac{1}{2}} + \frac{h^5}{5! \times 2^4} \sum_{k=0}^{n-1} f^{(4)}_{k+\frac{1}{2}}$$

$$+ \frac{h^7}{7! \times 2^6} \sum_{k=0}^{n-1} f^{(6)}_{k+\frac{1}{2}} + \cdots,$$

$$T_n - I = \frac{h^3}{2! \times 6} \sum_{k=0}^{n-1} f''_{k+\frac{1}{2}} + \frac{h^5}{4! \times 20} \sum_{k=0}^{n-1} f^{(4)}_{k+\frac{1}{2}} + \cdots,$$

$$\int_a^b f''(x)\,dx = f'(b) - f'(a),$$

$$h \sum_{k=0}^{n-1} f''_{k+\frac{1}{2}} = f'(b) - f'(a) - \frac{h^3}{3! \times 2^2} \sum_{k=0}^{n-1} f^{(4)}_{k+\frac{1}{2}} - \cdots,$$

$$T_n = I + \frac{h^2}{2! \times 6}(f'(b) - f'(a)) - \frac{h^5}{4! \times 30} \sum_{k=0}^{n-1} f^{(4)}_{k+\frac{1}{2}} + \cdots.$$

So, we have

$$T_n = I + \frac{h^2}{2! \times 6}(f'(b) - f'(a)) - \frac{h^4}{4! \times 30}(f'''(b) - f'''(a))$$

$$+ \frac{h^6}{6! \times 42} \sum_{k=0}^{n-1} f^{(6)}_{k+\frac{1}{2}} - \cdots.$$

4.4.2 Richardson Extrapolation

Note that

$$T_n = I + \tau_1 h^2 + \tau_2 h^4 + O(h^6),$$

$$T_{2n} = I + \tau_1 \left(\frac{h}{2}\right)^2 + \tau_2 \left(\frac{h}{2}\right)^4 + O(h^6),$$

$$4T_{2n} - T_n = 3I - \frac{3}{4}\tau_2 h^4 + O(h^6),$$

$$\frac{4T_{2n} - T_n}{3} = I - \frac{1}{4}\tau_2 h^4 + O(h^6),$$

where $I = \int_a^b f(x)\,dx$.

Richardson extrapolation:

$$S_n = I - \frac{T_2}{4}h^4 + O(h^6),$$

$$S_{2n} = I - \frac{T_2}{4}\left(\frac{h}{2}\right)^4 + O(h^6),$$

$$16S_{2n} - S_n = 15I + O(h^6),$$

$$C_n = I + O(h^6),$$

$$C_n = (16S_{2n} - S_n)/15.$$

4.4.3 Romberg Integration

Step length k-th bisection composite trapezoidal rule:

$$T_{0,k} = I + \sum_{i=1}^{m} \tau_{0,i} h_k^{2i} + O(h_k^{2m+2}).$$

Taking $h_{k+1} = \frac{1}{2}h_k = \frac{b-a}{2^{k+1}} = 2^{-1}h_k$, then

$$T_{1,k} = I + \sum_{i=2}^{m} \tau_{1,i} h_{k+1}^{2i} + O(h_{k+1}^{2m+2}),$$

$$T_{1,k} = (4T_{0,k+1} - T_{0,k})/3,$$

$$= \frac{4^1}{4^1-1}T_{0,k+1} - \frac{1}{4^1-1}T_{0,k},$$

$\tau_{1,i}$ is a constant that doesn't depend on h_{k+1}.

$$T_{2,k} = I + \sum_{i=3}^{m} \tau_{2,i} h_{k+2}^{2i} + O(h_{k+2}^{2m+2})$$

$$= \frac{4^2}{4^2-1}T_{1,k+1} - \frac{1}{4^2-1}T_{1,k},$$

where

$$T_{1,k+1} = I + \sum_{i=2}^{m} \tau_{1,i} h_{k+2}^{2i} + O(h_{k+2}^{2m+2}), \quad \cdots, \quad T_{j,k} = I + \sum_{i=j+1}^{m} \tau_{j,i} h_{k+j}^{2i} + O(h_{k+j}^{2m+2}),$$

$$h_{k+j} = \frac{1}{2}h_{k+j-1}, \quad T_{j,k} = (4^j T_{j-1,k+1} - T_{j-1,k})/(4^j - 1).$$

As $m = j$, $T_{j,k} - I = O(h_{j+k}^{2j+2})$.

Chapter 4　Numerical Integration and Differentiation

Table 4.4.1　Romberg integration method

	h^2	h^4	h^6	h^8
h_0	$T_{0,0}$			
h_1	$T_{0,1}$	$T_{1,0}$		
h_2	$T_{0,2}$	$T_{1,1}$	$T_{2,0}$	
h_3	$T_{0,3}$	$T_{1,2}$	$T_{2,1}$	$T_{3,0}$
$\vdots$				

Provide the algorithm in the table 4.4.1, the following algorithm only processes $\{T_{0,k}\}$ (h^2) to the magnitude of error h^6 of $\{T_{2,k}\}$ (h^6).

Denote

$T_{0,k}$, $T_{0,k+1}$ by T_1, T_2;
$T_{1,k}$, $T_{1,k+1}$ by S_1, S_2;
$T_{2,k}$, $T_{2,k+1}$ by C_1, C_2.

$$T_{0,k} = \frac{h_k}{2}(f(a) + 2\sum_{k=1}^{n-1} f(x_k) + f(b)),$$

$$T_{0,k+1} = \sum_{k=0}^{n} \frac{\frac{h_k}{2}}{2}[f(x_k) + f(x_{k+\frac{1}{2}})] + \frac{\frac{h_k}{2}}{2}[f(x_{k+1}) + f(x_{k+\frac{1}{2}})]$$

$$= \frac{h_k}{2} \sum_{k=0}^{n} [f(x_k) + 2f(x_{k+\frac{1}{2}}) + f(x_{k+1})]$$

$$= \frac{h_k}{2}[f(a) + 2\sum_{k=0}^{n-1} f(x_{k+\frac{1}{2}}) + 2\sum_{k=0}^{n-1} f(x_k) + f(b)]$$

$$= \frac{1}{2}T_{0,k} + \frac{h_k}{2}\sum_{i=0}^{n-1} f(x_{i+\frac{1}{2}}).$$

Romberg algorithm:

Step 1: $h := b - a$, $T_1 := \frac{h}{2}[f(a) + f(b)]$.

Step 2: $S := \sum_{i=0}^{n-1} f[a + (i + \frac{1}{2})h]$, $T_2 := \frac{T_1}{2} + \frac{h}{2} \cdot S$.

Step 3: $S_2 := T_2 + \frac{T_2}{4^1 - 1} - \frac{T_1}{4^1 - 1}$.

Step 4: $k := k + 1$, $h := \frac{h}{2}$, $T_1 := T_2$, $S_1 := S_2$.

Step 5: $C_2 := S_2 + \dfrac{1}{15}(S_2 - S_1)$.

Step 6: $C_1 := C_2, |C_2 - C_1| < \varepsilon$. Stop.

§4.5   Gaussian Quadrature

The Newton-Cotes formulas were derived by integrating interpolating polynomials, the formula of this type is exact less than or equal to n.

All the Newton-Cotes formulas use values of the function at equally-spaced points.

4.5.1   Gaussian Quadrature

$I = \displaystyle\int_a^b \rho(x)f(x)\,dx$ is called by weighted integral.

Consider

$$\int_a^b \rho(x)f(x)\,dx \approx \sum_{k=1}^n A_k f(x_k), \qquad (4.5.1)$$

where $x_i \neq x_j \, (i \neq j)$.

If A_k satisfies

$$A_k = \int_a^b \rho(x) l_k(x)\,dx, \quad l_k(x) = \prod_{\substack{j=1 \\ j \neq k}}^n \dfrac{(x - x_j)}{(x_k - x_j)}, \quad k = 0,1,2,\cdots,n,$$

then (4.5.1) is interpolating quadrature formula.

Theorem 4.5.1   (4.5.1) has at least $(n-1)$-th degree of accuracy if and only if (4.5.1) is interpolating quadrature.

Question   Are there $\{x_k\}, \{A_k\}$, such that (4.5.1) has $(2n-1)$-th degree of accuracy?

Definition 4.5.1   If (4.5.1) has $(2n-1)$-th degree of accuracy, then (4.5.1) is called by Gaussian quadrature, $\{x_k\}$ is called Gaussian points.

Remark 4.5.1   Taking $f(x) = x^i, i = 1,2,\cdots,2n-1$, we get

$$\sum_{k=1}^n A_k x_k^i = \int_a^b \rho(x) x^i dx, \quad i = 0,1,\cdots,2n-1. \qquad (4.5.2)$$

For example, if $n = 1$, then

$$A_1 = \int_a^b \rho(x)\,dx, \quad A_1 x_1 = \int_a^b x\rho(x)\,dx.$$

So

$$x_1 = \frac{\int_a^b x\rho(x)\,dx}{\int_a^b \rho(x)\,dx}, \quad A_1 = \int_a^b \rho(x)\,dx.$$

If $\rho(x) \equiv 1$, then

$$x_1 = \frac{\frac{b^2 - a^2}{2}}{b - a} = \frac{b + a}{2}, \quad A_1 = b - a.$$

The formula $\int_a^b f(x)\,dx \approx (b - a) f\left(\frac{b + a}{2}\right)$ is middle rectangle rule.

Remark 4.5.2 n points Gaussian quadrature is interpolating quadrature. So one should give $\{x_k\}$, then $A_k = \int_a^b \rho(x) l_k(x)\,dx$ or (4.5.2).

Theorem 4.5.2 n distinct points $x_k(k = 0, 1, 2, \cdots, n)$ are Gaussian points of Gaussian quadrature if and only if $\omega_n(x) = \prod_{k=1}^n (x - x_k)$ is orthogonal to less than $(n - 1)$-th polynomial with weighted function $\rho(x)$, i.e.

$$\int_a^b \rho(x) \omega_n(x) x^j\,dx = 0, \quad j = 0, 1, \cdots, n - 1. \tag{4.5.3}$$

Proof If $\{x_k\}_{k=1}^n$ are Gaussian points, then

$$\int_a^b \rho(x) f(x)\,dx \approx \sum_{k=1}^n A_k f(x_k)$$

is exact for $(2n - 1)$-th polynomial $\omega_n(x) x^j$, $j = 0, \cdots, n - 1$. That is

$$\int_a^b \rho(x) \omega_n(x) x^j\,dx = \sum_{k=1}^n A_k \omega_n(x_k) x_k^j.$$

Note $\omega_n(x_k) = 0$ ($k = 1, 2, \cdots, n$), so we have

$$\int_a^b \rho(x) \omega_n(x) x^j\,dx = 0, \quad j = 0, \cdots, n - 1.$$

Assume that $\{x_k\}_{k=1}^n$ and $\int_a^b \rho(x) f(x)\,dx \approx \sum_{k=1}^n A_k f(x_k)$, then

$$f(x) = \omega_n(x) p(x) + q(x),$$
$$f(x_k) = \omega_n(x_k) p(x_k) + q(x_k) = q(x_k),$$

and the degree of $p(x)$, $q(x)$ satisfies $\leq n - 1$. So

$$\int_a^b \rho(x)f(x)\,dx = \int_a^b \rho(x)\omega_n(x)p(x)\,dx + \int_a^b \rho(x)q(x)\,dx$$

$$= \int_a^b \rho(x)q(x)\,dx$$

$$= \sum_{k=1}^n A_k q(x_k)$$

$$= \sum_{k=1}^n A_k f(x_k).$$

Therefore, $\{x_k\}_{k=1}^n$ are Gaussian points.

4.5.2 Orthogonal Polynomial

(1) Orthogonal polynomial $\{\varphi_m(x)\}$ with $\rho(x)$, $\varphi_m(x)$ has only m zeroes, and $q(x) \leqslant m-1$,

$$\int_a^b \rho(x)\varphi_m(x)q(x)\,dx = 0.$$

(2) $\{g_m(x)\}$ is another orthogonal polynomial with $\rho(x)$, then $g_m(x) = c_m \varphi_m(x)$, $m = 0,1,2,\cdots$.

Given $x_1, x_2, \cdots, x_n$ are n zeroes of $\varphi_n(x)$ and $\omega_n(x) = \prod_{k=1}^n (x - x_k)$, then $\varphi_n(x) = a_n \omega_n(x)$, and

$$\int_a^b \rho(x)\omega_n(x)q(x)\,dx = a_n^{-1}\int_a^b \rho(x)\varphi_n(x)q(x)\,dx = 0.$$

So $x_1, x_2, \cdots, x_n$ are Gaussian points.

If $x_1, x_2, \cdots, x_n$ are Gaussian points, then

$$\int_a^b \rho(x)\omega_n(x)q(x)\,dx = 0,$$

the degree of $q(x)$ satisfies $\leqslant n-1$,

$$(\omega_n, \varphi_k) = \int_a^b \rho(x)\omega_n(x)\varphi_k(x)\,dx = 0, \quad 0 \leqslant k \leqslant n-1$$

and $\omega_n(x) = \sum_{j=0}^n a_j \varphi_j(x).$

So $(\omega_n, \varphi_k) = \alpha_k(\varphi_k, \varphi_k)$, namely $\alpha_n = \dfrac{(\omega_n, \varphi_n)}{(\varphi_n, \varphi_n)}$, $\alpha_k = 0, 0 \leqslant k \leqslant n-1$,

$$\omega_n(x) = \alpha_n \varphi_n(x).$$

It shows that $x_1, x_2, \cdots, x_n$ are zeroes of $\varphi_n(x)$.

Theorem 4.5.3 n points Gaussian quadrature exists, and the Gaussian points are the zeroes of $\varphi_n(x)$ of the orthogonal polynomial of $\{\varphi_m(x)\}$.

4.5.3 Error of Gaussian Quadrature

$$E_n(f) = \int_a^b \rho(x)f(x)\,dx - \sum_{k=1}^n A_k f(x_k).$$

Denote $\omega_n(x) = \prod_{k=1}^n (x - x_k)$, we have

Theorem 4.5.4 If $f(x) \in C^{2n}[a,b]$, then

$$E_n(f) = \frac{f^{(2n)}(\xi)}{(2n)!}(\omega_n, \omega_n), \tag{4.5.4}$$

where $\xi \in [a,b]$, $(\omega_n, \omega_n) = \int_a^b \rho(x)\omega_n^2(x)\,dx$.

Proof $(2n-1)$-th Hermite interpolation $h(x)$ satisfies

$$h(x_i) = f(x_i), \quad h'(x_i) = f'(x_i), \quad i = 1, 2, \cdots, n.$$

So

$$h(x) = \sum_{i=1}^n l_i^2(x)(\alpha_i x + \beta_i)f(x_i) + \sum_{i=1}^n l_i^2(x)(x - x_i)f'(x_i),$$

where $\alpha_i = -2l_i'(x_i), \beta_i = 1 - \alpha_i x_i, i = 1, 2, \cdots, n$.

Letting $r(x) = f(x) - h(x)$, then we have

$$r(x) = \frac{f^{(2n)}(\tilde{\xi})}{(2n)!}\omega_n^2(x), \quad a < \tilde{\xi} < b,$$

$$\int_a^b \rho(x)r(x)\,dx = \frac{1}{(2n)!}\int_a^b \rho(x)f^{(2n)}(\tilde{\xi})\omega_n^2(x)\,dx = \frac{f^{(2n)}(\xi)}{(2n)!}(\omega_n, \omega_n).$$

Since $h(x)$ is $(2n-1)$-th polynomial, then

$$\int_a^b \rho(x)r(x)\,dx = \int_a^b \rho(x)f(x)\,dx - \int_a^b \rho(x)h(x)\,dx$$

$$= \int_a^b \rho(x)f(x)\,dx - \sum_{k=1}^n A_k h(x_k)$$

$$= E_n(f).$$

Theorem 4.5.5 A_k of Gaussian quadrature is positive.

Proof Define $q_j(x) = \prod_{\substack{k=1 \\ k \neq j}}^n \frac{(x - x_k)^2}{(x_j - x_k)^2}, j = 1, 2, \cdots, n$, then

$$\int_a^b \rho(x) q_j(x) \, dx = \sum_{i=1}^n A_i q_j(x) = A_j > 0.$$

The error of $f(x_k)$ is $\xi_k, k = 1, 2, \cdots, n$,

$$E = \sum_{k=1}^n A_k \xi_k,$$

$$|E| \leq \sum_{k=1}^n A_k |\xi_k| \leq \xi \left(\sum_{k=1}^n A_k \right) = \xi \int_a^b \rho(x) \, dx,$$

where $\xi = \max_{1 \leq k \leq n} |\xi_k|$.

Therefore, if $[a,b]$ is finite, then Gaussian quadrature is stable.

4.5.4 Special Gaussian Quadrature

Letting $x = \dfrac{a+b}{2} + \dfrac{b-a}{2} t$, the interval from $[a,b]$ to $[-1,1]$, then

$$\int_a^b f(x) \, dx = \frac{b-a}{2} \int_{-1}^1 f\left(\frac{a+b}{2} + \frac{b-a}{2} t \right) dt.$$

So Gaussian quadrature in $[-1,1]$ is important.

Example 4.5.1 2 points Gauss-Legendre quadrature:

$$\int_{-1}^1 f(x) \, dx \approx A_0 f(x_0) + A_1 f(x_1),$$

$$L_2(x) = \frac{1}{2}(3x^2 - 1),$$

$$x_0 = -\frac{1}{\sqrt{3}}, \quad x_1 = \frac{1}{\sqrt{3}}.$$

Use the definition of degree of accuracy, we have $A_0 = A_1 = 1$.

a) Gauss-Legendre Quadrature

Legendre polynomial:

$$L_n(x) = \frac{1}{2^n n!} \frac{d^n}{dx^n} (x^2 - 1)^n, \quad n \geq 1,$$

$$L_0(x) = 1, \quad x \in [-1,1], \quad \rho(x) \equiv 1.$$

Gauss-Legendre quadrature:

$$\int_{-1}^1 f(x) \, dx \approx \sum_{k=1}^n A_k f(x_k),$$

where x_k is zero of $L_k(x)$, $A_k = \int_{-1}^1 l_k(x) \, dx$,

$$l_k(x) = \prod_{\substack{i=1 \\ k \neq i}}^{n} \frac{x - x_i}{x_k - x_i}, \quad k = 1, 2, \cdots, n.$$

The Gaussian points and coefficients of Gauss-Legendre rule are given in the following table 4.5.1.

Table 4.5.1 The Gaussian points and coefficients for Gauss-Legendre quadrature

n	x_k	A_k
1	$x_1 = 0.0$	$A_1 = 2$
2	$x_1 = -x_2 = -0.57735$	$A_1 = A_2 = 1$
3	$x_1 = -x_3 = -0.7745906692, x_2 = 0$	$A_1 = A_3 = \frac{5}{9}, A_2 = \frac{8}{9}$
4	$x_1 = -x_4 = -0.8611363116$	$A_1 = A_4 = 0.3478548451$
	$x_2 = -x_3 = -0.3399810436$	$A_2 = A_3 = 0.6521451549$
5	$x_1 = -x_5 = -0.9061798459$	$A_1 = A_5 = 0.2369268851$
	$x_2 = -x_4 = -0.5384693101, x_3 = 0$	$A_2 = A_4 = 0.4786286705, A_3 = 0.5688888889$

b) Gauss-Chebyshev Quadrature

Chebyshev polynomial $T_n(x) = \cos(n \arccos x)$, $-1 \leq x \leq 1$ is orthogonal polynomial with $\rho(x) = (1 - x^2)^{-\frac{1}{2}}$ in $[-1, 1]$.

n zeroes: $x_k = \cos \frac{2k-1}{2n} \pi, k = 1, 2, \cdots, n.$

n points Gauss-Chebyshev quadrature:

$$\int_{-1}^{1} \frac{1}{\sqrt{1-x^2}} f(x) \, dx \approx \sum_{k=1}^{n} A_k f(x_k) = \frac{\pi}{n} \sum_{k=1}^{n} f(x_k),$$

$$A_k = \int_{-1}^{1} \frac{1}{\sqrt{1-x^2}} l_k(x) \, dx$$

$$\xlongequal{x = \cos\theta} \int_{\pi}^{0} \frac{1}{\sin\theta} (-\sin\theta) \prod_{\substack{i=1 \\ i \neq k}}^{n} \frac{\cos\theta - \cos\frac{2i-1}{2n}\pi}{\cos\frac{2k-1}{2n}\pi - \cos\frac{2i-1}{2n}\pi} \, d\theta,$$

$$l_k(x) = \prod_{\substack{i=1 \\ i \neq k}}^{n} \frac{x - x_i}{x_k - x_i}, \quad k = 1, 2, \cdots, n.$$

Example 4.5.2 5 points Gauss quadrature: $I = \int_{-1}^{1} \frac{e^x}{\sqrt{1-x^2}} dx.$

Solution
$$f(x) = e^x, \quad \rho(x) = \frac{1}{\sqrt{1-x^2}},$$

$$I \approx \frac{\pi}{5} \sum_{k=1}^{n} e^{\cos\frac{2k-1}{2n}\pi} \approx 3.977463,$$

$$|R(f)| \leq \frac{n}{2^9 \times 10!} \leq 4.6 \times 10^{-9}.$$

Example 4.5.3 Use Gauss quadrature: $I = \int_0^{\frac{\pi}{2}} x^2 \cos x \, dx.$

Solution
$$x = \frac{a+b}{2} + \frac{b-a}{2}t = \frac{\pi}{4} + \frac{\pi}{4}t,$$

$$I = \int_{-1}^{1} \frac{\pi^2}{4^2}(1+t)^2 \cos\frac{\pi}{4}(1+t) \frac{\pi}{4} dt$$

$$= \int_{-1}^{1} \left(\frac{\pi}{4}\right)^3 (1+t)^2 \cos\frac{\pi}{4}(1+t) dt.$$

Use 4 points Gauss-Legendre quadrature:

$$I \approx \sum_{k=1}^{4} A_k f(x_k)$$

$$= 0.3478548 \times [f(-0.8611363) + f(0.8611363)]$$
$$+ 0.6521451 \times [f(-0.3399810436) + f(0.3399810436)]$$
$$\approx 0.467402 \, (I = 0.467401\cdots),$$

$$f(t) = \left(\frac{\pi}{4}\right)^3 (1+t)^2 \cos\frac{\pi}{4}(1+t).$$

c) Gauss-Laguerre Quadrature

Laguerre polynomial: $x \in [0, +\infty]$, $\rho(x) = e^{-x}$,

$$L_n(x) = e^x \frac{d^n}{dx^n}(x^n e^{-x}),$$

$$\int_0^{+\infty} e^{-x} f(x) dx \approx \sum_{k=1}^{n} A_k f(x_k),$$

$x_1, x_2, \cdots, x_n$ are zeroes of $L_n(x)$,

$$A_k = \frac{(n!)^2}{[L_n'(x_k)]^2 x_k}, \quad k = 1, 2, \cdots, n.$$

The Gaussian points and coefficients of Gauss-Laguerre rule are given in the following table 4.5.2.

Table 4.5.2 The Gaussian points and coefficients for Gauss-Laguerre quadrature

n	x_k		A_k	
1	1		1	
2	0.585786438	3.414213562	0.853553391	0.146446609
3	0.415774557	2.294280360	0.711093010	0.278517734
	6.289945083		0.010389257	
⋮	⋮		⋮	

Example 4.5.4 $I = \int_0^{+\infty} e^{-x}\sin x\, dx$, $f(x) = \sin x$.

Solution 2 points Gauss-Laguerre quadrature:

$$I \approx \int_0^{+\infty} e^{-x}\sin x\, dx, \quad f(x) = \sin x,$$

$I = 0.853553391 \times \sin(0.585786438) + 0.146446609 \times \sin(3.414213562)$.

d) Gauss-Hermite Quadrature

$$x \in (-\infty, +\infty), \quad \rho(x) = e^{-x^2},$$

$$H_n(x) = (-1)^n e^{x^2}\frac{d^n}{dx^n}e^{-x^2}, \quad n = 0, 1, \cdots,$$

$$\int_{-\infty}^{+\infty} e^{-x^2}f(x)\, dx \approx \sum_{k=1}^{n} A_k f(x_k),$$

$$A_k = 2^{n+1} n! \frac{\sqrt{\pi}}{[H_n'(x_k)]^2}.$$

The Gaussian points and coefficients of Gauss-Hermite rule are given in the following table 4.5.3.

Table 4.5.3 The Gaussian points and coefficients for Gauss-Hermite quadrature

n	x_k	A_k
1	0	1.772453851
2	±0.707106781	0.886226926
3	±1.224744871	0.295408975
	0	1.181635901
⋮	⋮	⋮

Example 4.5.5 Use 2 points Gauss-Hermite quadrature calculate $\int_{-\infty}^{+\infty} x^2 e^{-x^2} dx$.

Solution

$$H_2(x) = 4x^2 - 2 \Rightarrow A_1 = 2^3 \times 2 \times \frac{\sqrt{\pi}}{2^6 \times \frac{1}{2}},$$

$$x_1 = -\frac{\sqrt{2}}{2}, \quad x_2 = \frac{\sqrt{2}}{2}, \quad A_1 = A_2 = \frac{\sqrt{\pi}}{2},$$

$$\int_{-\infty}^{+\infty} e^{-x^2} x^2 \, dx \approx \frac{\sqrt{\pi}}{2}\left[\left(-\frac{\sqrt{2}}{2}\right)^2 + \left(\frac{\sqrt{2}}{2}\right)^2\right] = \frac{\sqrt{\pi}}{2}.$$

e) General Gaussian Quadrature

When the weight function is not special function.

Example 4.5.6 $\int_0^1 \sqrt{x} f(x) \, dx \approx A_0 f(x_0) + A_1 f(x_1).$

Solution 1 $f(x) = 1, x, x^2, x^3$ are exact.

$$\begin{cases} A_0 + A_1 = \frac{2}{3}, \\ A_0 x_0 + A_1 x_1 = \frac{2}{5}, \\ A_0 x_0^2 + A_1 x_1^2 = \frac{2}{7}, \\ A_0 x_0^3 + A_1 x_1^3 = \frac{2}{9} \end{cases} \Rightarrow \begin{cases} x_0 = 0.821162, \\ x_1 = 0.289949, \\ A_0 = 0.389111, \\ A_1 = 0.277556. \end{cases}$$

$$\int_0^1 \sqrt{x} f(x) \, dx \approx 0.389111 \times f(0.821162) + 0.277556 \times f(0.289949).$$

Solution 2

$$w_2(x) = (x - x_0)(x - x_1) = x^2 + bx + c,$$

$$\int_0^1 \sqrt{x}(x^2 + bx + c) \, dx = 0,$$

$$\int_0^1 \sqrt{x}(x^2 + bx + c) x \, dx = 0,$$

$$\Rightarrow \begin{cases} \frac{2}{7} + \frac{2}{5}b + \frac{2}{3}c = 0, \\ \frac{2}{9} + \frac{2}{7}b + \frac{2}{5}c = 0 \end{cases} \Rightarrow b = -\frac{10}{9}, c = \frac{5}{21}, w_2(x) = x^2 - \frac{10}{9}x + \frac{5}{21},$$

$$\Rightarrow x_0 = 0.289949, x_1 = 0.821162.$$

Taking $f(x) = 1, x$, we have

$$\begin{cases} A_0 + A_1 = \int_0^1 \sqrt{x}\,dx = \dfrac{2}{3}, \\ A_0 x_0 + A_1 x_1 = \int_0^1 \sqrt{x} \cdot x\,dx = \dfrac{2}{5} \end{cases}$$

$$\Rightarrow A_0 = 0.277556, A_1 = 0.389111.$$

§4.6 Numerical Differentiation

If $f'(a)$ exists, then the derivative of the function f at a is

$$\lim_{h \to 0} \frac{f(a+h) - f(a)}{h} = f'(a),$$

$$\lim_{h \to 0} \frac{f(a) - f(a-h)}{h} = f'(a),$$

$$\lim_{h \to 0} \frac{f(a+h) - f(a-h)}{2h} = f'(a).$$

Forward divided difference:

$$G_1(h) = \frac{f(a+h) - f(a)}{h}.$$

Backward divided difference:

$$G_{-1}(h) = \frac{f(a) - f(a-h)}{h}.$$

$$G_0(h) = f'(a) + \sum_{i=1}^{m} c_i h^{2i} + o(h^{2(m+1)}).$$

$$f(a+h) = f(a) + hf'(a) + \frac{h^2}{2}f''(a) + \frac{h^3}{3!}f'''(a) + \cdots,$$

$$f(a-h) = f(a) + (-h)f'(a) + \frac{h^2}{2}f''(a) - \frac{h^3}{3!}f'''(a) + \cdots,$$

$$G_0(h) = \frac{2hf'(a) + \dfrac{2h^3}{3!}f'''(a) + \cdots}{2h} = f'(a) + \frac{h^2}{3!}f'''(a) + \cdots.$$

Richardson extrapolation: as for Romberg

$$G_0^1(h) = \frac{4G_0\left(\dfrac{h}{2}\right) - G_0(h)}{4 - 1}, \quad \text{"}h\text{: the length of step"}.$$

Centre divided difference:

$$G_0(h) = \frac{f(a+h) - f(a-h)}{2h}.$$

By Taylor's formula, we have

$$E_1 = f'(a) - G_1(h) = -\frac{h}{2}f''(a) - \frac{h^2}{6}f'''(\xi_1),$$

$$E_{-1} = f'(a) - G_{-1}(h) = \frac{h}{2}f''(a) - \frac{h^2}{6}f'''(\xi_2).$$

Richardson extrapolation $f'(a) - G_m(h) = o(h^{2m+2})$.

$$E_0 = f'(a) - G_0(h) = -\sum_{i=1}^{m} c_i h^{2i} - \frac{h^{2m+2}}{(2m+3)!} f^{(2m+3)}(\xi).$$

$$f''(a) \approx \frac{1}{h^2}[f(a+h) + f(a-h) - 2f(a)],$$

$$g_1(h) = \frac{G_1(h) - G_{-1}(h)}{h},$$

$$f''(a) - g_1(h) = \frac{h^2}{12} f^{(4)}(\xi).$$

Interpolating numerical differentiation:

$$x_0, x_1, \cdots, x_n,$$
$$f(x_0), f(x_1), \cdots, f(x_n),$$
$$f(x) \approx P_n(x).$$

n-th Lagrange interpolation polynomial:

$$f'(x) \approx P_n'(x),$$

$$f'(x) - P_n'(x) = \frac{f^{(n+1)}(\xi)}{(n+1)!} w_n'(x) + \frac{w_n(x)}{(n+1)!} \frac{d}{dx} f^{(n+1)}(\xi),$$

$$f'(x_k) - P_n'(x_k) = \frac{f^{(n+1)}(\xi)}{(n+1)!} w_n'(x_k).$$

Letting $x = a + \lambda h$, then three points

$$x_0 = a - h, \quad x_1 = a, \quad x_2 = a + h,$$

$$P_2(x) = P_2(a + \lambda h)$$
$$= \frac{\lambda}{2}(\lambda - 1)f(x_0) + (1 - \lambda^2)f(x_1) + \frac{\lambda}{2}(\lambda + 1)f(x_2)$$
$$+ \frac{1}{3!}(x - x_0)(x - x_1)(x - x_2) + \frac{h^3}{3!}\lambda(\lambda + 1)(\lambda - 1),$$

$$P_2'(x) = \frac{1}{h}\left[\left(\lambda - \frac{1}{2}\right)f(x_0) - 2\lambda f(x_1) + \left(\lambda + \frac{1}{2}\right)f(x_2)\right],$$

$$P_2''(x) = \frac{1}{h^2}[f(x_0) - 2f(x_1) + f(x_2)].$$

When $x = x_1$, $\lambda = 0$, then we have

$$f'(a) \approx P_2'(a) = \frac{f(a+h) - f(a-h)}{2h},$$

$$f''(a) \approx P_2''(a) = \frac{1}{h^2}[f(a+h) + f(a-h) - 2f(a)].$$

Three points formula: $x = x_0$, $\lambda = -1$,

$$f'(x_0) = \frac{1}{h}\left[-\frac{3}{2}f(x_0) + 2f(x_1) - \frac{1}{2}f(x_2)\right],$$

$$f'(x_0) \approx \frac{1}{2h}[-3f(x_0) + 4f(x_1) - f(x_2)] + \frac{h^2}{3}f'''(\xi_1),$$

$$f'(x_2) \approx \frac{1}{2h}[f(x_0) - 4f(x_1) + 3f(x_2)] + \frac{h^2}{3}f'''(\xi_2).$$

Excises 4

4.1 Determine the undetermined coefficients and the values of the nodes in the following quadrature formula so that the algebraic precision of the formula is as high as possible and that the formula has several algebraic precision.

(1) $\int_{-2h}^{2h} f(x) dx \approx Af(-h) + Bf(0) + Cf(h);$

(2) $\int_{-1}^{1} f(x) dx \approx \frac{1}{3}[f(-1) + 2f(x_1) + 3f(x_2)];$

(3) $\int_{-h}^{h} f(x) dx \approx Af(-h) + Bf(x_1).$

4.2 Let n be an even number, and the node is symmetric about the origin of the coordinates on interval $[-1,1]$. If the formula

$$\int_{-1}^{1} f(x) dx \approx \sum_{k=0}^{n} A_k f(x_k)$$

for all polynomial functions of degree n, prove that it is also true for all polynomial functions of degree $n+1$.

4.3 Calculating the following integral with trapezoidal formula and Simpson formula.

(1) $\int_0^1 \dfrac{x}{4+x^2}dx, n=8$;

(2) $\int_1^9 \sqrt{x}\,dx, n=4$;

(3) $\int_0^{\frac{\pi}{6}} \sqrt{4-\sin^2\varphi}\,d\varphi, n=6$.

4.4 Use the trapezoidal formula and the Simpson formula to calculate
$\int_{-1}^1 f(x)\,dx \approx A_1 f(-1) + A_2 f(-\dfrac{1}{3}) + A_3 f(\dfrac{1}{3})$ and analyze the error bounds and the error bounds estimated by the remainder of the integral formula.

4.5 Solve the coefficients A_1, A_2 and A_3, such that the integration formula
$$\int_{-1}^1 f(x)\,dx \approx A_1 f(-1) + A_2 f(-\dfrac{1}{3}) + A_3 f(\dfrac{1}{3})$$
is exact for all polynomials whose degrees are not less than 2.

4.6 (The error of the trapezoidal quadrature formula) Give the proof of the residual expression of the trapezoidal quadrature formula. i.e. To prove that if $f \in C^2[a,b]$, then there is $\eta \in [a,b]$, such that
$$\int_a^b f(x)\,dx - \dfrac{b-a}{2}[f(a)+f(b)] = -\dfrac{(b-a)^3}{12}f''(\eta).$$

4.7 Using the Simpson formula to calculate $\int_0^1 e^{-x}\,dx$ and estimate the error.

4.8 Calculate $\int_1^{15} x^2 \ln x\,dx$ by the adaptive integral of Simpson formula, and make the error does not exceed 10^{-3}.

4.9 (Simpson quadrature formula error) Prove that: if $f \in C^4[a,b]$, then there is $\eta \in [a,b]$ such that
$$\int_a^b f(x)\,dx - \dfrac{b-a}{6}[f(a)+4f(\dfrac{a+b}{2})+f(b)] = -\dfrac{(b-a)^3}{2880}f^{(4)}(\eta).$$

4.10 If using the compound trapezoidal formula to calculate the integral $\int_0^1 e^x\,dx$, how many equal part should be divided with the interval $[0,1]$ to make the truncation error does not exceed $\dfrac{1}{2} \times 10^{-5}$?

If switching to composite Simpson formula, how many should be divided to achieve the same accuracy?

4.11 Prove that the results obtained by using the trapezoidal formula are larger than the exact value if $f''(x) > 0$ and explain the geometric significance.

4.12 If the composite trapezoidal formula and compound Simpson formula are used to calculate the integral

$$\int_1^3 e^x \sin x \, dx,$$

request truncation error does not exceed 10^{-4} (rounding error), ask the number of function value on the nodes need to be calculated.

4.13 Let $f \in C^2[a,b]$, $[a, b]$ be divided into n subintervals, the length of which is $h = \dfrac{b-a}{n}$, the midpoint of the subinterval is

$$x_k = a + \left(k - \frac{1}{2}\right)h, \quad k = 1, 2, \cdots, n.$$

Try to deduce the following compound midpoint formula:

$$\int_a^b f(x) \, dx = h \sum_{k=1}^n f(x_k) + \frac{(b-a)h^2}{24} f''(\eta), \quad \eta \in [a,b].$$

4.14 (1) The composite trapezoidal formula divides $[a, b]$ into n subintervals, $h = \dfrac{b-a}{n}$, indicating that when n is a large integer, the error is approximately equal to $-\dfrac{h^2}{12}[f'(b) - f'(a)]$.

(2) For the composite midpoint formula and the composite Simpson formula, we derive the error approximation similar to (1).

4.15 Let $f \in C^4[a,b]$, prove the following formula with derivative values

$$\int_a^b f(x) \, dx = \frac{b-a}{2}[f(a) + f(b)] + \frac{(b-a)^2}{12}[f'(a) - f'(b)]$$

$$+ \frac{(b-a)^5}{720} f^{(4)}(\eta),$$

where $\eta \in [a,b]$.

4.16 Supposed that the error of the integration formula has the asymptotic expansion

$$I - I_n = \frac{c_1}{n\sqrt{n}} + \frac{c_2}{n^2} + \frac{c_3}{n^2\sqrt{n}} + \frac{c_4}{n^3} + \cdots.$$

Try to promote Richardson extrapolation. If we know the value I_n, I_{2n}, I_{4n}, compute the estimate value of I by using this such that the errors have the order of $1/(n^2\sqrt{n})$.

4.17 Using the Romberg algorithm to calculate $\int_0^1 e^x dx$.

4.18 Calculated the following integral by the Romberg quadrature method, and make the error does not exceed 10^{-5}.

(1) $\dfrac{2}{\sqrt{\pi}} \int_0^1 e^{-x} dx$;

(2) $\int_0^{2\pi} x\sin x dx$;

(3) $\int_0^3 x\sqrt{1+x^2} dx$.

4.19 Prove the equation

$$n\sin\frac{\pi}{n} = \frac{\pi}{n} - \frac{\pi^3}{3! n^2} + \frac{\pi^5}{5! n^4} - \cdots.$$

Approximately π by extrapolation algorithm with the value of $n\sin\dfrac{\pi}{n}(n=3,6,12)$.

4.20 Using the following method to calculate integral $\int_1^3 \dfrac{dy}{y}$ and compare the results.

(1) Romberg method;

(2) Gauss formula with three points and five point;

(3) Using two points compound Gaussian formula when the interval divided into four equal parts.

4.21 Use the extrapolation method to calculate the derivative value of $f(x) = xe^x$ at $x = 2.0$, $h = 0.2$.

4.22 Calculate by the Gauss type quadrature formula with $n=1$ and $n=2$:

$$I = \int_1^{1.5} e^{-x^2} dx.$$

And compare that with the Romberg method.

4.23 Constructing the Gaussian quadrature formula

$$\int_0^1 \frac{1}{\sqrt{x}} f(x) dx \approx A_0 f(x_0) + A_1 f(x_1).$$

4.24 Calculate the integral

$$I = \int_{-1}^{1} (1 - x^2)^{\frac{3}{2}} \cos x \, dx.$$

(1) With three points Gauss-Legendre formula;

(2) With three points Gauss-Chebyshev formula.

4.25 Calculate the integral $\int_{1}^{3} e^x \sin x \, dx$ using the Gaussian-Legendre formula when $n = 2, 3$.

4.26 Calculate the integral $\int_{0}^{+\infty} \dfrac{e^{-x}}{1 + e^{-2x}} dx$ using the Gauss-Laguerre formula when $n = 2$.

4.27 Prove that the algebraic precision of the quadrature formula of $n + 1$ nodes:

$$\int_{a}^{b} \rho(x) f(x) \, dx \approx \sum_{k=0}^{n} A_k f(x_k)$$

(where $\rho(x)$ is the weight function) does not exceed $2n + 1$.

4.28 Let $x_0, x_1, \cdots, x_n$ as nodes on the interval $[a, b]$, then Gauss type quadrature formula is

$$\int_{a}^{b} \rho(x) f(x) \, dx \approx \sum_{k=0}^{n} A_k f(x_k).$$

Prove that:

(1) $A_k > 0, k = 0, 1, \cdots, n$.

(2) $\sum_{k=0}^{n} A_k = \int_{a}^{b} \rho(x) \, dx.$

(3) If there is error ε_k, $\varepsilon_k \leq \varepsilon, k = 0, 1, \cdots, n$ when calculate $f(x_k)$, then the error of the formula $\sum_{k=0}^{n} A_k f(x_k)$ does not exceed $\varepsilon \int_{a}^{b} \rho(x) \, dx$.

4.29 Determine the nodes x_0, x_1 and coefficients A_0, A_1 of the quadrature formula

$$\int_{0}^{1} \sqrt{x} f(x) \, dx \approx A_0 f(x_0) + A_1 f(x_1),$$

such that the quadrature formula has the highest algebraic accuracy.

4.30 Prove that if $f \in C^{2n+2}[a, b]$, then there is $\eta \in [a, b]$ such that the remainder of the Gaussian quadrature formula

$$\int_{a}^{b} \rho(x) f(x) \, dx - \sum_{k=0}^{n} A_k f(x_k) = \frac{f^{(2n+2)}(\eta)}{(2n+2)!} \int_{a}^{b} \rho(x) [\omega_{n+1}(x)]^2 \, dx,$$

where $\omega_{n+1}(x) = (x - x_0)(x - x_1)\cdots(x - x_n)$.

4.31 Suppose that $f \in C^3[a,b]$, $x_0 - h, x_0, x_0 + h$ are in $[a, b]$, try to derive the central difference scheme for calculating $f'(x_0)$ and its errors:
$$f'(x_0) = \frac{1}{2h}[f(x_0 + h) - f(x_0 - 2h)] - \frac{h^2}{6}f'''(\eta),$$
where $\eta \in [x_0 - h, x_0 + h]$.

4.32 Using the three formulas to find derivative values of $f(x) = \dfrac{1}{(1+x)^2}$ at point $x = 1.0, 1.1, 1.2$ and estimate errors, where the value of $f(x)$ as follows:

x	1.0	1.1	1.2
$f(x)$	0.250	0.2268	0.2066

4.33 Derive the numerical differential formula by interpolation formula:
$$f'(x_0) = \frac{1}{2h}[-3f(x_0) + 4f(x_0 + h) - f(x_0 + 2h)] + \frac{h^2}{3}f'''(\eta),$$
where $\eta \in [a,b]$, suppose that $x_0, x_0 + 2h$ are in $[a, b]$, $f \in C^3[a,b]$.

Chapter 5 Solving Linear System of Equations

Linear system of equations is associated with many problems in engineering and science, as well as with application of mathematics to the social sciences and the quantitative study of business and economic problems.

The linear system of equations is

$$\begin{cases} a_{11}x_1 + a_{12}x_2 + \cdots + a_{1n}x_n = b_1, \\ a_{21}x_1 + a_{22}x_2 + \cdots + a_{2n}x_n = b_2, \\ \cdots\cdots \\ a_{n1}x_1 + a_{n2}x_2 + \cdots + a_{nn}x_n = b_n. \end{cases}$$

Then the system can be written in the matrix form as

$$AX = b,$$

where

$$A = \begin{pmatrix} a_{11} & a_{12} & \cdots & a_{1n} \\ a_{21} & a_{22} & \cdots & a_{2n} \\ \vdots & \vdots & & \vdots \\ a_{n1} & a_{n2} & \cdots & a_{nn} \end{pmatrix}, \quad X = \begin{pmatrix} x_1 \\ \vdots \\ x_n \end{pmatrix}, \quad b = \begin{pmatrix} b_1 \\ \vdots \\ b_n \end{pmatrix}.$$

We have direct methods and iterative methods. Direct techniques are methods that give an answer in a fixed number of steps, subject only to round-off errors.

§5.1 Elementary Notions and Results of Linear Algebra

5.1.1 Norms of Vector

Definition 5.1.1 A vector norm on $\mathbf{R}^n$ is a function $\|\cdot\|$, from $\mathbf{R}^n$ to $\mathbf{R}$ with the following properties:

(I) $\|x\| \geq 0$ for all $x \in \mathbf{R}^n$;
(II) $\|x\| = 0$ if and only if $x = \mathbf{0}$;
(III) $\|\alpha x\| = |\alpha| \cdot \|x\|$ for all $\alpha \in \mathbf{R}$ and $x \in \mathbf{R}^n$;
(IV) $\|x + y\| \leq \|x\| + \|y\|$ for all $x, y \in \mathbf{R}^n$.

Definition 5.1.2 p-norm of vector $x = (x_1, x_2, \cdots, x_n)^T$ is defined by

$$\|x\| = \left(\sum_{i=1}^{n} |x_i|^p \right)^{1/p}, p \in [1, +\infty). \qquad (5.1.1)$$

For example, p are taken as 1 and 2, we have

$$1\text{-norm}: \|x\| = \sum_{i=1}^{n} |x_i|; \qquad (5.1.2)$$

$$2\text{-norm}: \|x\| = \left(\sum_{i=1}^{n} |x_i|^2 \right)^{1/2}; \qquad (5.1.3)$$

$$\infty\text{-norm}: \|x\|_\infty = \max\{|x_1|, \cdots, |x_n|\}. \qquad (5.1.4)$$

The images of 2-dimensional vectors for $\|x\|_2 \leq 1$ and $\|x\|_\infty \leq 1$ are shown in figure 5.1.1.

2-norm is called **the Euclidean norm** of the vector x since it represents the usual notion of distance from the origin in case x is $\mathbf{R}, \mathbf{R}^2$ or $\mathbf{R}^3$.

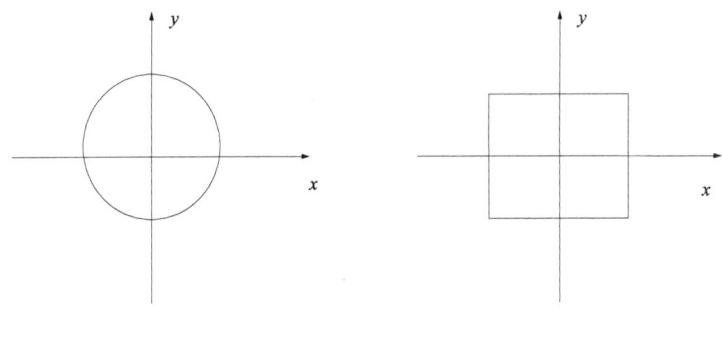

$\|x\|_2 \leq 1$ $\qquad\qquad\qquad$ $\|x\|_\infty \leq 1$

Figure 5.1.1 The images of 2-dimensional vectors x for $\|x\|_2 \leq 1$ and $\|x\|_\infty \leq 1$

The inner product of $\mathbf{R}^n$ is defined by

$$\|x\|_2 = (x, x)^{1/2}.$$

Cauchy-Schwarz is

$$x \cdot y = \sum_{i=1}^{n} (x_i \cdot y_i) \leq \left(\sum_{i=1}^{n} |x_i|^2 \right)^{1/2} \cdot \left(\sum_{i=1}^{n} |y_i|^2 \right)^{1/2} = \|x\| \cdot \|y\|.$$

Namely,
$$|(x,y)| \leq (x,x)^{1/2}(y,y)^{1/2}.$$

Suppose that A is a symmetric and position definition matrix. A-norm: $\|x\|_A = \sqrt{(x,x)_A}$. $(x,x)_A = (Ax,x)$ is inner product.

Theorem 5.1.1 $\|x\|_p$, $\|x\|_q$ are norms of $\mathbf{R}^n$, then there are m and M, such that $x \in \mathbf{R}^n$,
$$m\|x\|_q \leq \|x\|_p \leq M\|x\|_q. \tag{5.1.5}$$

Proof We will prove that $\|x\|_p$ and $\|x\|_2$ are equivalent.

Denote $S = \{y \in \mathbf{R}^n, \|y\|_2 = 1\}$, then S is bounded and completed. Set $\|y\|_p$ is continuous in $\mathbf{R}^n$, then $\|y\|_p$ can reach min and max in S. $\forall x \in \mathbf{R}^n$, $x \neq 0$, then $\dfrac{x}{\|x\|_2} \in S$. So we have
$$m \leq \left\|\frac{x}{\|x\|_2}\right\|_p \leq M.$$

Namely,
$$m\|x\|_2 \leq \|x\|_p \leq M\|x\|_2.$$

Remark 5.1.1 For the norm $\|x\|_p (p = 1, 2, \infty)$, then
$$\|x\|_1/\sqrt{n} \leq \|x\|_2 \leq \|x\|_1,$$
$$\|x\|_\infty \leq \|x\|_1 \leq n\|x\|_\infty, \tag{5.1.6}$$
$$\|x\|_\infty \leq \|x\|_2 \leq \sqrt{n}\|x\|_\infty.$$

5.1.2 Convergence of Vector Sequence

Letting $\{x^{(k)}\}$ ($k = 1, 2, \cdots$) is a sequence of vectors, where
$$x^{(k)} = (x_1^{(k)}, \cdots, x_2^{(k)})^\mathrm{T} \in \mathbf{R}^n.$$

If $\lim\limits_{k \to \infty} x_i^{(k)} = x_i$ ($i = 1, 2, \cdots, n$), then call $\{x^{(k)}\} \to x = (x_1, \cdots, x_n)^\mathrm{T}$.

Namely, $x^{(k)} \to x(k \to \infty)$ if and only if $\lim\limits_{k \to \infty} \|x^{(k)} - x\|_\infty = 0$, where
$$\|x^{(k)} - x\|_\infty = \max\{|x_1^{(k)} - x_1|, \cdots, |x_n^{(k)} - x_n|\}.$$

Theorem 5.1.2 Suppose that $\|x\|$ is a norm of $\mathbf{R}^n$, then $x^{(k)} \to x(k \to \infty)$ if and only if $\|x^{(k)} - x\| \to 0(k \to \infty)$.

5.1.3 Krylov Subspace

Give r_0 and A, k-dimension Krylov Space:

$$K(A, r_0, k) = \text{space}\{r_0, Ar_0, \cdots, A^{k-1} r_0\}.$$

5.1.4 Some Remarks of Matrix

Definition 5.1.3 If $\|x\|$ is a norm of $\mathbf{R}^n$, then

$$\forall A \in \mathbf{R}^{n \times n}, \quad \|A\| = \max_{x \neq 0} \frac{\|Ax\|}{\|x\|} = \max_{\|x\|_1} \|Ax\| \qquad (5.1.7)$$

is called the nature or induced matrix norm associated with the vector norm.

Theorem 5.1.3 The natural matrix norm satisfies:
(I) $\|A\| \geq 0$, $\|A\| = 0$ if and only if $A = \mathbf{0}$;
(II) $\|\alpha A\| = |\alpha| \cdot \|A\|$, $\forall \alpha \in \mathbf{R}$;
(III) $\|A + B\| \leq \|A\| + \|B\|$, $\forall A, B \in \mathbf{R}^{n \times n}$;
(IV) $\|A \cdot x\| \leq \|A\| \cdot \|x\|$, $\forall x \in \mathbf{R}^n$;
(V) $\|A \cdot B\| \leq \|A\| \cdot \|B\|$, $\forall A, B \in \mathbf{R}^{n \times n}$.

Proof (I) ~ (III) are easy to check.
(IV): By $\|A\| = \max\limits_{x \neq 0} \frac{\|Ax\|}{\|x\|}$, we obtain $\|A\| \geq \frac{\|Ax\|}{\|x\|}$. So

$$\|Ax\| \leq \|A\| \|x\|.$$

(V): By (IV), then $\|AB\| = \max\limits_{\|x\|} \|ABx\| \leq \|A\| \max\limits_{\|x\|=1} \|Bx\| \leq \|A\| \|B\|$. Therefore

$$\|AB\| \leq \|A\| \|B\|.$$

Remark 5.1.2 Frobenius norm: $\|A\|_F = \left(\sum\limits_{i=1}^{n} \sum\limits_{j=1}^{n} a_{ij}^2\right)^{1/2}$ is not nature matrix norm, but the matrix norm satisfies (I) ~ (III), except for (IV) ~ (V).

Vector norm: $\|x\|_1$, $\|x\|_2$, $\|x\|_\infty$. From the above vector norms, we can give the natural matrix norm:

$$\|A\|_1 = \max_j \sum_{i=1}^{n} |a_{ij}|. \qquad (5.1.8)$$

Proof For any $x \in \mathbf{R}^n$ and $\|x\|_1 = 1$, then

$$\|Ax\|_1 = \sum_{i=1}^{n} \left| \sum_{j=1}^{n} a_{ij} \cdot x_j \right| \leq \sum_{i=1}^{n} \sum_{j=1}^{n} |a_{ij}| \cdot |x_j| = \sum_{j=1}^{n} |x_j| \cdot \sum_{i=1}^{n} |a_{ij}|$$

$$\leq \left(\max_j \sum_{i=1}^{n} |a_{ij}| \right) \cdot \|x\|_1.$$

So

$$\|A\|_1 \leq \max_j \sum_{i=1}^n |a_{ij}|.$$

Letting $\max_j \sum_{i=1}^n |a_{ij}| = \sum_{i=1}^n |a_{ik}|$ and e_k is the k column of the unit matrix I_n. Then $\|e_k\| = 1$ and

$$\|A\|_1 = \max_{\|x\|_1 = 1} \|Ax\|_1 \geq \|Ae_k\|_1 = \sum_{i=1}^n |a_{ik}| = \max_j \sum_{i=1}^n |a_{ij}|.$$

So, we have

$$\|A\|_1 = \max_j \sum_{i=1}^n |a_{ij}|.$$

Similarly, we can prove the following conclusions:

$$\|A\|_\infty = \max_i \sum_{j=1}^n |a_{ij}|, \tag{5.1.9}$$

$$\|A\|_2 \leq \sqrt{\lambda_{max}},$$

where λ_{max} is the max eigenvalue of $A^T A$.

Example 5.1.1 Assume that $A = \begin{pmatrix} 1 & -2 \\ -3 & 4 \end{pmatrix}$, calculate $\|A\|_p (p = 1,2,\infty)$.

Solution By definition, we have $\|A\|_1 = 6$ and $\|A\|_\infty = 7$.

Since $A^T A = \begin{pmatrix} 10 & -14 \\ -14 & 20 \end{pmatrix}$, so $|\lambda I - A^T A| = \lambda^2 - 30\lambda + 4 = 0$.

Namely, $\lambda = 15 \pm \sqrt{221}$. Therefore

$$\|A\|_2 = \sqrt{15 + \sqrt{221}} \approx 5.46.$$

We introduce the definition of spectral radius for a matrix A.

The spectral radius $\rho(A)$ of a matrix A is defined by

$$\rho(A) = \max\{|\lambda| : \lambda \in \sigma(A)\},$$

where $\sigma(A)$ is the set of all the eigenvalues of A.

Remark 5.1.3 If A is a symmetric matrix, then

$$\|A\|_2 = \sqrt{\rho(A^T A)} = \rho(A). \tag{5.1.10}$$

Theorem 5.1.4 Suppose that $A \in \mathbf{R}^{n \times n}$, then

(1) $\rho(A) \leq \|A\|$ for any the nature norm $\|A\|$ of matrix A.

(2) For any $\varepsilon > 0$, there is a natural norm $\|\cdot\|_\varepsilon$ such that

$$\|A\|_{\varepsilon} \leq \rho(A) + \varepsilon.$$

Proof (1) If $\|\cdot\|$ is the nature matrix norm of A, then $\|Ax\| \leq \|A\| \cdot \|x\|$ for any $x \in \mathbf{R}^n$.

Letting λ is eigenvalue of A, then $Av = \lambda v$. So
$$|\lambda| \cdot |v| = \|\lambda v\| = \|Av\| \leq \|A\| \cdot \|v\|.$$

That is $|\lambda| \leq \|A\|$, therefore
$$\rho(A) \leq \|A\|.$$

(2) Suppose that $A = pJp^{-1}$, where $J = \begin{pmatrix} J_1 & & & \\ & J_2 & & \\ & & \ddots & \\ & & & J_s \end{pmatrix}$ is a Jordan

matrix and $J_i = \begin{pmatrix} \lambda_1 & 1 & & \\ & \lambda_2 & 1 & \\ & & \ddots & \\ & & & \lambda_s \end{pmatrix}_{n_i \times n_i}$, $\sum_{i=1}^{s} n_i = n$.

Letting $D = \begin{pmatrix} 1 & & & \\ & \varepsilon & & \\ & & \ddots & \\ & & & \varepsilon^{n-1} \end{pmatrix}_{n \times n}$, then $\tilde{J} = D^{-1}JD$ and $\|\tilde{J}\| \leq \rho(A) + \varepsilon$.

Setting $Q = pD$ and $\|x\| = \|Q^{-1}x\|_{\infty}$, then
$$\|A\| = \max_{\|x\|=1} \|Ax\| = \max_{\|Q^{-1}x\|_{\infty}=1} \|Q^{-1}Ax\|_{\infty}.$$

Letting $y = Q^{-1}x$, then
$$\|A\| = \max_{\|y\|_{\infty}=1} \|Q^{-1}AQy\|_{\infty} = \max_{\|y\|_{\infty}=1} \|\tilde{J}y\|_{\infty} = \|\tilde{J}\|_{\infty} \leq \rho(A) + \varepsilon.$$

5.1.5 Convergence of Sequence of Matrix

Definition 5.1.4 If there is $A = (a_{ij}) \in \mathbf{R}^{n \times n}$, such that
$$\lim_{k \to \infty} a_{ij}^{(k)} = a_{ij}, \quad i,j = 1,2,\cdots,n,$$
the matrix sequence $A^{(k)} = (a_{ij}^{(k)}) \in \mathbf{R}^{n \times n}$ is convergent and setting
$$\lim_{k \to \infty} A^{(k)} = A.$$

Theorem 5.1.5 Suppose that $A \in \mathbf{R}^{n \times n}$, then $A^{(k)} \to \mathbf{0}(k \to \infty)$ if and only if $\rho(A) < 1$.

Proof If $\rho(A) < 1$, there exists a norm $\|\cdot\|$, such that $\|A\| < 1$. Thus $\|A^k\| < \|A\|^k \to 0$. Namely,
$$\lim_{k \to \infty} A^k = 0.$$
Assume that $\rho(A) \geq 1$. Since $\|A^k x\| = \|\lambda^k x\| \geq |x|$, then $\|A^k\| \geq 1$.

Theorem 5.1.6 $\sum_{k=0}^{\infty} A^k$ is convergent if and only if $\rho(A) < 1$, and if $\rho(A) < 1$, then we have
$$I + A + \cdots + A^k + \cdots = (I - A)^{-1}. \tag{5.1.11}$$

Proof If $\sum_{k=0}^{\infty} A^k$ is convergent, then $A^k \to 0$. So
$$\rho(A) < 1.$$
If $\rho(A) < 1$, then $|I - A| \neq 0$, and
$$(I - A)(I + A + \cdots + A^k) = I - A^{k+1}.$$
In fact,
$$I + A + \cdots + A^k = (I - A)^{-1}(I - A^{k+1}).$$
If $\rho(A) < 1$, then $A^{(k)} \to 0$. We have
$$I + A + \cdots + A^k + \cdots = (I - A)^{-1}.$$

Remark 5.1.4
$$\|(I - A)^{-1}\| = \|I + A + \cdots + A^k + \cdots\|$$
$$\leq \|I\| + \|A\| + \cdots + \|A^k\| + \cdots = \frac{1}{1 - \|A\|} \tag{5.1.12}$$
and
$$A + E = A(I + A^{-1}E). \tag{5.1.13}$$

Theorem 5.1.7 If $\|A\| \neq 0$, $E \in \mathbf{R}^{n \times n}$ and $\|A^{-1}\| \cdot \|E\| < 1$, then $\|A + E\| \neq 0$ and $\|(A + E)^{-1}\| \leq \dfrac{\|A^{-1}\|}{1 - \|A^{-1}\| \cdot \|E\|}$.

Proof It can be checked that
$$\|(A + E)^{-1}\| = \|(I + A^{-1}E)^{-1} \cdot A^{-1}\| \leq \|A^{-1}\| \cdot \|(I + A^{-1}E)^{-1}\|.$$
By $\|A^{-1}E\| < 1$, we obtain
$$|I + A^{-1}E| \neq 0 \text{ and } |I + A^{-1}E| \leq \frac{1}{1 - \|A^{-1}E\|} \leq \frac{1}{1 - \|A^{-1}\|\|E\|}.$$
So $\|A + E\| \neq 0$ and $\|(A + E)^{-1}\| \leq \dfrac{\|A^{-1}\|}{1 - \|A^{-1}\|\|E\|}$.

5.1.6 Condition Number of Matrix

Definition 5.1.5 If $|A| \neq 0$, Then $\|A^{-1}\| \cdot \|A\|$ is called the condition number of A.

Remark 5.1.5 If A is a symmetric and positive definite matrix, then the condition number of A satisfies

$$\text{cond}(A) = \|A^{-1}\| \cdot \|A\| \geq \|A^{-1} \cdot A\| = 1. \tag{5.1.14}$$

Assume that $\lambda_{\min}$ and $\lambda_{\max}$ with $0 < \lambda_{\min} \leq \lambda_{\max}$ are the smallest eigenvalue and the largest eigenvalue, respectively. We see that

$$\|A\|_2 = \rho(A) = \lambda_{\max}, \quad \|A^{-1}\|_2 = \rho(A^{-1}) = \frac{1}{\lambda_{\min}}. \tag{5.1.15}$$

Hence,

$$\text{cond}_2(A) = \frac{\lambda_{\max}}{\lambda_{\min}}. \tag{5.1.16}$$

5.1.7 Special Matrix

Definition 5.1.6 A is called strictly diagonal dominant matrix if

$$\sum_{\substack{j=1 \\ j \neq i}}^{n} |a_{ij}| < |a_{ii}|, \quad i = 1, 2, \cdots, n.$$

Theorem 5.1.8 If A is a diagonal dominant matrix, then $|A| \neq 0$.

Proof If $\sum_{\substack{j=1 \\ j \neq i}}^{n} |a_{ij}| < |a_{ii}|, i = 1, 2, \cdots, n$. Assume that the system $Ax = 0$ has solution $x = (x_1, \cdots, x_n)^T \neq 0$. Then there exists $1 \leq i \leq n$, such that

$$|x_i| = \max_{1 \leq j \leq n} |x_j| > 0.$$

Then we have

$$|a_{ii}| \cdot |x_i| \leq \sum_{\substack{j=1 \\ j \neq i}}^{n} |a_{ij}| \cdot |x_j| \leq |x_i| \cdot \sum_{\substack{j=1 \\ j \neq i}}^{n} |a_{ij}|.$$

Consequently,

$$|a_{ii}| \leq \sum_{\substack{j=1 \\ j \neq i}}^{n} |a_{ij}|.$$

Definition 5.1.7 If the most of elements of A is zero, then $A \in \mathbf{R}^{n \times n}$ is called **sparse matrix**.

Definition 5.1.8 A is called non-negative matrix, if $a_{ij} \geq 0$, then setting $A \geq 0$.

§5.2 Direct Methods for Solving Linear System of Equations

5.2.1 Gaussian Elimination

In this section we introduce Gaussian elimination in a general system $AX = b$ with n equations and n unknowns. The goal is to construct an equivalent upper-triangular system.

If $a_{11} \neq 0, a_{22}^{(2)} \neq 0, \cdots, a_{k-1,k-1}^{(k-1)} \neq 0$, we arrive at the equivalent system

$$\begin{cases} a_{11}^{(1)} x_1 + a_{12}^{(1)} x_2 + \cdots + a_{1n}^{(1)} x_n = b_1^{(1)}, \\ \quad\quad a_{22}^{(2)} x_2 + \cdots + a_{2n}^{(2)} x_n = b_2^{(2)}, \\ \quad\quad\quad\quad \cdots\cdots \\ \quad\quad\quad\quad a_{kk}^{(k)} x_k + \cdots + a_{kn}^{(k)} x_n = b_k^{(k)}, \\ \quad\quad\quad\quad \cdots\cdots \\ \quad\quad\quad\quad a_{nk}^{(n)} x_k + \cdots + a_{nn}^{(n)} x_n = b_n^{(n)}, \end{cases} \quad (5.2.1)$$

where

$$\begin{cases} a_{ij}^{(k)} = a_{ij}^{(k-1)} - \dfrac{a_{i,k-1}^{(k-1)}}{a_{k-1,k-1}^{(k-1)}} \cdot a_{k-1,j}^{(k-1)}, & i,j = k,\cdots,n, \\ b_i^{(k)} = b_i^{(k-1)} - \dfrac{a_{i,k-1}^{(k-1)}}{a_{k-1,k-1}^{(k-1)}} \cdot b_{k-1}^{(k-1)}, & i = k,\cdots,n. \end{cases}$$

The final result after x_{n-1} has been eliminated is

$$\begin{cases} a_{11}^{(1)} x_1 + a_{12}^{(1)} x_2 + \cdots + a_{1n}^{(1)} x_n = b_1^{(1)}, \\ \quad\quad a_{22}^{(2)} x_2 + \cdots + a_{2n}^{(2)} x_n = b_2^{(2)}, \\ \quad\quad\quad\quad \cdots\cdots \\ \quad\quad\quad\quad\quad\quad a_{nn}^{(n)} x_n = b_n^{(n)}, \end{cases} \quad (5.2.2)$$

where $a_{kk}^{(k)} \neq 0$ for $k = 1, 2, \cdots, n$.

Hence the system can be solved by back substitution. We obtain

$$x_n = b_n^{(n)}/a_{nn}^{(n)}, \quad x_i = \frac{b_i^{(i)} - \sum_{j=i+1}^{n} a_{ij}^{(i)} x_j}{a_{ii}^{(i)}} (i = n-1, \cdots, 1). \quad (5.2.3)$$

5.2.2 Gaussian Elimination with Pivoting Strategies

Condition of Gaussian elimination is $a_{kk}^{(k)} \neq 0, k = 1, 2, \cdots, n-1$. If A is a sparse matrix or $a_{kk}^{(k)} \neq 0$ but small enough, then the results of calculation are not ideal.

(1) Gaussian elimination with column pivoting strategies.

Suppose step k Gaussian elimination, letting $a_k = \max\limits_{k \leq i \leq n} |a_{ik}^{(k)}|$. And take $a_j = a_k$ for $j \geq k$. If $j > k$, then interchange row j and row k such that $l_{ik} = \dfrac{a_{ik}^{(k)}}{a_{kk}^{(k)}}$ satisfies $|l_{ik}| \leq 1$.

(2) Pivoting strategies for all elements.

Define $\alpha_k = \max\limits_{k \leq i, j \leq n} |a_{ij}^{(k)}|$, then interchange row below k or column after k, such that absolute value of the main element arrive at α_k.

Example 5.2.1 Consider the linear system
$$\begin{cases} x_1 - x_2 + 2x_3 - x_4 = -8, \\ 2x_1 - 2x_2 + 3x_3 - 3x_4 = -20, \\ x_1 + x_2 + x_3 = -2, \\ x_1 - x_2 + 4x_3 + 3x_4 = 4. \end{cases}$$

Solution The augmented matrix
$$\tilde{A}^{(1)} = (A, b) = \begin{pmatrix} 1 & -1 & 2 & -1 & \vdots & -8 \\ 2 & -2 & 3 & -3 & \vdots & -20 \\ 1 & 1 & 1 & 0 & \vdots & -2 \\ 1 & -1 & 4 & 3 & \vdots & 4 \end{pmatrix}$$
$$\to \tilde{A}^{(2)} = \begin{pmatrix} 1 & -2 & 3 & -3 & \vdots & -20 \\ 0 & 0 & -1 & -1 & \vdots & -4 \\ 0 & -4 & 1 & -3 & \vdots & -16 \\ 0 & 0 & -5 & -9 & \vdots & -28 \end{pmatrix}$$

$$\rightarrow \tilde{A}'^{(2)} = \begin{pmatrix} 1 & -2 & 3 & -3 & \vdots & -20 \\ 0 & -4 & -1 & -3 & \vdots & -16 \\ 0 & 0 & -1 & -1 & \vdots & -4 \\ 0 & 0 & -5 & -9 & \vdots & -28 \end{pmatrix}$$

$$\rightarrow \tilde{A}^{(3)} = \begin{pmatrix} 2 & -2 & 3 & -3 & \vdots & -20 \\ 0 & -4 & 1 & -3 & \vdots & -16 \\ 0 & 0 & -1 & -1 & \vdots & -4 \\ 0 & 0 & 0 & -4 & \vdots & -8 \end{pmatrix}.$$

So the solution to the linear system is

$$\begin{cases} x_1 = -7, \\ x_2 = 3, \\ x_3 = 2, \\ x_4 = 2. \end{cases}$$

5.2.3 Matrix Factorization and Gaussian Elimination

Main result: The essential thought of Gaussian elimination is $A = LU$, where L is a unit lower triangular matrix, U is an upper-triangular matrix.

Suppose $(k-1)$-th Gaussian elimination for $AX = b$, we obtain the equivalent system $A_k x = b_k$, where

$$A_k = \begin{pmatrix} a_{11}^{(1)} & \cdots & \cdots & \cdots & a_{1n}^{(1)} \\ & \ddots & & & \vdots \\ & & a_{kk}^{(k)} & \cdots & a_{kn}^{(k)} \\ & & \vdots & & \vdots \\ & & a_{nk}^{(n)} & \cdots & a_{nn}^{(n)} \end{pmatrix}, \quad b_k = \begin{pmatrix} b_1^{(1)} \\ \vdots \\ b_k^{(k)} \\ \vdots \\ b_n^{(n)} \end{pmatrix}. \qquad (5.2.4)$$

The k-th elimination: $A_{k+1} = L_k \cdot A_k$, $b_{k+1} = L_k \cdot b_k$, where

$$L_k = \begin{pmatrix} 1 & & & & & \\ & \ddots & & & & \\ & & 1 & & & \\ & & -l_{k+1,k} & 1 & & \\ & & \vdots & & \ddots & \\ & & -l_{n,k} & \cdots & \cdots & 1 \end{pmatrix}, \quad l_{ik} = \frac{a_{ik}^{(k)}}{a_{kk}^{(k)}}, i = k+1, \cdots, n.$$

$$(5.2.5)$$

Denote $l_k = (0,\cdots,0,l_{k+1,k},\cdots,l_{n,k})^T (k = 1,2,\cdots,n-1)$, then
$$L_k = I - l_k \cdot e_k^T, \quad A_k = L_{k-1}\cdots L_1 A, \quad b_k = L_{k-1}\cdots L_1 b, \quad k = 2,\cdots,n.$$
And so on, the equivalent system is
$$A_n x = b_n,$$
where $A_n = L_{n-1}\cdots L_1 A, b_n = L_{n-1}\cdots L_1 b$.

That is $A = (L_{n-1}\cdots L_1)^{-1} A_n$ and $L = (L_{n-1}\cdots L_1)^{-1} = L_1^{-1}\cdots L_{n-1}^{-1} = I + \sum_{k=1}^{n-1} l_k \cdot e_k^T$, $L_k^{-1} = I + l_k \cdot e_k^T$. So

$$A = LU = \begin{pmatrix} 1 & 0 & \cdots & 0 \\ l_{21} & 1 & \cdots & \vdots \\ \vdots & \vdots & & \vdots \\ l_{n1} & \cdots & \cdots & 1 \end{pmatrix} \cdot \begin{pmatrix} n_{11} & n_{12} & \cdots & n_{1n} \\ 0 & n_{22} & \cdots & n_{2n} \\ \vdots & \vdots & & \vdots \\ 0 & \cdots & \cdots & n_{nn} \end{pmatrix}. \quad (5.2.6)$$

Therefore Gaussian elimination:

① $A = LU \Rightarrow LUx = b$;

② Letting $Ux = y$, $Ly = b \Rightarrow y$;

③ $x = U^{-1}y$.

Theorem 5.2.1 $A = LU$ if and only if the order principal submatrix of A is non-singular, i.e. $|A_i| \neq 0$ for $i = 1,2,\cdots,n$.

Proof By $A_k = L_{k-1}\cdots L_1 A$, we have $A = L_1^{-1}\cdots L_{k-1}^{-1} A_k$, where A_k is

$$\begin{pmatrix} a_{11}^{(1)} & \cdots & \cdots & \cdots & a_{1n}^{(1)} \\ & \ddots & & & \vdots \\ & & a_{kk}^{(k)} & \cdots & a_{kn}^{(k)} \\ & & \vdots & & \vdots \\ & & a_{nk}^{(n)} & \cdots & a_{nn}^{(n)} \end{pmatrix} \quad \text{and} \quad \tilde{L}_k = \begin{pmatrix} M_k & 0 \\ H_k & I_{n-k} \end{pmatrix}.$$

Then
$$\begin{pmatrix} A_{11} & A_{12} \\ A_{21} & A_{22} \end{pmatrix} = \begin{pmatrix} M_k & 0 \\ H_k & I_{n-k} \end{pmatrix} \cdot \begin{pmatrix} A_{11}^{(k)} & A_{12}^{(k)} \\ A_{21}^{(k)} & A_{22}^{(k)} \end{pmatrix},$$

where A_{11} is the leading principal submatrix of A, $A_{11}^{(k)}$ is the leading principal submatrix of A_k.

So
$$A_{11} = M_k \cdot A_{11}^{(k)},$$

and
$$\det(A_{11}) = \det(M_k) \cdot \det(A_{11}^k) = \det(A_{11}^{(k)}) = a_{11}^{(1)} a_{22}^{(2)} \cdots a_{kk}^{(k)}.$$
Therefore $a_{kk}^{(k)} \neq 0, k = 1, 2, \cdots, n-1$ if and only if $|A_i| \neq 0$ for $i = 1, 2, \cdots, n$.

Assume $L_1 U_1 = L_2 U_2 = A$, then $B = L_1^{-1} L_2 = U_1 U_2^{-1}$. We have
$$B = I.$$
Namely,
$$L_1 = L_2, \quad U_1 = U_2.$$

Theorem 5.2.2 If $|A| \neq 0$, then there is trans-formation matrix P such that $PL = LU$.

Remark 5.2.1 (1) Doolittle factorization $A = LU$, L is unit lower triangular.

$$\begin{pmatrix} a_{11} & \cdots & \cdots & a_{1n} \\ \vdots & & & \vdots \\ \vdots & & & \vdots \\ a_{n1} & \cdots & \cdots & a_{nn} \end{pmatrix} = \begin{pmatrix} 1 & & & \\ l_{21} & \ddots & & \\ \vdots & & \ddots & \\ l_{n1} & \cdots & \cdots & 1 \end{pmatrix} \cdot \begin{pmatrix} n_{11} & n_{12} & \cdots & n_{1n} \\ & \ddots & & \vdots \\ & & \ddots & \vdots \\ & & & n_{nn} \end{pmatrix}.$$

(5.2.7)

(2) Crount factorization: $A = LU$, U is unit upper triangular matrix.

$$L = \begin{pmatrix} l_{11} & & & \\ l_{21} & \ddots & & \\ \vdots & & \ddots & \\ l_{n1} & \cdots & \cdots & l_{nn} \end{pmatrix}, \quad U = \begin{pmatrix} 1 & \cdots & \cdots & n_{1n} \\ & \ddots & & \vdots \\ & & \ddots & \vdots \\ & & & 1 \end{pmatrix}.$$

(3) $A = LDU$, L and U are unit lower and upper triangular matrix, $D = \text{diag}(d_1, \cdots, d_n)$.

5.2.4 Factorization of Special Types of Matrixs

Definition 5.2.1 Matrix A is positive definite, if it is symmetric and if $X^T A X > 0$ for every n-dimension vector $X \neq 0$.

(1) Cholesky factorization of positive matrix.

Proof By $A = LDU$ and $A^T = A$, then
$$U^T D L^T = A = LDU.$$
We have $U = L^T$. So
$$A = LDL^T,$$

where $D = \text{diag}(d_1, \cdots, d_n)$.

Since A is a positive matrix, so $d_i^{1/2} > 0, i = 1, 2, \cdots, n$. Take
$$D^{1/2} = \text{diag}(d_1^{1/2}, \cdots, d_n^{1/2}),$$
we obtain
$$A = LD^{1/2}D^{1/2}L^T = (LD^{1/2})(D^{1/2}L^T) = \tilde{L} \cdot \tilde{L}^T,$$
where $\tilde{L} = LD^{1/2}$.

Suppose that
$$\begin{pmatrix} a_{11} & \cdots & \cdots & a_{1n} \\ \vdots & & & \vdots \\ \vdots & & & \vdots \\ a_{n1} & \cdots & \cdots & a_{nn} \end{pmatrix} = \begin{pmatrix} l_{11} & & & \\ l_{21} & \ddots & & \\ \vdots & & \ddots & \\ l_{n1} & \cdots & \cdots & l_{nn} \end{pmatrix} \cdot \begin{pmatrix} l_{11} & l_{21} & \cdots & l_{n1} \\ & \ddots & & \vdots \\ & & \ddots & \vdots \\ & & & l_{nn} \end{pmatrix},$$

we find $l_{11} = \sqrt{a_{11}}$, and

$$\begin{cases} l_{ij} = \dfrac{(a_{ij} - \sum\limits_{k=1}^{j-1} l_{ik} l_{jk})}{l_{jj}}, & j = 1, 2, \cdots, i-1. \\ l_{ii} = \left[a_{ii} - \sum\limits_{k=1}^{i-1} l_{ik}^2 \right]^{1/2}, \end{cases} \quad (5.2.8)$$

(2) Tridiagonal matrix.

Assume that linear system $Ax = b$, where $A = \begin{pmatrix} e_1 & f_1 & & & \\ d_2 & \ddots & \ddots & & \\ & \ddots & \ddots & f_{n-1} \\ & & d_n & e_n \end{pmatrix}$ is a

tridiagonal matrix.

Step I: Assume that $A = LU = \begin{pmatrix} 1 & & & \\ l_2 & \ddots & & \\ & \ddots & \ddots & \\ & & l_n & 1 \end{pmatrix} \begin{pmatrix} r_1 & f_1 & & \\ & \ddots & \ddots & \\ & & \ddots & f_{n-1} \\ & & & r_n \end{pmatrix}$, we

have
$$r_1 = e_1, \quad l_i = \dfrac{d_i}{r_{i-1}}, \quad r_i = e_i - l_i \times f_{i-1}, \quad i = 2, 3, \cdots, n.$$

Step Ⅱ : $Ly = B$, $\begin{cases} y_1 = b_1, \\ y_i = b_i - l_i \times y_{i-1}, i = 2,3,\cdots,n. \end{cases}$

Step Ⅲ : $Ux = y$, $\begin{cases} x_n = \dfrac{y_n}{r_n}, \\ x_i = \dfrac{y_i - f_i \times x_{i+1}}{r_i}, i = n-1, n-2, \cdots, 1. \end{cases}$

§5.3 Error of Gaussian Elimination

Example 5.3.1 $(A): \begin{cases} x_1 + 5x_2 = 6, \\ x_1 + 5.001x_2 = 6.001. \end{cases}$

$(B): \begin{cases} x_1 + 5x_2 = 6, \\ x_1 + 4.999x_2 = 6.002. \end{cases}$

The solution of $(A): \begin{cases} x_1 = 1, \\ x_2 = 1 \end{cases}$ and $(B): \begin{cases} x_1 = 16, \\ x_2 = -2. \end{cases}$ (A) or (B) is an ill system.

(1) Perturbation of right term.

Denote the error of right term by δb, the error of solution is δx, then
$$A(x + \delta x) = b + \delta b. \tag{5.3.1}$$

So
$$A\delta x = \delta b.$$

Namely,
$$\delta x = A^{-1}\delta b.$$

Thus
$$\|\delta x\| \le \|A^{-1}\| \cdot \|\delta b\|.$$

By $\|b\| \le \|A\| \cdot \|x\|$, if $b \ne 0$, then $x \ne 0$. Therefore

$$\frac{\|\delta x\|}{\|x\|} \le \frac{\|A^{-1}\| \cdot \|\delta x\|}{\|x\|} = \frac{\|b\|}{\|b\|} \cdot \frac{\|A^{-1}\| \cdot \|\delta x\|}{\|x\|} \le \|A^{-1}\| \cdot \|A\| \cdot \frac{\|\delta b\|}{\|b\|},$$

where $\text{cond}(A) = \|A\| \cdot \|A^{-1}\|$.

(2) Error of Matrix A.

Suppose the error of A is δA, and the error of solution is δx, then we have

$$(A + \delta A)(x + \delta x) = b. \qquad (5.3.2)$$

Assume that $\|A^{-1}\| \cdot \|\delta A\| < 1$, then $|A + \delta A| \neq 0$. So

$$A\delta x = -\delta A x - \delta A \cdot \delta x.$$

Namely,

$$\delta x = -A^{-1}\delta A x - A^{-1}\delta A \cdot \delta x.$$

Then

$$\|\delta x\| \leq \|A^{-1}\| \cdot \|\delta A\| \cdot \|x\| + \|A^{-1}\| \cdot \|\delta A\| \cdot \|\delta x\|,$$
$$(1 - \|A^{-1}\| \cdot \|\delta A\|) \cdot \|\delta x\| \leq \|A^{-1}\| \cdot \|\delta A\| \cdot \|x\|.$$

$$\frac{\|\delta x\|}{\|x\|} \leq \frac{\|A^{-1}\| \cdot \|\delta A\|}{1 - \|A^{-1}\| \cdot \|\delta A\|} = \frac{\|A^{-1}\| \cdot \|A\| \cdot \frac{\|\delta A\|}{\|A\|}}{1 - \|A^{-1}\| \cdot \|A\| \cdot \frac{\|\delta A\|}{\|A\|}}$$

$$= \frac{\operatorname{cond}(A) \cdot \frac{\|\delta A\|}{\|A\|}}{1 - \operatorname{cond}(A) \cdot \frac{\|\delta A\|}{\|A\|}}.$$

§5.4 Iterative Methods for Solving Linear Systems

For large systems with a high percentage of 0 entries, however, these techniques are efficient in terms of both computer storage and computation. Systems of this type arise frequently in circuit analysis and in the numerical solution of boundary-value problems and partial differential equations.

5.4.1 Iterative Methods

An iterative technique to solve the $n \times n$ linear system $Ax = b$ starts with an initial approximation $x^{(0)}$ to the solution x and generates a sequence of vectors $\{x^{(k)}\}_{k=0}^{\infty}$ that converges to x.

Iterative technique involves a process that converts the system $Ax = b$ into an equivalent system of the form

$$X = TX + C.$$

For some fixed matrix T and vector C. After the initial vector $x^{(0)}$ is selected

the sequence of approximation solution vector is generated by computing
$$x^{(k)} = Tx^{(k-1)} + C$$
for each $k = 1, 2, 3, \cdots$.

Example 5.4.1 Consider the system of equations
$$\begin{cases} a_{11}x_1 + a_{12}x_2 + a_{13}x_3 = b_1, \\ a_{21}x_1 + a_{22}x_2 + a_{23}x_3 = b_2, \\ a_{31}x_1 + a_{32}x_2 + a_{33}x_3 = b_3. \end{cases}$$

The system can be written in the form
$$\begin{cases} x_1 = \dfrac{b_1 - a_{12}x_2 - a_{13}x_3}{a_{11}}, \\ x_2 = \dfrac{b_2 - a_{21}x_1 - a_{23}x_3}{a_{22}}, \\ x_3 = \dfrac{b_3 - a_{31}x_1 - a_{32}x_2}{a_{33}}. \end{cases}$$

Then
$$\begin{cases} x_1^{(k+1)} = \dfrac{b_1 - a_{12} x_2^{(k)} - a_{13} x_3^{(k)}}{a_{11}}, \\ x_2^{(k+1)} = \dfrac{b_2 - a_{21} x_1^{(k)} - a_{23} x_3^{(k)}}{a_{22}}, \\ x_3^{(k+1)} = \dfrac{b_3 - a_{31} x_1^{(k)} - a_{32} x_2^{(k)}}{a_{33}}, \end{cases}$$

for $k = 0, 1, 2, \cdots$.

The above formula is called Jacobi iterative method.

For $n \times n$ linear system $Ax = b$, we have
$$x_i = \sum_{\substack{j=1 \\ j \neq i}}^{n} \left(-\frac{a_{ij} \cdot x_j}{a_{ii}} \right) + \frac{b_i}{a_{ii}}, \quad i = 1, 2, \cdots, n.$$

Generating $x_i^{(k)}$ from components of $x_i^{(k-1)}$ by
$$x_i^{(k)} = \sum_{\substack{j=1 \\ j \neq i}}^{n} \left(-\frac{a_{ij} \cdot x_j^{(k-1)}}{a_{ii}} \right) + \frac{b_i}{a_{ii}}, \quad i = 1, 2, \cdots, n.$$

The formula is written in the matrix form $x^{(k)} = Tx^{(k-1)} + C$.

$$A = \begin{pmatrix} a_{11} & a_{12} & \cdots & a_{1n} \\ a_{21} & a_{22} & \cdots & a_{2n} \\ \vdots & \vdots & & \vdots \\ a_{n1} & a_{n2} & \cdots & a_{nn} \end{pmatrix}$$

is split into $A = D - L - U$, where

$$D = \begin{pmatrix} a_{11} & & & \\ & a_{22} & & \\ & & \ddots & \\ & & & a_{nn} \end{pmatrix}, \quad L = \begin{pmatrix} 0 & & & & \\ -a_{21} & \ddots & & & \\ \vdots & \ddots & \ddots & & \\ -a_{n1} & \cdots & -a_{n,n-1} & 0 \end{pmatrix},$$

$$U = \begin{pmatrix} 0 & -a_{12} & \cdots & -a_{1n} \\ & \ddots & \ddots & \vdots \\ & & \ddots & -a_{n-1,n} \\ & & & 0 \end{pmatrix}.$$

So system $Ax = b$ can be written in the form
$$(D - L - U)x = b.$$

Namely,
$$Dx = (L + U)x + b.$$

So
$$x = D^{-1}(L + U)x + D^{-1}b.$$

Then we have
$$x^{(k)} = D^{-1}(L + U)x^{(k-1)} + D^{-1}b, \quad k = 1, 2, \cdots.$$

The formula is called **Jacobi iterative formula**.

The bad of Jacobi iterative method:

(1) $a_{ii} \neq 0$;

(2) Speed of convergence is slow.

The good of Jacobi iterative method: compute $x_i^{(k)}$ independently.

The iterative formula

$$x_i^{(k+1)} = \frac{b_i - \sum_{j=1}^{i-1} a_{ij} \cdot x_j^{(k+1)} - \sum_{j=i+1}^{n} a_{ij} \cdot x_j^{(k)}}{a_{ii}}, \quad i = 1, 2, \cdots, n \quad (5.4.1)$$

is called **Gauss-Seidel iterative method**.

The iterative formula

$$x_i^{(k)} = w\frac{b_i - \sum_{j=1}^{i-1} a_{ij} \cdot x_j^{(k)} - \sum_{j=i+1}^{n} a_{ij} \cdot x_j^{(k-1)}}{a_{ii}} + (1-w)x_i^{(k-1)}, i = 1,2,\cdots,n$$

(5.4.2)

is called **Gauss-Seidel relaxation iterative method**. w is relaxation factor. $w > 1$, over-relaxation method; $w < 1$, under-relaxation method.

G-S iterative formula can be written in the matrix form

$$x^{(k+1)} = D^{-1}Lx^{(k+1)} - D^{-1}Ux^{(k)} + D^{-1}b, \quad k = 0,1,2,\cdots.$$

SOR iterative formula can be written in the matrix form

$$x^{(k+1)} = wD^{-1}Lx^{(k)} + (1-w)x^{(k)} + wD^{-1}Ux^{(k)} + wD^{-1}b, \quad k = 0,1,2,\cdots.$$

5.4.2 Convergence

Theorem 5.4.1 For any initial value $x^{(0)}$, the iterative method $x^{(k)} = Tx^{(k-1)} + C$ is convergent if and only if $\rho(T) < 1$.

Proof Letting x^* is the solution of $Ax = b$ and $\varepsilon_k = x^{(k)} - x^*$, by $x^* = Tx^* + C$ and $x^{(k)} = Tx^{(k-1)} + C$, then

$$\varepsilon_k = x^{(k)} - x^* = T(x^{(k-1)} - x^*).$$

Namely,

$$\varepsilon_{k+1} = T\varepsilon_k, \quad k = 0,1,2,\cdots$$

or

$$\varepsilon_{k+1} = T^k\varepsilon_0.$$

For any ε_0, $T^k \to 0$ if and only if $\rho(T) < 1$.

Remark 5.4.1 Since $\rho(G) \leq \|G\|$, so as $\|G\| < 1$, $x^{(k)} = Gx^{(k-1)} + C$ is convergent.

Theorem 5.4.2 If $\|G\| = q < 1$, then

$$\|x^{(k)} - x^*\| \leq \frac{q^k}{1-q}\|x^{(0)} - x^{(1)}\|.$$

Proof By $\varepsilon_k = G^k\varepsilon_0$, we have

$$\|\varepsilon_k\| = \|G^k\| \cdot \|\varepsilon_0\| \leq q^k\|\varepsilon_0\|.$$

Since $\rho(G) \leq \|G\| < 1$, so there is $(I-G)^{-1}$, $x^* = (I-G)^{-1}d$ and $d = M^{-1}b$. Thus

$$x^{(0)} - x^* = x^{(0)} - (I-G)^{-1}d = (I-G)^{-1}[(I-G)x^{(0)} - d]$$
$$= (I-G)^{-1}[x^{(0)} - Gx^{(0)} - d] = (I-G)^{-1}[x^{(0)} - x^{(1)}].$$

Therefore
$$\|\varepsilon_0\| \leq \|(I-G)^{-1}\| \cdot \|x^{(0)} - x^{(1)}\| \leq \frac{1}{1-q} \cdot \|x^{(0)} - x^{(1)}\|.$$

Hence
$$\|\varepsilon_k\| \leq \frac{q^k}{1-q} \cdot \|x^{(0)} - x^{(1)}\| \Rightarrow \|x^{(k)} - x^*\| \leq \frac{q^k}{1-q} \cdot \|x^{(0)} - x^{(1)}\|.$$

Example 5.4.2 Assume that the iterative formula is $x^{(k)} = Bx^{(k-1)} + f$, where $B = \begin{pmatrix} 0.9 & 0 \\ 0.3 & 0.8 \end{pmatrix}$ and $f = \begin{pmatrix} 1 \\ 2 \end{pmatrix}$.

Solution It is easy to check that $\|B\|_\infty = 1.1$, $\|B\|_1 = 1.2$, $\|B\|_2 = 1.043$ and $\|B\| > 1$. However, $\rho(B) = 0.9 < 1$, $\{x^{(k)}\}_{k=1}^\infty$ is convergent.

According to $\varepsilon_k = T^k \varepsilon_0$, where $\varepsilon_0 = x^{(0)} - x^*$, we obtain
$$\|\varepsilon_k\| = \|T^k\| \cdot \|\varepsilon_0\| \text{ for any } \varepsilon_0 \neq 0.$$

So
$$\frac{\|\varepsilon_k\|}{\|\varepsilon_0\|} \leq \|T_k\|,$$

$$\|T_k\| = \max_{\varepsilon_0 \neq 0} \frac{\|T^k \varepsilon_k\|}{\|\varepsilon_0\|} \leq \max_{\varepsilon_0 \neq 0} \frac{\|\varepsilon_k\|}{\|\varepsilon_0\|}.$$

Definition 5.4.1 The average speed of convergence is defined by
$$R_k(B) = \ln \|B^k\|^{1/k}, \quad \lim_{k \to \infty} \|B^k\|^{1/k} = \rho(B).$$

Definition 5.4.2 The asymptotic speed of convergence is $R(B) = \ln \rho(B)$.

Theorem 5.4.3 If A is a strictly diagonal dominated matrix, then Jacobi iterative method and SOR iterative method are convergent and $0 < w \leq 1$.

Proof Assume that $A = D - L - U$.
Jacobi: $x^{(k)} = D^{-1}(L+U)x^{(k-1)} + D^{-1}b$,

$$\|D^{-1}(L+U)\|_\infty = \max \frac{\sum_{\substack{j=1 \\ j \neq i}}^n |a_{ij}|}{|a_{ii}|}, \quad \rho(D^{-1}(L+U)) < 1.$$

SOR: the iterative matrix G, suppose the eigenvalue
$$\lambda, |\lambda| \geq 1, |D - wL| \neq 0.$$
$$\det(\lambda I - G) = \det(\lambda I - (D-wL)((1-w)D + wU))$$
$$= \det(D-wL)^{-1} \cdot \det(\lambda(D-wL) - (1-w)D - wU)$$

$$= \det(D - wL)^{-1} \cdot \det((\lambda + w - 1)D - w\lambda L - wU).$$

Setting $B = (\lambda + w - 1)D - w\lambda L - wU)$, to prove $|B| \neq 0$.

As $0 < w \leq 1, |\lambda| \geq 1$, then

$$|\lambda w| \leq |(\lambda + w - 1)|.$$

$$\sum_{\substack{j=1 \\ j \neq i}}^{n} |b_{ij}| = |\lambda w| \cdot \sum_{j=1}^{i-1} |a_{ij}| + |w| \cdot \sum_{j=i+1}^{n} |a_{ij}| \leq |\lambda w| \cdot \sum_{j=1}^{i-1} |a_{ij}| + |\lambda w| \cdot \sum_{j=i+1}^{n} |a_{ij}|$$

$$= |\lambda w| \cdot \sum_{\substack{j=1 \\ j \neq 1}}^{n} |a_{ij}| \leq |(\lambda + w - 1)| \cdot \sum_{\substack{j=1 \\ j \neq 1}}^{n} |a_{ii}| = |b_{ii}|.$$

Thus

$$|B| \neq 0,$$
$$\det(\lambda I - G) = \det(D - wL)^{-1} \cdot \det(B) \neq 0,$$
$$\rho(G) < 1.$$

So, SOR iterative method is convergent.

Lemma 5.4.1 B_1, B_2 are positive definite, then $\exists \sigma > 0$ s.t. $B_1 - \sigma B_2$ is a positive definite matrix.

Proof By $\lambda_{\min}(B_1) = \min_{\substack{x \in R^n \\ x \neq 0}} \frac{(B_1 x, x)}{(x, x)}$ and $\lambda_{\max}(B_2) = \max_{\substack{x \in R^n \\ x \neq 0}} \frac{(B_2 x, x)}{(x, x)}$ for $x \in R^n$, then

$$((B_1 - \sigma B_2)x, x) = (B_1 x, x) - \sigma(B_2 x, x)$$
$$\geq \lambda_{\min}(B_1) \cdot (x, x) - \sigma \lambda_{\max}(B_2)(x, x)$$
$$= [\lambda_{\min}(B_1) - \sigma \lambda_{\max}(B_2)](x, x).$$

Taking $0 < \sigma < \dfrac{\lambda_{\min}(B_1)}{\lambda_{\max}(B_2)}$, then $((B_1 - \sigma B_2)x, x) > 0$.

Lemma 5.4.2 If A is a positive definite matrix, D is a diagonal matrix, $|B| \neq 0, G = I - Q^{-1}A, \sigma > 0$. Then $A_Q^\sigma = (Q + Q^T - A) - \sigma Q^T D^{-1} Q$ is positive definite if and only if for any $x \in R^n, x \neq 0$,

$$\|Gx\|_A^2 \leq \|x\|_A^2 - \sigma \|x\|_{A^2}^2, \|\cdot\|_A^2 : (x, x)^{1/2}, \|x\|_{A^2} = (D^{-1}Ax, Ax)^{1/2}.$$

Proof For any $x \in R^n, x \neq 0, \tilde{x} = Q^{-1}Ax$, then

$$\|Gx\|_A^2 = (AGx, Gx) = (A(I - Q^{-1}A)x, (I - Q^{-1}A)x)$$
$$= (Ax, x) - (Ax, Q^{-1}Ax) - (AQ^{-1}Ax, x) + (AQ^{-1}Ax, Q^{-1}Ax)$$
$$= \|x\|_A^2 - ((Q + Q^T - A)\tilde{x}, \tilde{x}).$$

So $A_Q^\sigma = (Q + Q^T - A) - \sigma Q^T D^{-1} Q$ is positive definite if and only if for any $x \in \mathbf{R}^n, x \neq 0$, $\|Gx\|_A^2 < \|x\|_A^2 - \sigma \|x\|_A^2$, $\|\cdot\|_A^2 : (x,x)^{1/2}$, $\|\cdot\|_{A^2} = (D^{-1} Ax, Ax)^{1/2}$.

Corollary 5.4.1 Assume that A is a positive definite matrix, $G = I - Q^{-1} A$. If $A_Q = Q + Q^T - A$ is a positive definite matrix, then $\rho(G) < 1$.

Proof From lemma 5.4.1, $\exists \sigma > 0$ so that $A_Q^\sigma = A_Q - \sigma Q^T D^{-1} Q$. Then

$$\|Gx\|_A^2 \leq \|x\|_A^2 - \sigma \|x\|_A^2.$$

Thus

$$\|Gx\|_A^2 < \|x\|_A.$$

So

$$\|G\|_A = \max_{x \neq 0} \frac{\|Gx\|_A}{\|x\|_A} < 1.$$

Namely,

$$\rho(G) \leq \|G\|_A < 1.$$

The matrices of correction formulas for the three iterative methods are

$$B = \begin{cases} D, & \text{Jacobi}, \\ \frac{1}{w} D - L, & \text{SOR}; \end{cases} \qquad A_B = \begin{cases} 2D - A, & \text{Jacobi}, \\ \frac{2-w}{w} D, & \text{SOR}. \end{cases}$$

Theorem 5.4.4 Assume that A is a positive definite matrix, then

(1) If $2D - A$ is positive definite, then Jacobi iterative method is convergent.

(2) As $0 < w < 2$, SOR is convergent.

For the positive definite matrix A, G-S is convergent, Jacobi iterative method is not convergent. However, for general matrix, Jacobi iterative method is convergent, G-S iterative method is not convergent.

Example 5.4.3 Assume that linear system is $Ax = B$, where

$$A = \begin{pmatrix} 1 & -2 & 2 \\ -1 & 1 & -1 \\ -2 & -2 & 1 \end{pmatrix}.$$

The Jacobi iterative matrix is $G_1 = D^{-1}(L+U) = \begin{pmatrix} 0 & 2 & 2 \\ 1 & 0 & 1 \\ 2 & 2 & 0 \end{pmatrix}$, and $\rho(G_1) = 0$.

The G-S iterative matrix is $G_2 = (D-L)^{-1}U = \begin{pmatrix} 0 & 2 & -2 \\ 0 & 2 & -1 \\ 0 & 8 & -6 \end{pmatrix}$, and $\rho(G_2) = 2 + 2\sqrt{2}$.

Jacobi iterative method is convergent, however, G-S is not convergent.

How to choose w?

Choose w^* s.t. $\rho(G_{w^*}) = \min_{0<w<2} \rho(G_w)$. w^* is called optimal relaxation coefficient.

Remark 5.4.2 If $\exists p$, s.t.

$$pAp^T = \begin{pmatrix} D_1 & H \\ R & D_2 \end{pmatrix}, \quad \rho(G_J) < 1,$$

then SOR is convergent and the optimal relaxation factor

$$w^* = \frac{2}{1 + \sqrt{1 - \rho^2(G_J)}} \text{ for } w \in (0,2).$$

§5.5 Conjugate Gradient Method

The conjugate gradient method of Hestenes and Stiefel were originally developed a direct method designed to solve an $n \times n$ positive definite linear system.

As a direct method it is generally inferior to Gaussian elimination with pivoting since both methods require n steps to determine a solution, and the steps of the conjugate gradient method are more computationally expensive than those in Gaussian elimination. However, the CG method is very useful when employed as an iterative approximation method for solving large sparse systems with nonzero.

Assume that

$$Ax = b,$$

where A is positive definite.

Theorem 5.5.1 If A is positive definite, then $Ax = b$ is equivalent to

find $x \in \mathbf{R}^n$ such that
$$\varphi(x) = \min_{w \in \mathbf{R}^n} \varphi(w),$$
where quadratic functional $\varphi(w) = \frac{1}{2}(Aw, w) - (b, w), \forall w \in \mathbf{R}^n$.

Proof Letting $x = A^{-1}b$, then
$$\varphi(x) = \frac{1}{2}(Ax, x) - (b, x) = -\frac{1}{2}(Ax, x).$$
$\forall w \in \mathbf{R}^n$, we have
$$\varphi(w) - \varphi(x) = \frac{1}{2}(Aw, w) - (b, w) + \frac{1}{2}(Ax, x)$$
$$= \frac{1}{2}[(Aw, w) - 2(Ax, w) + (Ax, x)]$$
$$= \frac{1}{2}(A(w - x), w - x)$$
$$= \frac{1}{2}\|w - x\|_A^2 \geq 0.$$

So $w = x$ is minimum point.

Construct CG method:
$\{x^{(k)}\}$ s.t. $\varphi(x^{(k)}) \to \varphi(x), x^{(k+1)} = x^{(k)} + \alpha_k q^{(k)}, k = 0, 1, 2, \cdots$.
$q^{(k)}$: the iterative direction from $x^{(k)}$ to $x^{(k+1)}$. It is key to choose α_k and $q^{(k)}$.
$$\varphi(x) = \frac{1}{2}(Ax, x) - (b, x) = \frac{1}{2}\sum_{i=1}^{n}\sum_{j=1}^{n} a_{ij}x_i x_j - \sum_{j=1}^{n} b_j x_j,$$
$$\nabla \varphi(x) = Ax - b, \quad r^k = b - Ax^k = -\nabla \varphi(x^k) = q^k.$$
Taking $q^k = r^k$, $\min_{\alpha \in \mathbf{R}} \varphi(x^k + \alpha r^k) = \varphi(x^k + \alpha_k r^k)$.

Denote $f(\alpha) = \varphi(x^k + \alpha r^k)$, then
$$f(\alpha) = \frac{1}{2}(A(x^k + \alpha r^k), x^k + \alpha r^k) - (b, x^k + \alpha r^k)$$
$$= \varphi(x^k) - \alpha(r^k, r^k) + \frac{1}{2}\alpha^2(Ar^k, r^k).$$

The min point $\alpha_k = \frac{(r^k, r^k)}{(Ar^k, r^k)}, k = 0, 1, 2, \cdots$.

The method of steepest descent:
$$\begin{cases} \alpha_k = \dfrac{(r^k, r^k)}{(Ar^k, r^k)}, \\ x^{(k+1)} = x^{(k)} + \alpha_k q^{(k)}, \quad k = 0,1,2,\cdots. \\ r^k = b - Ax^k = r^{k-1} - \alpha_{k-1} Ar^{k-1}. \end{cases}$$
(5.5.1)

x^0: initial vector, $r^0 = b - Ax^0$.

Theorem 5.5.2 Suppose A is positive definite, $x = A^{-1}b$, then $\forall x^0 \in \mathbf{R}^n$, the method of steepest descent is convergent, and

$$\| x^k - x \|_A \leq \left(\dfrac{\text{cond}_2(A) - 1}{\text{cond}_2(A) + 1} \right)^k \cdot \| x^0 - x \|_A. \qquad (5.5.2)$$

CG Method: p^k s.t. $(p^i, p^j) = (Ap^i, p^j) = 0, \forall i \neq j$. To be easy to prove: $\{p^{(k)}\}_{k=0}^m$,

(1) $\forall m < n, \{p^{(k)}\}_{k=0}^\infty$ linear independent;

(2) $\forall m < n, p^m$ is zero vector.

Assume: x^0 is the initial vector, $r^0 = b - Ax^0$ is the initial residual vector, $x^0 = r^0 x^{k+1}, p^{k+1}, k \geq 0$,

$x^0, x^1, \cdots, x^k,\quad r^0, r^1, \cdots, r^k,\quad p^0, p^1, \cdots, p^k,\quad x^{(k+1)} = x^{(k)} + \alpha_k p^{(k)}$,

α_k satisfies $\varphi(x^{k+1}) = \min \varphi(x^k + \alpha p^k)$, $\alpha_k = \dfrac{(r^k, p^k)}{(Ap^k, p^k)}$, $r^k = b - Ax^k$.

Letting $p^{k+1} = r^{k+1} + c_0 p^0 + c_1 p^1 + \cdots + c_k p^k, p^{k+1} = r^{k+1} + \beta_k p^k$,

$$0 = (Ap^k, p^{k+1}) = (Ap^k, r^{k+1} + \beta_k p^k),$$

then

$$\beta_k = -\dfrac{(r^{k+1}, Ap^k)}{(Ap^k, p^k)}.$$

So

$$\begin{cases} \alpha_k = -\dfrac{(r^k, p^k)}{(Ap^k, p^k)}, \\ x^{(k+1)} = x^{(k)} + \alpha_k q^{(k)}, \\ r^k = b - Ax^k = r^{k-1} - \alpha_k Ar^{k-1}, \\ \beta_k = -\dfrac{(r^{k+1}, Ap^k)}{(Ap^k, p^k)}, \\ p^{k+1} = r^{k+1} + \beta_k p^k, \end{cases} \qquad (5.5.3)$$

where $r^0 = b - Ax^0$ and $p^0 = r^0$ for x^0.

Theorem 5.5.3 $\{r^k\}$ and $\{p^k\}$ of CG are orthogonal and A-orthogonal.

Theorem 5.5.4 Let A be positive definite, $x = A^{-1}b$, then CG method:

$$\|x^k - x\|_A \leq 2 \left(\frac{\sqrt{\text{cond}_2(A)} - 1}{\sqrt{\text{cond}_2(A)} + 1} \right)^k \cdot \|x^0 - x\|_A. \quad (5.5.4)$$

Remark 5.5.1 Conjugate Gradient method is a direct method, because $\{r^k\}$ is orthogonal, and

$$r^{n+1}, r^{n+2}, \cdots$$

are zero.

Excises 5

5.1 Let A be a symmetric matrix and $a_{11} \neq 0$, after a step Gaussian elimination method, A become $\begin{pmatrix} a_{11} & \alpha_1^T \\ 0 & A_2 \end{pmatrix}$, proof A_2 is a symmetric matrix.

5.2 Let $A = (a_{ij})_n$ be a symmetric matrix, after a step Gaussian elimination method, A become $\begin{bmatrix} a_{11} & \alpha_1^T \\ 0 & A_2 \end{bmatrix}$, where $A_2 = (a_{ij}^{(2)})_{n-1}$.

Prove: (1) The diagonal elements of A satisfy $a_{ii} > 0, i = 1, 2, \cdots, n$;

(2) A_2 is a symmetric matrix.

5.3 Let L_k be the lower triangular matrix of the index k (L_k and the unit matrix I are the same except for the following elements in the k-th diagonal element):

$$L_k = \begin{pmatrix} 1 & & & & & \\ & \ddots & & & & \\ & & 1 & & & \\ & & m_{k+1,k} & 1 & & \\ & & \vdots & & \ddots & \\ & & m_{n,k} & & & 1 \end{pmatrix}.$$

Prove $\tilde{L}_k = I_{ij}L_k I_{ij}$ is the lower triangular matrix of the index k when $i,j > k$, where I_{ij} is an elementary permutation matrix.

5.4 Calculating the Count decomposition of A, namely $A = LU$ where L is lower triangular matrix, U is unit upper triangular matrix.

5.5 Letting $Ux = d$ where U is triangular matrix.

(1) Deducing the solving equation and writing out the algorithm when U is the upper triangular matrix and lower triangular matrix.

(2) Calculating the multiplication and division times when solving $Ux = d$.

(3) U is a nonsingular matrix, calculating U^{-1}.

5.6 Proof:

(1) If A is a symmetric positive definite matrix, then A^{-1} also too.

(2) If A is a symmetric positive definite matrix, then A can be uniquely written as $A = L^T L$, where L is the lower triangular matrix with positive diagonal elements.

5.7 Using Gaussian elimination with maximal column pivoting to solving the equations

$$\begin{cases} 12x_1 - 3x_2 + 3x_3 = 15, \\ -18x_1 + 3x_2 - x_3 = -15, \\ x_1 + x_2 + x_3 = 6, \end{cases}$$

and calculate det$A$, where A is the coefficient matrix.

5.8 Using Doolittle decomposition to solve the solution of

$$\begin{cases} \dfrac{1}{4}x_1 + \dfrac{1}{5}x_2 + \dfrac{1}{6}x_3 = 9, \\ \dfrac{1}{3}x_1 + \dfrac{1}{4}x_2 + \dfrac{1}{5}x_3 = 8, \\ \dfrac{1}{2}x_1 + x_2 + 2x_3 = 8. \end{cases}$$

5.9 Using LU method to solve the equations of $Ax = b$, where

$$A = \begin{pmatrix} 2 & -1 & 0 & 0 & 0 \\ -1 & 2 & -1 & 0 & 0 \\ 0 & -1 & 2 & -1 & 0 \\ 0 & 0 & -1 & 2 & -1 \\ 0 & 0 & 0 & -1 & 2 \end{pmatrix}, \quad b = \begin{pmatrix} 1 \\ 0 \\ 0 \\ 0 \\ 0 \end{pmatrix}.$$

5.10 Using the improved square root method to solve the linear equations

$$\begin{pmatrix} 2 & -1 & 1 \\ -1 & -2 & 3 \\ 1 & 3 & 1 \end{pmatrix} \begin{pmatrix} x_1 \\ x_2 \\ x_3 \end{pmatrix} = \begin{pmatrix} 4 \\ 5 \\ 6 \end{pmatrix}.$$

5.11 Can the following matrix be decomposed into LU? Where L is unit lower triangular matrix, U is unit upper triangular matrix.

If decomposition, then the decomposition is unique?

$$A = \begin{pmatrix} 1 & 2 & 3 \\ 2 & 4 & 1 \\ 4 & 6 & 7 \end{pmatrix}, \quad B = \begin{pmatrix} 1 & 1 & 1 \\ 2 & 2 & 1 \\ 3 & 3 & 1 \end{pmatrix}, \quad C = \begin{pmatrix} 1 & 2 & 6 \\ 2 & 5 & 15 \\ 6 & 15 & 46 \end{pmatrix}.$$

5.12 Calculating the row norm, column norm, 2-norm and F-norm when

$$A = \begin{pmatrix} 0.6 & 0.5 \\ 0.1 & 0.3 \end{pmatrix}.$$

5.13 Prove:

(1) $\|x\|_\infty \leq \|x\|_1 \leq n \|x\|_\infty$; (2) $\frac{1}{\sqrt{n}} \|x\|_F \leq \|x\|_2 \leq n \|x\|_F$.

5.14 Letting $P \in \mathbf{R}^{n \times n}$ and nonsingular, if $\|x\|$ is a vector norm in $\mathbf{R}^n$, then $\|x\|_P$ also is a vector norm where $\|x\|_P = \|Px\|$.

5.15 Letting A is a symmetric positive definite matrix and $\|x\|_A = (Ax, x)^{\frac{1}{2}}$, prove $\|x\|_A$ is a norm of a vector in $\mathbf{R}^n$.

5.16 If A is a nonsingular matrix, then prove

$$\frac{1}{\|A^{-1}\|_\infty} = \min_{y \neq 0} \frac{\|Ay\|_\infty}{\|y\|_\infty}.$$

5.17 The first row of a matrix is multiplied by a number and become $A = \begin{pmatrix} 2\lambda & \lambda \\ 1 & 1 \end{pmatrix}$, prove $\mathrm{cond}(A)_\infty$ has the minimum value when $\lambda = \pm \frac{2}{3}$.

5.18 Calculating $\mathrm{cond}(A)_\nu (\nu = 2, \infty)$ when $A = \begin{pmatrix} 100 & 99 \\ 99 & 98 \end{pmatrix}$.

5.19 Prove $\mathrm{cond}(A)_2 = 1$ when A is an orthogonal matrix.

5.20 Prove $\mathrm{cond}(AB) \leq \mathrm{cond}(A)\mathrm{cond}(B)$ when $A, B \in \mathbf{R}^{n \times n}$ and $\|\cdot\|$ is the operator norm of matrix in $\mathbf{R}^{n \times n}$.

5.21 Prove:

(1) A^TA is a symmetric positive definite matrix;

(2) $\text{cond}_2(A^TA) = (\text{cond}_2(A))^2$, when $Ax = b$ and $A \in R^{n \times n}$ is a nonsingular matrix.

5.22 Letting linear equations
$$\begin{cases} 5x_1 + 2x_2 + x_3 = -12, \\ -x_1 + 4x_2 + 2x_3 = 20, \\ 2x_1 - 3x_2 + 10x_3 = 3. \end{cases}$$

(1) The convergence of this system is studied by Jacobi iterative method and Gauss-Seidel iterative method.

(2) Solving the equations by Jacobi iterative method and Gauss-Seidel iterative method and stop with $\|x^{(k+1)} - x^{(k)}\|_\infty < 10^{-4}$.

5.23 Letting linear equations

$$(1)\begin{cases} x_1 + 0.4x_2 + 0.4x_3 = 1, \\ 0.4x_1 + x_2 + 0.8x_3 = 2, \\ 0.4x_1 - 0.8x_2 + x_3 = 3; \end{cases} \qquad (2)\begin{cases} x_1 + 2x_2 - 2x_3 = 1, \\ x_1 + x_2 + x_3 = 1, \\ 2x_1 - 2x_2 + x_3 = 1. \end{cases}$$

And studies the convergence of these systems by Jacobi iterative method and Gaussian-Seidel iterative method.

5.24 Letting linear equations
$$\begin{cases} a_{11}x_1 + a_{12}x_2 = b_1, \\ a_{21}x_1 + a_{22}x_2 = b_2, \end{cases} \quad a_{11}, a_{12} \neq 0,$$

and prove that the Jacobi iterative method and the Gauss-Seidel iterative method converge or diverge at the same time and find the ratio of the convergence rate of the two methods.

5.25 Using a, b denote the necessary and sufficient condition for the Jacobian iteration and Gaussian-Seidel iteration convergence with the equation $Ax = f$ when $A = \begin{pmatrix} 10 & a & 0 \\ b & 10 & b \\ 0 & a & 5 \end{pmatrix}$, $\det A \neq 0$.

5.26 Using iterative method $x^{(k+1)} = x^{(k)} + \alpha(Ax^{(k)} - b), k = 0, 1, \cdots$ to solve $\begin{pmatrix} 3 & 2 \\ 1 & 2 \end{pmatrix}\begin{pmatrix} x_1 \\ x_2 \end{pmatrix} = \begin{pmatrix} 3 \\ -1 \end{pmatrix}$. Ask α in what range of values can make the iteration convergence, and what value does α make the iteration converge fastest?

5.27 Solving linear equations $Ax = b$ with Jacobi iteration and Gauss-Seidel iterative method. Prove both methods are converge when $A = \begin{pmatrix} 3 & 0 & -2 \\ 0 & 2 & 1 \\ -2 & 1 & 2 \end{pmatrix}$, and compare which method to converge quickly.

5.28 Using SOR method ($\omega = 1.03, \omega = 1, \omega = 1.1$) to solving linear equations
$$\begin{cases} 4x_1 - x_2 = 1, \\ -x_1 + 4x_2 - x_3 = 4, \\ -x_2 + 4x_3 = -3. \end{cases}$$
Its exact solution is $x^* = \left(\frac{1}{2}, 1, -\frac{1}{2}\right)^T$, and iteration is terminated when $\|x^* - x^{(k)}\| < 5 \times 10^{-6}$, determine the number of iteration for each ω.

5.29 Using SOR method ($\omega = 0.9$) to solving linear equations
$$\begin{cases} 5x_1 + 2x_2 + x_3 = -12, \\ -x_1 + 4x_2 + 2x_3 = 20, \\ 2x_1 - 3x_2 + 10x_3 = 3, \end{cases}$$
and stop with $\|x^{(k+1)} - x^{(k)}\| < 10^{-4}$.

5.30 Using iterative formula $x^{(k+1)} = x^{(k)} + \omega(b - Ax^{(k)}), k = 0, 1, 2, \cdots$ to solving linear equations $Ax = b$, where A is a symmetric positive definite matrix, prove the iterative formula is convergence when $0 < \omega < \frac{2}{\beta}$.

5.31 Letting $x^{(0)} = 0$, solving the following linear equations by conjugate gradient method:

(1) $\begin{pmatrix} 6 & 3 \\ 3 & 2 \end{pmatrix} \begin{pmatrix} x_1 \\ x_2 \end{pmatrix} = \begin{pmatrix} 0 \\ -1 \end{pmatrix}$; (2) $\begin{pmatrix} 4 & 3 & 0 \\ 3 & 4 & -1 \\ 0 & -1 & 4 \end{pmatrix} \begin{pmatrix} x_1 \\ x_2 \\ x_3 \end{pmatrix} = \begin{pmatrix} 3 \\ 5 \\ -5 \end{pmatrix}$.

5.32 Proving that there is $\varphi(x^{(k+1)}) \leq \varphi(x^{(k)})$ in the conjugate gradient method, if $r^{(k)} \neq 0$, then the strict inequality holds.

Chapter 6 Approximating Eigenvalues

§6.1 Linear Algebra and Eigenvalues

Theorem 6.1.1 If A is an $n \times n$ symmetric matrix, then

(1) the eigenvalue λ of A is a real number;

(2) A has n linearly independent eigenvectors;

(3) there exist orthogonal matrix P, such that

$$P^{-1}AP = \mathrm{diag}(\lambda_1, \lambda_2, \cdots, \lambda_n) = \begin{pmatrix} \lambda_1 & & \\ & \ddots & \\ & & \lambda_n \end{pmatrix},$$

where $\lambda_i (i = 1, 2, \cdots, n)$ is an eigenvalue of A.

Theorem 6.1.2 If A is an $n \times n$ matrix, then

(1) there exist unitary matrix U, such that

$$U^{-1}AU = \begin{pmatrix} r_{11} & \cdots & r_{1n} \\ & \ddots & \vdots \\ & & r_{nn} \end{pmatrix},$$

where $r_{ii} (i = 1, 2, \cdots, n)$ is an eigenvalue of A;

(2) there exist orthogonal matrix Q, such that

$$Q^{-1}AQ = \begin{pmatrix} R_{11} & \cdots & R_{1n} \\ & \ddots & \vdots \\ & & R_{nn} \end{pmatrix},$$

where $R_{ii} (i = 1, 2, \cdots, n)$ is an eigenvalue of A.

§6.2 The Power Method and the Inverse Power Method

6.2.1 The Power Method

The power method is an iterative technique used to determine the dominant eigenvalue of a matrix.

Suppose that the eigenvalues of matrix A are
$$\lambda_1, \lambda_2, \cdots, \lambda_n$$
with the associated eigenvector
$$x_1, x_2, \cdots, x_n,$$
respectively.

Assume that the dominant eigenvalue of A is
$$\lambda_1: |\lambda_1| \geq |\lambda_2| \geq \cdots\cdots \geq |\lambda_n|.$$
How to calculate λ_1 and x_1?

If $z_0 \neq 0$ is chosen appropriately, we calculate
$$z_{k+1} = A z_k = A^{k+1} z_0, \quad k = 0, 1, 2, \cdots, \tag{6.2.1}$$
$$z_0 = \alpha_1 x_1 + \alpha_2 x_2 + \cdots + \alpha_n x_n. \tag{6.2.2}$$

For $\alpha_1 \neq 0$, then we have
$$z_k = A^k z_0 = \alpha_1 \lambda_1^k x_1 + \alpha_2 \lambda_2^k x_2 + \cdots + \alpha_n \lambda_n^k x_n$$
$$= \lambda_1^k \left[\alpha_1 x_1 + \sum_{i=2}^{n} \alpha_i \left(\frac{\lambda_i}{\lambda_1}\right)^k x_i \right] \equiv \lambda_1^k (\alpha_1 x_1 + \varepsilon_k), \tag{6.2.3}$$

where $\varepsilon_k = \sum_{i=2}^{n} \alpha_i \left(\frac{\lambda_i}{\lambda_1}\right)^k x_i$.

Since $\left|\frac{\lambda_i}{\lambda_1}\right| < 1 \, (i \geq 2)$, then $\lim_{k \to 0} \varepsilon_k = 0$. As k is large enough, then
$$z_k \approx \lambda_1^k \alpha_1 x_1, \tag{6.2.4}$$
z_k is approximating to x_1.

Denote $z_k^{(i)}$ is the i-th element of z_k, then
$$\frac{z_{k+1}^{(i)}}{z_k^{(i)}} = \frac{\lambda_1^{k+1}(\alpha_1 x_1 + \varepsilon_{k+1})^{(i)}}{\lambda_1^k (\alpha_1 x_1 + \varepsilon_k)^{(i)}} = \lambda_1 \frac{\alpha_1 x_1^{(i)} + \varepsilon_{k+1}^{(i)}}{\alpha_1 x_1^{(i)} + \varepsilon_k^{(i)}} \to \lambda_1 \, (k \to \infty).$$

So, k is large enough, $\dfrac{z_{k+1}^{(i)}}{z_k^{(i)}} \approx \lambda_1$, $\max(z) = \|z\|_\infty$, for any $z_0 \neq \mathbf{0}\,(\alpha_1 \neq 0)$.

$$\begin{cases} y_1 = Az_0, m_1 = \max(y_1), z_1 = \dfrac{y_1}{m_1}, \\ y_2 = Az_1, m_2 = \max(y_2), z_2 = \dfrac{y_2}{m_2}, \\ \quad\cdots\cdots \\ y_k = Az_{k-1}, m_k = \max(y_k), z_k = \dfrac{y_k}{m_k}. \end{cases} \quad (6.2.5)$$

Theorem 6.2.1 Suppose A has n linearly independent eigenvectors, λ_1 is the dominant eigenvalue, then $\forall z_0 \neq \mathbf{0}\,(\alpha_1 \neq 0)$, $\lim\limits_{k \to \infty} z_k = \dfrac{x_1}{\max(x_1)}$, $\lim\limits_{k \to \infty} m_k = \lambda_1$.

Proof From (6.2.5), we have $z_k = \dfrac{Az_{k-1}}{m_k} = \dfrac{A^2 z_{k-2}}{m_k m_{k-1}} = \cdots = \dfrac{A^k z_0}{m_k \cdots m_1}$.

Note $\max(z_k) = \dfrac{\max(y_k)}{\max(y_k)} = 1$, $z_k = \dfrac{A^k z_0}{\|A^k z_0\|_\infty}$.

For $k \to \infty$,

$$z_k = \dfrac{\lambda_1^k \left(\alpha_1 x_1 + \sum\limits_{i=2}^n \alpha_i \left(\dfrac{\lambda_i}{\lambda_1}\right)^k x_i\right)}{\max\left(\lambda_1^k \left(\alpha_1 x_1 + \sum\limits_{i=2}^n \alpha_i \left(\dfrac{\lambda_i}{\lambda_1}\right)^k x_i\right)\right)}$$

$$= \dfrac{\alpha_1 x_1 + \sum\limits_{i=2}^n \alpha_i \left(\dfrac{\lambda_i}{\lambda_1}\right)^k x_i}{\max\left(\alpha_1 x_1 + \sum\limits_{i=2}^n \alpha_i \left(\dfrac{\lambda_i}{\lambda_1}\right)^k x_i\right)} \to \dfrac{x_1}{\max(x_1)},$$

$$m_k = \max(y_k) = \max(Az_{k-1})$$

$$= \lambda_1 \dfrac{\max\left(\alpha_1 x_1 + \sum\limits_{i=2}^n \alpha_i \left(\dfrac{\lambda_i}{\lambda_1}\right)^k x_i\right)}{\max\left(\alpha_1 x_1 + \sum\limits_{i=2}^n \alpha_i \left(\dfrac{\lambda_i}{\lambda_1}\right)^{k-1} x_i\right)}$$

$$= \lambda_1 \left(1 + 0 \left|\frac{\lambda_2}{\lambda_1}\right|^k\right) \to \lambda_1.$$

Remark 6.2.1

(1) $\dfrac{|m_{k+1} - \lambda_1|}{|m_k - \lambda|} \approx \left|\dfrac{\lambda_2}{\lambda_1}\right| = \dfrac{\left|\lambda_1\left(1 + 0\left|\frac{\lambda_2}{\lambda_1}\right|^{k+1}\right) - \lambda_1\right|}{\left|\lambda_1\left(1 + 0\left|\frac{\lambda_2}{\lambda_1}\right|^k\right) - \lambda_1\right|} \approx \left|\dfrac{\lambda_2}{\lambda_1}\right|.$

(2) since x_1 is unknown, for $\alpha_1 = 0$, $y_1 = Az_0 = \sum_{i=1}^{n} \beta_i x_i$.

(3) If $\lambda_1 = \lambda_2 = \cdots = \lambda_r$ and $|\lambda_1| > |\lambda_{r+1}| \geq \cdots \geq |\lambda_n|$, so, we have

$$z_k = \frac{A^k z_0}{\|A^k z_0\|_\infty}$$

$$= \frac{\lambda_1^k(\alpha_1 x_1 + \alpha_2 x_2 + \cdots + \alpha_n x_n) + \sum_{i=r+1}^{n} \alpha_i \lambda_i^k x_i}{\|A^k z_0\|_\infty} \to \frac{x_1}{\|x_1\|_\infty},$$

$$m_k = \frac{\|A^k z_0\|_\infty}{\|A^{k-1} z_0\|_\infty} \to \lambda_1.$$

Example 6.2.1 Use the power method to find the dominant eigenvalue λ_1 and eigenvector x_1 for the matrix

$$A = \begin{pmatrix} 2 & 0 & 1 \\ 1 & -1 & 2 \\ 0 & 1 & 5 \end{pmatrix}.$$

Solution Start with $z_0 = (1,1,1)^T$ and use formulas to generate the sequence (see table below).

k	0	1	2	3	4	5	$\cdots$	10	11
y_k		3.0000	2.0000	1.7500	1.6474	1.6142	$\cdots$	1.5951	1.5951
		2.0000	2.1667	1.9688	1.9595	1.9418	$\cdots$	1.9364	1.9364
		6.0000	5.3333	5.4063	5.3642	5.3653	$\cdots$	5.3612	5.3612
m_k	6.0000	5.3333	5.3333	5.4063	5.3642	5.3653	$\cdots$	5.3612	5.3612
z_k	1.0000	0.5000	0.3750	0.3237	0.3071	0.3009	$\cdots$	0.2975	0.2975
	1.0000	0.3333	0.4063	0.3642	0.3653	0.3619	$\cdots$	0.3612	0.3612
	1.0000	1.0000	1.0000	1.0000	1.0000	1.0000	$\cdots$	1.0000	1.0000

So the dominant eigenvalue is

$$\lambda_1 = 5.3612$$

and the eigenvector is

$$x_1 = (1.5951, 1.9364, 5.3612)^T.$$

6.2.2 The Inverse Power Method

We will now discuss the inverse power method. Suppose that A is a nonsingular $n \times n$ matrix and has distinct eigenvalues $\lambda_1, \lambda_2, \cdots, \lambda_n$ with associated eigenvector $x_1, x_2, \cdots, x_n$, respectively. And the eigenvalues $\lambda_1, \lambda_2, \cdots, \lambda_n$ satisfy

$$|\lambda_1| \geqslant |\lambda_2| \geqslant \cdots \geqslant |\lambda_{n-1}| > |\lambda_n|,$$

then the dominant eigenvalue of A^{-1} is $\dfrac{1}{\lambda_n}$. For any $z_k (k = 0,1,2,\cdots)$, to compute z_{k+1} by solving the linear system

$$Az_{k+1} = z_k, \quad k = 0,1,2,\cdots. \tag{6.2.6}$$

As k is large enough, we have the eigenvalue

$$\lambda_n \approx \frac{z_k^{(i)}}{z_{k+1}^{(i)}}, \quad i = 0,1,2,\cdots,n \tag{6.2.7}$$

with associated eigenvector z_k.

The inverse power method is a modification of the power method that gives faster convergence. It is used to determine the eigenvalue of A that is closest to specified number q.

Assume $|A| \neq 0$,

$$|\lambda_1| \geqslant |\lambda_2| \geqslant \cdots \geqslant |\lambda_{n-1}| > |\lambda_n|,$$

$$x_1 \quad\quad x_2 \quad\quad\quad x_{n-1} \quad\quad x_n$$

then A^{-1} has the same eigenvectors: $x_1, \cdots, x_n$.

Then the eigenvalues of A^{-1}:

$$|\lambda_1^{-1}| \leqslant |\lambda_2^{-1}| \leqslant \cdots \leqslant |\lambda_{n-1}^{-1}| < |\lambda_n^{-1}|.$$

Therefore, λ_n^{-1} is the dominant eigenvalue of A^{-1}.

The inverse power method is the method of applying the power method to A^{-1} to calculate λ_n^{-1} and x_n.

$\forall Z_0 (\alpha_n \neq 0)$,

$$\begin{cases} Ay_1 = Z_0, \quad m_1 = \|y_1\|_\infty, \quad Z_1 = y_1/m_1, \\ \quad \cdots\cdots \\ Ay_k = Z_{k-1}, \quad m_k = \|y_k\|_\infty, \quad Z_k = y_k/m_k. \end{cases}$$

$\|y_1\|_\infty = \max(y_1), \quad \|y_k\|_\infty = \max(y_k), k = 2,3,\cdots.$

Then $\quad Z_k \to \dfrac{x_n}{\|x_n\|_\infty}, \quad k \to \infty,$

$$m_k \to \lambda_n^{-1}, \quad k \to \infty.$$

How to calculate y_k?

$$A = LU,$$

L is the lower triangular matrix, U is the upper triangular matrix.

$$\begin{cases} LU_k = Z_{k-1}, \\ Uy_k = u_k \end{cases} \to y_k.$$

Remark 6.2.2 $A:\lambda \approx \tilde{\lambda}.$

$$\begin{cases} (A - \tilde{\lambda}I)y_k = Z_{k-1}, \\ m_k = \|y_k\|_\infty, \\ Z_k = \dfrac{y_k}{m_k}, \end{cases} \quad k = 1,2,\cdots.$$

If

$$0 < |\lambda_i - \tilde{\lambda}| < |\lambda_j - \tilde{\lambda}|, \quad j \neq i,$$

then $(\lambda_i - \tilde{\lambda})^{-1}$ is the dominant eigenvalue of $(A - \tilde{\lambda}I)^{-1}$.

$$\begin{cases} Z_k \to x_i, k \to \infty, \\ m_k \to \dfrac{1}{\lambda_i - \tilde{\lambda}}, k \to \infty. \end{cases}$$

Then $\tilde{\lambda} + \dfrac{1}{m_k} \to \lambda_i, k \to \infty.$

§6.3 Householder's Method

Householder's method is to reducing an arbitrary symmetric matrix to a similar tridiagonal matrix.

A matrix and its similar matrix have the same eigenvalues.

6.3.1 Householder Matrix

Definition 6.3.1
$$H = I - 2\omega\omega^T$$
is called Householder matrix, $\omega = (\omega_1, \omega_2, \cdots, \omega_n)^T$, and $\|\omega\|_2 = \sqrt{\omega^T\omega} = 1$.

Remark 6.3.1 $H^T = H, H^2 = I$.
$(H^2 = (I - 2\omega\omega^T)(I - 2\omega\omega^T) = I - 4\omega\omega^T + 4\omega\underline{\omega^T\omega}\omega^T = I)$
$\forall x = (x_1, x_2, \cdots, x_n)^T \neq \mathbf{0}$,

$$\alpha_1 = \|x\|_2 \operatorname{sgn}(x_1) = \sqrt{\sum_{i=1}^{n} x_i^2} \operatorname{sgn}(x_1),$$

$$y = -\alpha_1 e_1,$$

$$(I - 2\omega\omega^T)x = -\alpha_1 e_1 \rightarrow \omega = \frac{x + \alpha_1 e_1}{2\omega^T x},$$

where $e_1 = (1, 0, \cdots, 0)^T \in \mathbf{R}^n$.

$$\omega = \frac{x + \alpha_1 e_1}{\|x + \alpha_1 e_1\|_2},$$

$$H = I - \frac{2}{\|x + \alpha_1 e_1\|_2^2}(x + \alpha_1 e_1)(x + \alpha_1 e_1)^T,$$

$$Hx = (-\alpha_1, 0, 0, \cdots, 0)^T,$$

$$\begin{cases} \alpha_1 = \operatorname{sgn}(x_1) \|x\|_2, \\ H = x + \alpha_1 e_1, \beta = \frac{1}{2}\|u\|_2^2 = \alpha_1(\alpha_1 + x_1), \\ H = I - \beta^{-1} uu^T. \end{cases}$$

Theorem 6.3.1 $\forall x, y \in \mathbf{R}^n$, if $\|x\|_2 = \|y\|_2$, then there exists Householder matrix H such that
$$Hx = y.$$

Proof If $x = y$, one can take $\omega \perp x$,
$$(I - 2\omega\omega^T)x = x - 2\omega\omega^T x = x.$$
If $x \neq y$,
$$(I - 2\omega\omega^T)x = y,$$

$$x - y = 2\omega\omega^T x$$

$$\omega = \frac{x-y}{2\omega^T x},$$

$$2\omega^T x = 2\frac{(x-y)^T x}{\|y-x\|_2} = \frac{2(x^T x - y^T x)}{\|y-x\|_2} = \frac{(y-x)^T(y-x)}{\|y-x\|_2} = \|y-x\|_2,$$

$$\omega = \frac{x-y}{\|y-x\|_2},$$

$$\|\omega\|_2 = 1.$$

Theorem 6.3.2 Suppose $x = (x_1, x_2, \cdots, x_n)^T \neq 0$, then $\exists H$ s.t.

$$Hx = -\alpha_1 e_1,$$

where
$$\begin{cases} H = I - \beta^{-1} uu^T, \\ \alpha_1 = \text{sgn}(x_1) \|x\|_2, \\ u = x + \alpha_1 e_1, \\ \beta = \frac{1}{2}\|u\|_2^2 = \alpha_1(\alpha_1 + x_1) = \alpha_1^2 + \alpha_1 x_1. \end{cases}$$

Example 6.3.1 $x = (3,5,1,1)^T$.

Solution $\|x\|_2 = 6$, $\sigma = \text{sgn}(x_1)\|x\|_2 = 6$,

$$Hx = -\sigma \cdot e_1, \quad e_1 = (1,0,0,0)^T,$$

$$u = x + \sigma e_1 = (9,5,1,1)^T,$$

$$\beta = \sigma(\sigma + x_1) = \frac{1}{2}\|u\|_2^2 = 54,$$

$$H = I - \beta^{-1} uu^T = \frac{1}{54}\begin{pmatrix} -27 & -45 & -9 & -9 \\ -45 & 29 & -5 & -5 \\ -9 & -5 & 53 & -1 \\ -9 & -5 & -1 & 53 \end{pmatrix},$$

$$Hx = (-6,0,0,0)^T.$$

Theorem 6.3.3 Suppose A is an $n \times n$ matrix, then $\exists$ orthogonal matrix $Q = H_1, \cdots, H_{n-2}$ s.t. $Q^T AQ$ is upper Hessenberg matrix.

If $A_{n \times n}$ is symmtrix, then $\exists$ orthogonal matrix Q s.t. $Q^T AQ$ is triangular diagonal matrix.

6.3.2 QR Factorization

Theorem 6.3.4 Suppose $A_{n \times n}: |A| \neq 0$, then $\exists$ orthogonal matrix Q

and upper triangular matrix R s.t. $A = QR$.

Definition 6.3.2 Givens' method

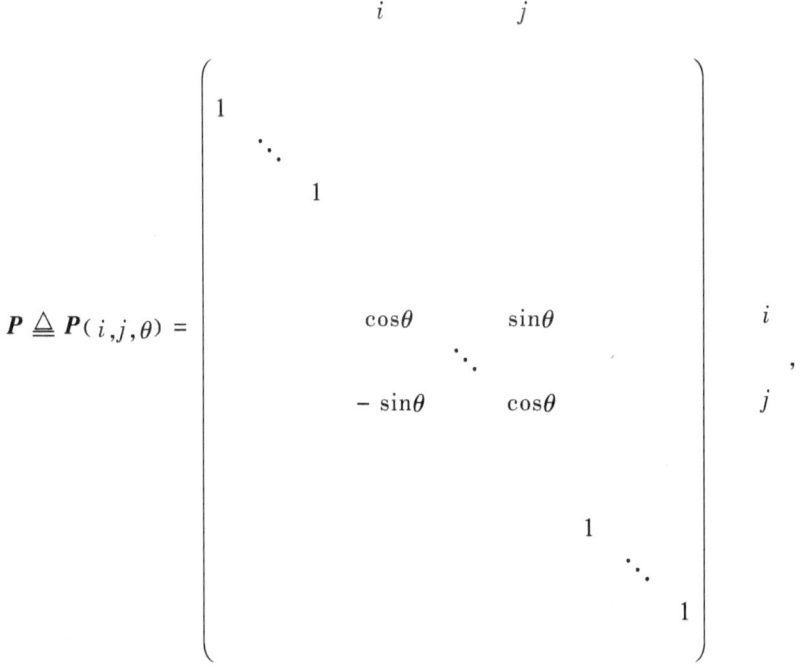

P is orthogonal matrix, $P^{-1} = P^{T}$.

Theorem 6.3.5 $|A_{n \times n}| \neq 0$, then $\exists$ orthogonal matrix $P_1, \cdots, P_{n-1}$ s.t. $P_{n-1} \cdots P_2 P_1 A = R$,

$$A = QR.$$

§6.4 QR Algorithm

1961, Francis gave QR algorithm.

Suppose $A_{n \times n}$ is a matrix, how to calculate Q_1?

$$A_1 = A = Q_1 R_1,$$

Q_1: orthogonal matrix; R_1: upper triangular matrix.

$$A_2 = R_1 Q_1 = Q_1^{T} A_1 Q_1, \quad Q_1^{-1} = Q^{T},$$
$$A_2 = Q_2 R_2,$$
$$A_3 = R_2 Q_2 = Q_2^{T} A_2 Q_2,$$

$$A_1 = A = Q_1 R_1, \quad A_{k+1} \sim A_k,$$

$$\begin{cases} A_k = Q_k R_k, \\ A_{k+1} = R_k Q_k = Q_k^T A_k Q_k, \end{cases} \quad k = 1, 2, \cdots.$$

$\{A_k\}_{k=1}^{\infty}$: "matrix sequence".

Theorem 6.4.1 Letting $\tilde{Q}_k = Q_1 Q_2 \cdots Q_k$, $\tilde{R}_k = R_1 R_2 \cdots R_k$, then

(1) $\{A_k\}$ is orthogonal and similar, $A_{k+1} = \tilde{Q}_k^T A \tilde{Q}_k$;

(2) $A^k = \tilde{Q}_k \tilde{R}_k$.

Theorem 6.4.2 Suppose $A_{n \times n}$ is a matrix.

(1) $|\lambda_1| > |\lambda_2| > \cdots > |\lambda_n| > 0$.

(2) $A = XDX^{-1}$, $D = \text{diag}(\lambda_1, \lambda_2, \cdots, \lambda_n)$, $X^{-1} = LU$, then

$$k \to \infty, \quad a_{ij}^{(k)} \text{ of } A_k \to \lambda_i (i = 1, 2, \cdots, n).$$

§6.5 Improved Power Method

The power method is linearly convergent by $\left|\dfrac{\lambda_2}{\lambda_1}\right|$.

a) Moving Origin Method

Suppose that the eigenvalues of matrix A are $\lambda_1, \lambda_2, \cdots, \lambda_n$ with associated eigenvector $x_1, x_2, \cdots, x_n$, respectively.

For any constant p, then the eigenvalues for the matrix $B = A - pI$ are $\lambda_1 - p, \lambda_2 - p, \cdots, \lambda_n - p$, and the matrix A and B have the same eigenvectors. Choosing appropriate constant p, such that

$$|\lambda_1 - p| > |\lambda_2 - p| \geqslant \cdots \geqslant |\lambda_n - p|, \quad (6.5.1)$$

and

$$\left|\frac{\lambda_2 - p}{\lambda_1 - p}\right| < \left|\frac{\lambda_2}{\lambda_1}\right|. \quad (6.5.2)$$

Applying the power method to B, calculate $\lambda_1 - p$ and the corresponding eigenvector.

Example 6.5.1 Suppose A has eigenvalues $\lambda_1 = 12, \lambda_2 = 10, \lambda_3 = 8$. Since $\left|\dfrac{\lambda_2}{\lambda_1}\right| = 0.8$, taking $p = 9$, then $\left|\dfrac{\lambda_2 - p}{\lambda_1 - p}\right| = \dfrac{1}{3}$.

b) Rayleigh Method

Theorem 6.5.1 Suppose that A is an $n \times n$ symmetric matrix and the eigenvalues for matrix A satisfy

$$|\lambda_1| > |\lambda_2| \geq \cdots\cdots \geq |\lambda_n|.$$

Then

$$\frac{(A^k z_k, z_k)}{(z_k, z_k)} = \lambda_1 + O\left(\left|\frac{\lambda_2}{\lambda_1}\right|^{2k}\right).$$

Proof Since A is symmetric, there are the orthogonal eigenvectors $x_1, x_2, \cdots, x_n$. We have

$$\frac{(Az_k, z_k)}{(z_k, z_k)} = \frac{(A^{k+1} z_0, A^k z_0)}{(A^k z_0, A^k z_0)} = \frac{\alpha_1^2 \lambda_1^{2k+1} + \sum_{j=2}^{n} \alpha_j^2 \lambda_j^{2k+1}}{\alpha_1^2 \lambda_1^{2k} + \sum_{j=2}^{n} \alpha_j^2 \lambda_j^{2k}}$$

$$= \lambda_1 + \frac{\sum_{j=2}^{n} \alpha_j^2 (\lambda_j - \lambda_1) \left(\frac{\lambda_j}{\lambda_1}\right)^{2k}}{\alpha_1^2 + \sum_{j=2}^{n} \alpha_j^2 \left(\frac{\lambda_j}{\lambda_1}\right)^{2k}}$$

$$= \lambda_1 \left[1 + \frac{-\sum_{j=2}^{n} \alpha_i^2 \left(\frac{\lambda_j}{\lambda_1}\right)^{2k} + \sum_{j=2}^{n} \alpha_i^2 \left(\frac{\lambda_j}{\lambda_1}\right)^{2k+1}}{\alpha_1^2 + \sum_{j=2}^{n} \alpha_j^2 \left(\frac{\lambda_j}{\lambda_1}\right)^{2k}} \right]$$

$$= \lambda_1 + \lambda_1 \left[1 + \frac{\sum_{j=2}^{n} \alpha_i^2 \left(\frac{\lambda_j}{\lambda_1}\right)^{2k} \left[\frac{\lambda_j}{\lambda_1} - 1\right]}{\alpha_1^2 + \sum_{j=2}^{n} \alpha_j^2 \left(\frac{\lambda_j}{\lambda_1}\right)^{2k}} \right]$$

$$= \lambda_1 + O\left(\left|\frac{\lambda_2}{\lambda_1}\right|^{2k}\right).$$

Excises 6

6.1 Estimation of the bounds of the following matrix eigenvalues using the Gerschgorin disk theorem:

$$(1)\begin{pmatrix} -1 & 0 & 0 \\ -1 & 0 & 1 \\ -1 & -1 & 2 \end{pmatrix}; \quad (2)\begin{pmatrix} 4 & -1 & & & \\ -1 & 4 & -1 & & \\ & \ddots & \ddots & & \\ & & -1 & 4 & -1 \\ & & & -1 & 4 \end{pmatrix}.$$

6.2 Calculate the eigenvalues and eigenvectors of the following matrices and whether they are similar to diagonal matrices or not.

$$(1)\begin{pmatrix} 2 & -3 & 6 \\ 0 & 3 & -4 \\ 0 & 2 & -3 \end{pmatrix}; \quad (2)\begin{pmatrix} 2 & 0 & 1 \\ 0 & 2 & 0 \\ 1 & 0 & 2 \end{pmatrix}; \quad (3)\begin{pmatrix} 1 & 0 & 0 \\ -1 & 0 & 1 \\ -1 & -1 & 2 \end{pmatrix}.$$

6.3 Calculate the main eigenvalues and corresponding eigenvectors of the following matrices by power method:

$$(1)A_1 = \begin{pmatrix} 7 & 3 & -2 \\ 3 & 4 & -1 \\ -2 & -1 & 3 \end{pmatrix}; \quad (2)A_2 = \begin{pmatrix} 3 & -4 & 3 \\ -4 & 6 & -1 \\ 3 & 3 & 1 \end{pmatrix}.$$

6.4 Using the inverse power method to find the eigenvalues closest to 6 and the corresponding eigenvectors of the matrix

$$\begin{pmatrix} 6 & 2 & 1 \\ 2 & 3 & 1 \\ 1 & 1 & 1 \end{pmatrix}.$$

6.5 Please find the eigenvector corresponding to the eigenvalue 4 of matrix

$$\begin{pmatrix} 4 & 0 & 0 \\ 0 & 3 & 1 \\ 0 & 1 & 3 \end{pmatrix}.$$

6.6 (1) Let A be a symmetric matrix, λ and $x(\|x\|_2 = 1)$ are an eigenvalue of A and the corresponding eigenvector. Let P be an orthogonal matrix, satisfied $Px = e_1 = (1,0,\cdots,0)^T = B$. Prove that the elements of the first column of $B = PAP^T$ are zero except λ.

(2) For matrix $A = \begin{pmatrix} 2 & 10 & 2 \\ 10 & 5 & -8 \\ 2 & -8 & 11 \end{pmatrix}$, $\lambda = 9$ is its eigenvalue, $x = $

$\left(\frac{2}{3},\frac{1}{3},\frac{2}{3}\right)^{T}$ is the eigenvector corresponding to 9, try to find an elementary reflection matrix P, satisfied $Px = e_1$, and calculate $B = PAP^T$.

6.7 Using the elementary reflection matrix $A = \begin{pmatrix} 1 & 3 & 4 \\ 3 & 1 & 2 \\ 4 & 2 & 1 \end{pmatrix}$, orthogonal similarity is reduced to a symmetric tridiagonal matrix.

6.8 Let A_{n-1} be a matrix obtained by the Housholder method and let y be an eigenvector of A_{n-1}.

(1) Prove the corresponding vector $x = P_1 P_2 \cdots P_{n-2} y$ of the matrix A;

(2) For the given y how to calculate x?

6.9 Calculate all the eigenvalues of the following matrices with the QR method with displacement.

$(1) A = \begin{pmatrix} 1 & 2 & 0 \\ 2 & -1 & 1 \\ 0 & 1 & 3 \end{pmatrix}$; $(2) B = \begin{pmatrix} 3 & 1 & 0 \\ 1 & 2 & 1 \\ 0 & 1 & 1 \end{pmatrix}$.

6.10 Try the elementary reflection matrix to decompose the matrix $A = \begin{pmatrix} 1 & 1 & 1 \\ 2 & -1 & -1 \\ 2 & -4 & 5 \end{pmatrix}$ into the form of QR, where Q is the orthogonal matrix and R is the upper triangular matrix.

6.11 Let $A = \begin{pmatrix} A_{11} & A_{12} \\ 0 & A_{22} \end{pmatrix} \begin{matrix} 3 \\ 2 \end{matrix}$, λ_i is the eigenvalue of A_{11}, λ_j is the eigenvalue of A_{22}, $x_i = (\alpha_1, \alpha_2, \alpha_3)^T$ is the eigenvector corresponding to λ_i and A_{11}, $y_j = (\beta_1, \beta_2)^T$ is the eigenvector corresponding to λ_j and A_{22}. Prove that:

(1) λ_i and λ_j are the eigenvalues of A.

(2) $x'_i = (\alpha_1, \alpha_2, \alpha_3, 0, 0)^T$ is the feature vector of A corresponding to λ_i, and $y'_j = (0, 0, 0, \beta_1, \beta_2)^T$ is the feature vector of A corresponding to λ_j.

Chapter 7 Numerical Solutions of Nonlinear Systems

§7.1 The Bisection Method

Example 7.1.1 $f(x) = e^{-\frac{x}{10}} \sin(10x) = 0$ and so on.

$p_n(x) = 0, n = 1,2,3,4$, the exact solution is easy to be found, however, for $n \geqslant 5$, there is no formula of the solution.

Definition 7.1.1 $f(x) = (x - x^*)^m g(x)$, m is a positive integer, $g(x^*) \neq 0$, then x^* is called the zero of multiplicity m; $m = 1$, x^* is called simple solution.

If $f(x^*) = f^{(1)}(x^*) = \cdots = f^{(m-1)}(x^*) = 0, f^{(m)}(x^*) \neq 0$, then x^* is the zero point of multiplicity m.

7.1.1 Bisection Method

If $f(x) = 0, x \in [a,b]$, and $f(a)f(b) < 0$, only one solution.

Bisection method (see Figure 7.1.1):

(1) $a_1 = a, b_1 = b$, letting $x_1 = \dfrac{a+b}{2}$. If $f(a_1) \cdot f(x_1) < 0$, then $a_2 = a_1, b_2 = x_1$, else $a_2 = x_1$.

(2) Letting $x_2 = \dfrac{a_1 + x_1}{2} = \dfrac{a_2 + b_2}{2}$. If $f(x_1) \cdot f(x_2) < 0$, then $a_3 = x_2, b_3 = x_1$.

Bisection method: $n = 1, a_1 = a, b_1 = b$.

Step 1: $x_n = \dfrac{a_n + b_n}{2}$.

Step 2: If $|f(x_n)| \leqslant \delta_n$ or $b_n - x_n \leqslant \varepsilon$, x_n, stop.

Step 3: If $f(a_n)f(x_n) > 0$, then $a_{n+1} = x_n, b_{n+1} = b_n$, else $a_{n+1} = a_n, b_{n+1} = x_n$.

Step 4: $n: = n+1$, step 1.

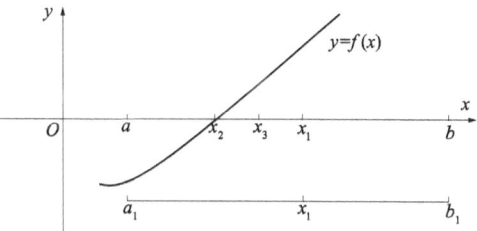

Figure 7.1.1 Bisection method

7.1.2 Error Estimation

Theorem 7.1.1 If $f \in C[a,b]$, $f(a)f(b) < 0$, then $\{x_n\}$ of the bisection method satisfies $|x_n - x^*| \leq \dfrac{b-a}{2^n}$.

Proof On the interval $[a_n, b_n]$,
$$b_n - a_n = \frac{b_{n-1} - a_{n-1}}{2} = \cdots = \frac{b-a}{2^{n-1}},$$

$$|x_n - x^*| = \left|\frac{b_n + a_n}{2} - x^*\right| \leq \frac{b_n + a_n}{2} = \frac{b-a}{2^{n-1}}.$$

Remark 7.1.1 The bisection method has clear formula, but it is slow to convergent. Moreover, it does not work for complex solution and multiplicity solution of the equation.

§7.2 Fixed Point Iterative Method

7.2.1 Fixed Point Iterative Method

$$f(x) = 0 \Leftrightarrow x = \varphi(x).$$

If $f(x^*) = 0 \Rightarrow x^* = \varphi(x^*)$, x^* is a fixed point.

Fixed point iterative method:
$$\begin{cases} x_{k+1} = \varphi(x_k), \\ x_0. \end{cases}$$

$\varphi(x)$ is called by iterative function. $\{x_n\} \to x^*$, x^* is a zero of $f(x)$.

How to choose the iterative function $\varphi(x)$?

7.2.2 General Results of the Fixed Point Iterative Method

Theorem 7.2.1 (1) If $\varphi(x) \in C[a,b]$, and $a \leq \varphi(x) \leq b$, $\forall x \in (a,b)$, then $\varphi(x)$ has one fixed point in (a,b).

(2) If $\varphi(x) \in C^1[a,b]$, $\exists\ 0 < L < 1$, s.t. $|\varphi'(x)| \leq L$ for all $x \in [a,b]$, then $\varphi(x)$ has a unique fixed point.

Proof (1) $\psi(x) = \varphi(x) - x$, then $\psi(x) \in C[a,b]$, $\psi(a) = \varphi(a) - a \geq 0$, $\psi(b) = \varphi(b) - b \leq 0$.

(2) Assume x_1^*, x_2^* are two fixed points, then we have
$$|x_1^* - x_2^*| = |\varphi(x_1^*) - \varphi(x_2^*)| = |\varphi'(\xi) \cdot (x_1^* - x_2^*)|$$
$$\leq L |x_1^* - x_2^*| < |x_1^* - x_2^*|.$$

Therefore, x^* is unique.

Theorem 7.2.2 Suppose $\varphi(x) \in C[a,b] \cap C'[a,b]$, and satisfies

(i) $a \leq \varphi(x) \leq b$, $\forall x \in (a,b)$;

(ii) $\exists\ 0 < L < 1, |\varphi(x)| \leq L, \forall x \in (a,b)$, then we get

(1) $\forall x_0 \in (a,b), x_k \to x^*\ (k \to \infty)$;

(2) the error of $\{x_k\}$, $|x_k - x^*| \leq \dfrac{1}{1-L}|x_{k+1} - x_k| \leq \dfrac{L^k}{1-L}|x_1 - x_0|$.

Proof The conditions (i) and (ii) imply x^* is unique.
$$|x_k - x^*| = |\varphi(x_{k-1}) - \varphi(x^*)| = |\varphi'(\xi)| \cdot |x_{k-1} - x^*|.$$
(1) $|x_k - x^*| \leq L^k |x_0 - x^*|$.
(2) $\quad |x_{k+1} - x_k| = |\varphi(x_k) - \varphi(x_{k-1})| \leq L|x_k - x_{k-1}|$

and
$$|x_{k+1} - x_k| = |x_{k+1} - x^* + x^* - x_k| \geq |x_k - x^*| - |x_{k+1} - x^*|$$
$$\geq |x_k - x^*| - L|x_k - x^*| = (1-L)|x_k - x^*|,$$
$$\Rightarrow |x_k - x^*| \leq \frac{1}{1-L}|x_{k+1} - x_k| \leq \cdots \leq \frac{L^k}{1-L}|x_1 - x_0|.$$

7.2.3 Locally Convergence

Definition 7.2.1 If there exists $N(x^*) = [x^* - \delta, x^* + \delta]$, $\delta > 0$ for $\forall x_0 \in N(x^*)$, $\{x_k\}$ convergent, then $\{x_k\}$ is locally convergent.

Theorem 7.2.3 If x^* is a fixed point, $\varphi'(x)$ is continuous in $U(x^*,\delta)$ and $|\varphi'(x^*)| \leq L < 1$, then the fixed point iterative method is locally convergent.

Proof $\varphi'(x)$ is continuous, so, $\forall \varepsilon \in (0, 1-L)$, $\exists N(x^*) = [x^* - \delta, x^* + \delta]$, s.t. $|\varphi'(x)| \leq L + \varepsilon < 1$ and
$$|\varphi(x) - x^*| = |\varphi(x) - \varphi(x^*)| \leq (L+\varepsilon)|x - x^*| < \delta,$$
$\forall x \in N(x^*)$, $x^* - \delta < \varphi(x) < x^* + \delta$.

Definition 7.2.2 $\{x_k\}$ convergents to x^*, $e_k = x_k - x^*$.

If $p \geq 1$ and $c > 0$, s.t. $\lim\limits_{k \to \infty} \dfrac{|e_{k+1}|}{|e_k|^p} = c$, then $\{x_n\}$ is called p-order convergent;

If $p = 1$ and $0 < c < 1$, s.t. $\lim\limits_{k \to \infty} \dfrac{|e_{k+1}|}{|e_k|^p} = c$, then $\{x_n\}$ is called linearly convergent.

Here, $e_{k+1} = x_{k+1} - x^* = \varphi(x_k) - \varphi(x^*) = \varphi'(\xi) e_k$, $\lim\limits_{k \to \infty} \dfrac{|e_{k+1}|}{|e_k|} = |\varphi'(x^*)| \neq 0$.

Theorem 7.2.4 $x_{k+1} = \varphi(x_k)$, If $\varphi^p(x)$ ($p > 1$) is continuous in $U(x^*, \delta)$, then $\varphi(x_k) = x_{k+1}$ ($k = 0, 1, 2, \cdots$) is p-order convergent $\Leftrightarrow \varphi(x^*) = x^*$, $\varphi^{(l)}(x^*) = 0$, $l = 1, 2, \cdots, p-1$, $\varphi^{(p)}(x^*) \neq 0$ and $\lim\limits_{k \to \infty} \dfrac{e_{k+1}}{e_k^p} = \dfrac{1}{p!} \varphi^{(p)}(x^*) \neq 0$.

Proof $\Leftarrow$) : $p > 1$, $\varphi'(x^*) = 0$, $\varphi'(x)$ is continuous, and $x_0 \neq x^*$, $x_k \neq x^*$.
$$\varphi(x_k) = \varphi(x^*) + \varphi'(x^*)(x_k - x^*) + \cdots$$
$$+ \dfrac{1}{(p-1)!} \varphi^{(p-1)}(x^*)(x_k - x^*)^{p-1} + \dfrac{1}{p!} \varphi^{(p)}(\xi)(x_k - x^*)^p,$$
$$x_{k+1} - x^* = \dfrac{1}{p!} \varphi^{(p)}(\xi)(x_k - x^*)^p, \text{ so, } \lim\limits_{k \to \infty} \dfrac{|e_{k+1}|}{|e_k|^p} = \dfrac{1}{p!} \varphi^{(p)}(x^*).$$

$\Rightarrow$) : Suppose $x_{k+1} = \varphi(x_k)$ is p-order convergent, then
$$\lim\limits_{k \to \infty} x_k = x^*, \text{ so } \varphi(x) = x^*.$$
Assume that $\exists p_0$ s.t. $\varphi^{(l)}(x^*) = 0$, $l = 1, 2, \cdots, p-1$, $\varphi^{(p_0)}(x^*) \neq 0$, and $p_0 \neq p$, $p_0 \leq p - 1$, then
$$\lim\limits_{k \to \infty} \dfrac{e_{k+1}}{e_k^{p_0}} = \dfrac{1}{p_0!} \varphi^{(p_0)}(x^*), \quad p_0 \leq p - 1, \quad \dfrac{e_{k+1}}{e_k^p} = \dfrac{e_{k+1}}{e_k^{p_0}} \cdot \dfrac{1}{e_k^{p-p_0}},$$
it does not exists $\varphi(x_k) = x_{k+1}$ ($k = 0, 1, 2, \cdots$), $\{x_k\}$ is p-order convergent.

7.2.4 Accelerating Convergence

(1) Aitken's Δ^2 method: $\begin{cases} x_{k+1} = \varphi(x_k), \\ x_0, \end{cases}$

$x_1 = \varphi(x_0)$, $x_1 - x^* = \varphi(x_0) - \varphi(x^*) = \varphi'(\xi)(x_0 - x^*)$.

Suppose $|\varphi'(\xi)|$ changes small, $\varphi'(\xi) \approx L$, $x_1 - x^* = L(x_0 - x^*)$,

$x_2 = \varphi(x_1)$, $x_2 - x^* = \varphi'(\xi_1)(x_1 - x^*)$.

So $\dfrac{x_1 - x^*}{x_2 - x^*} = \dfrac{x_0 - x^*}{x_1 - x^*}$, $x^* = \dfrac{x_0 x_2 - x_1^2}{x_2 - 2x_1 + x_0} = x_0 - \dfrac{(x_1 - x_0)^2}{x_2 - 2x_1 + x_0}$.

While $x_k \to x_{k+1}, x_{k+2}, \cdots$,

$$\bar{x}_{k+1} = x_k - \dfrac{(x_{k+1} - x_k)^2}{x_k - 2x_{k+1} + x_{k+2}} = x_k - \dfrac{(\Delta x_k)^2}{\Delta^2 x_k}.$$

Therefore, $\lim\limits_{k \to \infty} \dfrac{\bar{x}_{k+1} - x^*}{x_k - x^*} = 0$.

Forward difference Δx_k: $\Delta x_k = x_{k+1} - x_k$,

$\Delta x_{k+1} = x_{k+2} - x_{k+1}$,

$\Delta^2 x_k = x_{k+2} - 2x_{k+1} + x_k$.

(2) Steffensen's iterative method: Aitken's method + fixed point iterative.

x_{k+1}: $y_k = \varphi(x_k)$.

x_{k+2}: $z_k = \varphi(y_k)$.

$\bar{x}_{k+1}$: $x_{k+1} = x_k - \dfrac{(y_k - z_k)^2}{x_k - 2y_k + z_k}$.

§7.3 Newton's Iteration Method

7.3.1 Newton's Method

Newton's method is one of the most powerful and well-known numerical method for solving a root-finding problem.

Iterative method: $f(x) = 0 \Leftrightarrow x = \varphi(x)$,

$x_k = \varphi(x_k)$, $\{x_k\} \to x^*$.

Chapter 7 Numerical Solutions of Nonlinear Systems

The iterative function of Newton's method is chosen:
Suppose $f(x) \in C^2(U(\alpha,\delta))$, $\forall x_0 \in U(\alpha,\delta)$,

$$f(x) = f(x_0) + f'(x_0)(x-x_0) + \frac{f''(\xi_0)}{2!}(x-x_0)^2,$$

$$0 = f(\alpha) = f(x_0) + f'(x_0)(\alpha - x_0) + \frac{f''(\xi_0)}{2!}(\alpha - x_0)^2.$$

If $f'(x_0) \neq 0$ and omitting the term $(\alpha - x_0)^2$, then we have

$$0 = f(x_0) + f'(x_0)(\alpha - x_0),$$

$$\Rightarrow \alpha = x_0 - \frac{f(x_0)}{f'(x_0)}, \quad x_1 = x_0 - \frac{f(x_0)}{f'(x_0)}.$$

$x_{n+1} = x_n - \dfrac{f(x_n)}{f'(x_n)}$, $n = 0,1,2,\cdots$ is called Newton's method (See Figure 7.3.1).

$T_k: y - f(x_k) = f'(x_k)(x - x_k)$

$\Rightarrow x_{k+1} = x_k - \dfrac{f(x_k)}{f'(x_k)}.$

Theorem 7.3.1 Suppose $f(x) \in C^m[a,b]$ $(m>2)$, p is a simple zero solution of $f(x) = 0$, then, as $x_0 \to p$, Newton's method is convergent and the order is at least 2.

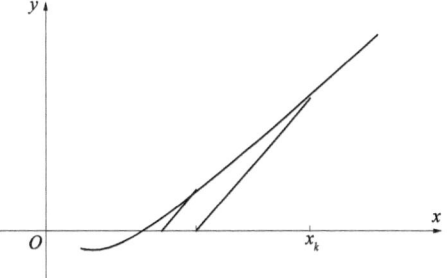

Figure 7.3.1 The Newton's method

Proof Letting $g(x) = x - \dfrac{f(x)}{f'(x)}$. Since $f(x) \in C^2[a,b]$, so we have

$$g'(x) = 1 - \frac{f'(x)f'(x) - f(x)f''(x)}{[f'(x)]^2} = \frac{f(x)f''(x)}{[f'(x)]^2}.$$

Because p is simple solution, $f(p) = 0$, $f'(p) \neq 0$, then $g'(p) = 0$ and $\exists r > 0$, $\forall x \in (p-r, p+r)$, $f'(x) \neq 0$. So $g'(x)$, $g''(x)$ are continuous in $(p-r, p+r)$.

Using theorem 7.3.1, we have $\{x_k\}$ is convergent and the order is at least 2.

Remark 7.3.1 x_0 is close to p, i.e. $x_0 \in (p-r, p+r)$. How to choose x_0?

Theorem 7.3.2 Suppose $f''(x)$ exists in $[a,b]$ and satisfying:

(1) $f(a)f(b) < 0$;

(2) $f'(x) \neq 0$, $x \in (a,b)$, $f''(x)$ remains sign;

(3) $\left|\dfrac{f(a)}{f'(a)}\right| < b - a$, $\left|\dfrac{f(b)}{f'(b)}\right| < b - a$.

Then the Newton's method is convergent for $x_0 \in [a,b]$ and the order is 2.

Example 7.3.1 Given $c > 0, x^2 - c = 0$.

$$x_{k+1} - \sqrt{c} = \frac{1}{2x_k}(x_k - \sqrt{c})^2,$$

$$x_{k+1} + \sqrt{c} = \frac{1}{2x_k}(x_k + \sqrt{c})^2,$$

$$\Rightarrow \frac{x_{k+1} - \sqrt{c}}{x_{k+1} + \sqrt{c}} = \left(\frac{x_k - \sqrt{c}}{x_k + \sqrt{c}}\right)^2,$$

$$\Rightarrow \frac{x_k - \sqrt{c}}{x_k + \sqrt{c}} = \left(\frac{x - \sqrt{c}}{x_0 + \sqrt{c}}\right)^{2^k}.$$

Denote $g = \dfrac{x_0 - \sqrt{c}}{x_0 + \sqrt{c}}$, then $x_k - \sqrt{c} = 2\sqrt{c}\dfrac{g^{2^k}}{1 - g^{2^k}}$, $\forall x_0 > 0$, $|g| < 1$. Therefore, $k \to \infty$, $x_k \to \sqrt{c}$.

Example 7.3.2 $\sqrt{115}$.

Solution $c = 115, x_0 = 10$,

$$\begin{cases} x_{k+1} = \dfrac{1}{2}\left(x_k + \dfrac{115}{x_k}\right), \\ x_0 = 10. \end{cases}$$

Example 7.3.3 $xe^x - 1 = 0$.

Solution $f(x) = xe^x - 1$,

$$\begin{cases} x_{k+1} = x_k - \dfrac{x_k e^{x_k} - 1}{x_k e^{x_k} + e^{x_k}} = x_k - \dfrac{x_k - e^{-x_k}}{x_k + 1}, \\ x_0 = 0.5. \end{cases}$$

7.3.2 Modified Newton's Method

Simplified Newton's method:

$$x_{n+1} = x_n - \frac{f(x_n)}{f'(x_0)}, \quad n = 0, 1, 2, \cdots.$$

$$x_{k+1} = x_k - cf(x_k).$$

The iterative function: $\varphi(x) = x - cf(x)$.

So
$$\varphi'(x) = 1 - cf'(x).$$

$$|\varphi'(x)| < 1 \Rightarrow |1 - cf'(x)| < 1 \Rightarrow 0 < cf'(x) < 2,$$

the order is 1.

7.3.3 The Case of Multiplicity m

Suppose α is zero of multiplicity $m\,(m\geqslant 2)$ of $f(x)$,
$$f(\alpha) = f'(\alpha) = \cdots = f^{(m-1)}(\alpha) = 0, f^{(m)}(\alpha) \neq 0.$$
The iterative function: $\varphi(x) = x - \dfrac{f(x)}{f'(x)}$.

Letting $x = \alpha + h$, we get

$$\varphi(\alpha + h) = \alpha + h - \frac{f(\alpha + h)}{f'(\alpha + h)}$$

$$= \alpha + h - \frac{f^{(m)}(\alpha)\dfrac{h^m}{m!} + O(h^{m+1})}{f^{(m)}(\alpha)\dfrac{h^{m-1}}{(m-1)!} + O(h^m)}$$

$$= \alpha + h - \frac{1}{m}h + O(h^2)$$

$$= \alpha + \left(1 - \frac{1}{m}\right)h + O(h^2),$$

$$\varphi'(\alpha) = \lim_{h\to\infty}\frac{\varphi(\alpha + h) - \varphi(\alpha)}{h}$$

$$= 1 - \frac{1}{m}.$$

If $m \geqslant 2$, then $\varphi'(\alpha) = 1 - \dfrac{1}{m} > 0$, and $|\varphi'(\alpha)| < 1$.

So, Newton's method is linearly convergent.

Remark 7.3.2 $f(x) = (x - \alpha)^m g(x), g(\alpha) \neq 0$,

$$u(x) = \frac{f(x)}{f'(x)}$$

$$= \frac{(x - \alpha)^m g(x)}{m(x-\alpha)^{m-1}g(x) + (x-\alpha)^m g'(x)}$$

$$= \frac{(x-\alpha)g(x)}{mg(x) + (x-\alpha)g'(x)},$$

then α is a simple zero of $u(x)$,

$$x_{n+1} = x_n - \frac{u(x_n)}{u'(x_n)}$$

$$= x_n - \frac{f(x_n)f'(x_n)}{[f'(x_n)]^2 - f(x_n)f''(x_n)}.$$

The iterative function

$$g(x) = x - \frac{f(x)f'(x)}{[f'(x)]^2 - f(x)f''(x)},$$

and the order is 2.

Example 7.3.4 $f(x) = x^3 + 2x^2 + 10x - 20 = 0$.

Solution

$$\begin{cases} x_{k+1} = x_k - \dfrac{x_k^3 + 2x_k^2 + 10x_k - 20}{3x_k^2 + 4x_k + 10}, \\ x_0 = 1. \end{cases}$$

Example 7.3.5 $f(x) = x^4 - 4x^2 + 4 = 0$.

$x = \sqrt{2}$ is zero of multiplicity 2.

Solution (1) Newton's method:

$$x_{n+1} = x_n - \frac{x_n^2 - 2}{4x_n}.$$

(2) $$\varphi(x) = x - m\frac{f(x)}{f'(x)},$$

letting $m = 2$, then $x_{n+1} = x_n - \dfrac{x_n^2 - 2}{2x_n}$.

(3) Modified Newton's method:

$$x_{n+1} = x_n - \frac{x_n(x_n^2 - 2)}{x_n^2 + 2}.$$

7.3.4 Newton's Downhill Method

$x_{n+1} = x_n - \lambda\dfrac{f(x_n)}{f'(x_n)}$, λ is downhill factor. How to choose λ?

$$|f(x_{n+1})| < |f(x_n)|, \quad n = 0,1,2,\cdots.$$

(1) $\lambda = 1$, if $|f(x_1)| < |f(x_0)|$, $\lambda \leftarrow 2\lambda$;

(2) If $|f(x_1)| \geq |f(x_0)|$, $\lambda \leftarrow \dfrac{\lambda}{2}$.

Example 7.3.6 Use Newton's method and Newton's downhill method to solve the solution of $2x^3 - 3x^2 + 1 = 0$ close to $x_0 = -0.4$ and 0.9, need $\varepsilon = 10^{-8}$.

Solution The numerical results are

k	Newton's method	Newton's downhill
0	-0.4	-0.4
1	-0.5167	-0.5167
2	-0.5004	-0.5004
3	-0.5000	-0.5000

k	Newton's method	Newton's downhill
0	0.9	0.9
1	0.9519	0.9519
2	0.9763	0.9763
3	0.9883	0.9883
4	0.9942	0.9942
5	0.9971	0.9971
6	0.9985	0.9985
7	0.9993	0.9993
8	0.9996	0.9996
9	0.9998	0.9999
10	0.9998	0.9999

§7.4 Numerical Solution for Nonlinear Systems of Equations

7.4.1 Fixed Points for Functions of Several Variables

$$\begin{cases} f_1(x_1, x_2, \cdots, x_m) = 0, \\ f_2(x_1, x_2, \cdots, x_m) = 0, \\ \cdots \cdots \\ f_m(x_1, x_2, \cdots, x_m) = 0, \end{cases} \quad (7.4.1)$$

where $f_1, \cdots, f_m$ are continuous functions of $x_1, x_2, \cdots, x_m$. And

$$x = (x_1, x_2, \cdots, x_m)^T \in \mathbf{R}^m,$$
$$f_i(x) = 0, \quad i = 1, 2, \cdots, m.$$

Denote the vector function F, $F(x) = (f_1(x), f_2(x), \cdots, f_m(x))^T$, then (7.4.1) is written as $F(x) = \mathbf{0}$.

The functions $f_1, \cdots, f_m$ are the coordinate functions of $\boldsymbol{F}$.

Definition 7.4.1 $D \subset \boldsymbol{R}^m, \boldsymbol{x}_0 \in D$,
$$\lim_{x \to x_0} f_i(\boldsymbol{x}) = A_i \Leftrightarrow \forall \varepsilon > 0, \exists \delta > 0, 0 < \|\boldsymbol{x} - \boldsymbol{x}_0\| < \delta, |f_i(\boldsymbol{x}) - A_i| < \varepsilon.$$
$$\lim_{x \to x_0} \boldsymbol{F}(\boldsymbol{x}) = \boldsymbol{A} = (A_1, \cdots, A_m)^T \Leftrightarrow \lim_{x \to x_0} f_i(\boldsymbol{x}) = A_i, i = 1, 2, \cdots, m.$$

If $\lim_{x \to x_0} \boldsymbol{F}(\boldsymbol{x}) = \boldsymbol{F}(\boldsymbol{x}_0)$, then call $\boldsymbol{F}$ is continuous at $\boldsymbol{x}_0$.

Suppose $\boldsymbol{x}^*$ satisfies $\boldsymbol{F}(\boldsymbol{x}^*) = \boldsymbol{0}, \boldsymbol{F}(\boldsymbol{x}) = \boldsymbol{0} \Leftrightarrow \boldsymbol{x} = \phi(\boldsymbol{x}), \boldsymbol{x}^* = \phi(\boldsymbol{x}^*), \boldsymbol{x}^*$ is fixed point.

And
$$\boldsymbol{x}^{n+1} = \phi(\boldsymbol{x}^n).$$

The sequence of vector $\{\boldsymbol{x}^{(k)}\}$ closed domain $D \subset \boldsymbol{R}^m$.

Theorem 7.4.1 $\phi(\boldsymbol{x})$ satisfies:

(1) $\exists 0 < k < 1, \forall \boldsymbol{x}, \boldsymbol{y} \in D,$ s.t. $\|\phi(\boldsymbol{x}) - \phi(\boldsymbol{y})\| \leq k \|\boldsymbol{x} - \boldsymbol{y}\|$;

(2) $\forall \boldsymbol{x} \in D$, we have $\phi(\boldsymbol{x}) \in D$.

Then, ϕ has unique fixed points $\boldsymbol{x}^* \in D$ and $\forall \boldsymbol{x} \in D, \{\boldsymbol{x}^{(k)}\}$ is convergent,

i.e. $\lim_{k \to \infty} \boldsymbol{x}^{(k)} = \boldsymbol{x}^*, \|\boldsymbol{x}^{(k)} - \boldsymbol{x}^*\| \leq \dfrac{k^n}{1-k} \|\boldsymbol{x}^{(1)} - \boldsymbol{x}^{(0)}\|$.

Proof $\forall \boldsymbol{x}^{(0)} \in D, \boldsymbol{x}^{(n)} \in D$,
$$\|\boldsymbol{x}^{(n)} - \boldsymbol{x}^{(n-1)}\| = \|\phi(\boldsymbol{x}^{(n-1)}) - \phi(\boldsymbol{x}^{(n-2)})\| \leq k \|\boldsymbol{x}^{(n-1)} - \boldsymbol{x}^{(n-2)}\|.$$

$\forall l > n$, we have
$$\|\boldsymbol{x}^{(l)} - \boldsymbol{x}^{(n)}\| \leq \|\boldsymbol{x}^{(l)} - \boldsymbol{x}^{(l-1)}\| + \cdots + \|\boldsymbol{x}^{(n+1)} - \boldsymbol{x}^{(n)}\|$$
$$\leq (k^{l-n} + \cdots + k^2 + k) \|\boldsymbol{x}^{(n)} - \boldsymbol{x}^{(n-1)}\|$$
$$\leq \dfrac{k^n}{1-k} \|\boldsymbol{x}^{(1)} - \boldsymbol{x}^{(0)}\|.$$

Using Cauchy theorem, we know $\{\boldsymbol{x}^{(n)}\}$ convergent and $\lim_{n \to \infty} \boldsymbol{x}^{(n)} = \boldsymbol{x}^*, \boldsymbol{x}^* \in D$.
$$\|\phi(\boldsymbol{x}^*) - \boldsymbol{x}^*\| \leq \|\phi(\boldsymbol{x}^*) - \phi(\boldsymbol{x}^{(n)})\| + \|\phi(\boldsymbol{x}^{(n)}) - \boldsymbol{x}^*\|$$
$$\leq k \|\boldsymbol{x}^* - \boldsymbol{x}^{(n)}\| + \|\boldsymbol{x}^{(n+1)} - \boldsymbol{x}^*\|,$$

$\|\boldsymbol{x}^* - \boldsymbol{x}^{(n)}\| \to 0$, so $\|\phi(\boldsymbol{x}^*) - \boldsymbol{x}^*\| = 0$, $\boldsymbol{x}^*$ is a fixed point of $\phi(\boldsymbol{x})$.

Assume that $\boldsymbol{y}^*$ is another fixed point, then
$$\|\boldsymbol{x}^* - \boldsymbol{y}^*\| = \|\phi(\boldsymbol{x}^*) - \phi(\boldsymbol{y}^*)\| \leq k \|\boldsymbol{x}^* - \boldsymbol{y}^*\|$$
and $0 < k < 1$.

So $\|\boldsymbol{x}^* - \boldsymbol{y}^*\| = 0, \boldsymbol{x}^* = \boldsymbol{y}^*$.

Denote: $\phi(\boldsymbol{x}) = (\varphi_1(\boldsymbol{x}), \cdots, \varphi_m(\boldsymbol{x}))^T$, Jacobi matrix of $\phi(\boldsymbol{x})$ is

$$\phi'(x^*) = \begin{pmatrix} \dfrac{\partial \varphi_1}{\partial x_1} & \cdots & \dfrac{\partial \varphi_1}{\partial x_m} \\ \vdots & & \vdots \\ \dfrac{\partial \varphi_m}{\partial x_1} & \cdots & \dfrac{\partial \varphi_m}{\partial x_m} \end{pmatrix}.$$

If ϕ has a fixed point x^*, $\phi'(x)$ is continuous, $\rho(\phi'(x^*)) < 1$, then $\{x^{(n)}\} \to x^*$. If $\exists\, 0 < k < 1$, s.t.

$$\left| \dfrac{\partial \varphi_i}{\partial x_j} \right| \leqslant \dfrac{k}{m}, \quad x \in D, \quad i,j = 1,\cdots,m,$$

then
$$\rho(\phi'(x^*)) < 1.$$

Example 7.4.1
$$\begin{cases} x_1^2 - 10x_1 + x_2^2 + 8 = 0, \\ x_1 x_2^2 + x_1 - 10x_2 + 8 = 0. \end{cases}$$

Solution $x = \begin{pmatrix} x_1 \\ x_2 \end{pmatrix}$,

$$G(x) = \begin{pmatrix} g_1(x) \\ g_2(x) \end{pmatrix} = \begin{pmatrix} \dfrac{x_1^2 + x_2^2 + 8}{10} \\ \dfrac{x_1 x_2^2 + x_1 + 8}{10} \end{pmatrix},$$

$$\|G(y) - G(x)\|_1 \leqslant 0.75 \|y - x\|_1,$$

$$G'(x) = \begin{pmatrix} \dfrac{\partial g_1}{\partial x_1} & \dfrac{\partial g_1}{\partial x_2} \\ \dfrac{\partial g_2}{\partial x_1} & \dfrac{\partial g_2}{\partial x_2} \end{pmatrix} = \begin{pmatrix} \dfrac{x_1}{5} & \dfrac{x_2}{5} \\ \dfrac{x_2^2 + 1}{10} & \dfrac{x_1 x_2}{5} \end{pmatrix},$$

$$G'(x^*) = \begin{pmatrix} 0.2 & 0.2 \\ 0.2 & 0.2 \end{pmatrix}, \quad \|G'(x^*)\|_1 = 0.4 < 1.$$

7.4.2 Newton's Method

$$g(x) = x - \phi(x) f(x),$$

$$\phi(x) = \dfrac{1}{f'(x)},$$

$$x^{(n)} = g(x^{(n-1)}),$$

$$f_j(x_1,\cdots,x_n) = f_j(x_1^{(0)},\cdots,x_n^{(0)}) + \sum_{k=1}^{n}(x_k - x_k^{(0)}) \dfrac{\partial}{\partial x_k} f_j + R_j,$$

$$R_j = \frac{1}{2}\sum_{k,l=1}^{n}(x_l - x_l^{(0)})(x_k - x_k^{(0)})\frac{\partial^2}{\partial x_l \partial x_k}f_j, \quad j = 1,2,\cdots,n,$$

$$\Rightarrow f_j(x_1^{(0)},\cdots,x_n^{(0)}) + \sum_{k=1}^{n}(x_k - x_k^{(0)})\frac{\partial}{\partial x_k}f_j(x_1^{(0)},\cdots,x_n^{(0)}) = 0, j = 1,2,\cdots,n.$$

(7.4.2)

(7.4.2) is a linear system of equations.

$$J(x) = J(x_1,\cdots,x_n) = \begin{pmatrix} \frac{\partial f_1}{\partial x_1} & \cdots & \frac{\partial f_1}{\partial x_n} \\ \vdots & & \vdots \\ \frac{\partial f_n}{\partial x_1} & \cdots & \frac{\partial f_n}{\partial x_n} \end{pmatrix},$$

$$f = (f_1,\cdots,f_n)^T.$$

(7.4.2) is written as $f(x^{(0)}) + J(x^{(0)})(x - x^{(0)}) = 0$,

$$R_j = \frac{1}{2}(x - x^{(0)})^T H_j(\xi)(x - x^{(0)}),$$

$$H_j = \frac{\partial^2 f_j}{\partial x_l \partial x_k}, \quad l,k = 1,2,\cdots,n.$$

Newton's method:

$$x^{(k+1)} = x^{(k)} - J^{-1}(x^{(k)})f(x^{(k)}), \quad k = 0,1,\cdots,$$

$$J(x^{(k)})(x^{(k+1)} - x^{(k)}) = -f(x^{(k)}).$$

Downhill method:

$$\|f(x^{(k+1)})\| \leq \|f(x^{(k)})\|, \quad k = 0,1,2,\cdots,$$

$$x^{(k+1)} = x^{(k)} - w_k J^{-1}(x^{(k)})f(x^{(k)}), \quad k = 0,1,2,\cdots.$$

Modified Newton's method:

$$\begin{cases} x^{(k+1)} = x^{(k)} - (J(x^{(k)}) + \mu_k I)^{-1}f(x^{(k)}), \\ x^{(k+1)} = x^{(k)} - J^{-1}(x^{(0)})f(x^{(k)}). \end{cases}$$

Excises 7

7.1 The bisection method is used to find the solution of the equation $x^2 - x - 1 = 0$ such that the error is less than 0.05.

7.2 Find the solution of the equation $x^3 - x^2 - 1 = 0$ near $x_0 = 1.5$, take the following equivalent form and establish the corresponding iterative formula.

(1) $x = 1 + 1/x^2$, iterative formula $x_{k+1} = 1 + 1/x_k^2$;

(2) $x^3 = x^2 + 1$, iterative formula $x_{k+1} = \sqrt[3]{x_k^2 + 1}$;

(3) $x^2 = \dfrac{1}{x-1}$, iterative formula $x_{k+1} = 1/\sqrt{x_k - 1}$.

Try to analyze the convergence of each iteration formula, and select a formula to give the approximate solution with four digits.

7.3 Compare the amount of computation required for the solution of $e^x + 10x - 2 = 0$ to three decimal places:

(1) Using dichotomy in the interval $[0,1]$;

(2) Using iterative method $x_{k+1} = (2 - e^{x_k})/10$, the initial value $x_0 = 0$.

7.4 Given a function $f(x)$, assuming that for all x, $f'(x)$ exists and $0 < m \leq f'(x) \leq M$, proving that the iterative procedure $x_{k+1} = x_k - \lambda f(x_k)$ converges to the solution x^* of $f(x) = 0$ for any fixed number λ in the range $0 < \lambda < 2/M$.

7.5 Set $\varphi(x) = x - p(x)f(x) - q(x)f^2(x)$, try to determine the function of $p(x)$ and $q(x)$, such that the solution of $f(x) = 0$ and $\varphi(x)$ iterative function for the iterative method at least three order convergence.

7.6 Use the following method to find the solution of $f(x) = x^3 - 3x - 1 = 0$ near $x_0 = 2$, the solution of the exact value $x^* = 1.87938524\cdots$, requires accurate result to four digits.

(1) Using Newton's method;

(2) Using chord-truncating method, take $x_0 = 2, x_1 = 1.9$;

(3) Using parabola method, take $x_0 = 2, x_1 = 3, x_2 = 2$.

7.7 Please try to find the minimum positive solution of $x - \tan x = 0$ using the method of Dichotomy and Newton's method respectively.

7.8 Researching on the Newton formula $x_{k+1} = \dfrac{1}{2}\left(x_k + \dfrac{a}{x_k}\right), x_0 > 0$ for $\sqrt{a}$, prove that for all $k = 1, 2, \cdots, x_k \geq \sqrt{a}$, the sequence $\{x_1, x_2, \cdots\}$ is decreasing.

7.9 For the Newton formula $x_{k+1} = x_k - f(x_k)/f'(x_k)$ of $f(x) = 0$, please prove that $R_k = (x_k - x_{k-1})/(x_{k-1} - x_{k-2})^2$ converges to $-f''(x^*)/[2f'(x^*)]$, where x^* is the solution of $f(x) = 0$.

7.10 Applying the Newton's method to the equation $x^3 - a = 0$, derive the iterative formula of the cubic root $\sqrt[3]{a}$ and discuss its convergence.

7.11 Applying the Newton's method to the equation $f(x) = 1 - \dfrac{a}{x^2} = 0$, derive the iterative formula for $\sqrt{a}$, and use this formula to find the value of $\sqrt{115}$.

7.12 Applying the Newton's method to the equation $f(x) = x^n - a = 0$ and $f(x) = 1 - \dfrac{a}{x^n} = 0$, derive the iterative formula for $\sqrt[n]{a}$ respectively, find the value of $\lim\limits_{k \to \infty} (\sqrt[n]{a} - x_{k+1})/(\sqrt[n]{a} - x_k)^2$.

7.13 Prove that the iterative formula $x_{k+1} = \dfrac{x_k(x_k^2 + 3a)}{3x_k^2 + a}$ is the third-order method of calculating $\sqrt{a}$. Assume that the initial value x_0 is sufficiently close to the solution x^*, please try to calculate $\lim\limits_{k \to \infty} (\sqrt{a} - x_{k+1})/(\sqrt{a} - x_k)^3$.

7.14 Use the parabola method to find the two zeros of polynomial $p(x) = 4x^4 - 10x^3 + 1.25x^2 + 5x + 1.5$, and then use the reduced order to find all the zeros.

7.15 The nonlinear system $\begin{cases} 3x_1^2 - x_2^2 = 0, \\ 3x_1 x_2^2 - x_1^3 - 1 = 0 \end{cases}$ has a solution in the neighborhood of $(0.4, 0.7)^T$. It constructs a fixed point iterative method such that it can converge to this solution and the calculation is accurate to 10^{-5} (by $\|\cdot\|_\infty$).

7.16 Using the Newton's method to solve the system $\begin{cases} x_1^2 + x_2^2 = 4, \\ x_1^2 - x_2^2 = 1, \end{cases}$ taking $x^{(0)} = (1.6, 1.2)^T$.

Chapter 8 Numerical Solutions of Ordinary Differential Equations

§8.1 Introduction

Initial value problem: given $y|_{x_0}, y'|_{x_0}, \cdots$.

Boundary value problem: given $y|_{x_0}, y|_{x_1}$ or $y'|_{x_0}, y'|_{x_1}, \cdots$.

The initial problem of ODE:

$$\begin{cases} y' = f(x,y), & a \leqslant x \leqslant b, |y| < \infty, \\ y(a) = y_0, & y_0 \in \mathbf{R}. \end{cases} \quad (8.1.1)$$

Suppose $f: G \to \mathbf{R}$ continuous, and $\exists L > 0$, s.t.

$$|f(x,y_1) - f(x,y_2)| \leqslant L|y_1 - y_2|, \forall (x,y_1), (x,y_2) \in G,$$

where $G = [a,b] \times \mathbf{R}$.

Theorem 8.1.1 The initial problem of (8.1.1) has unique solution $y \in C^1[a,b]$.

Definition 8.1.1 Problem (8.1.1) is well-posed in $[a,b]$, if $\exists k, \varepsilon_0 > 0$ s.t. $\forall \varepsilon \leqslant \varepsilon_0$ and given function $\tilde{f}(x,y)$, constant $\tilde{y}_0$, when

$$|y_0 - \tilde{y}_0| \leqslant \varepsilon, |f(x,y) - \tilde{f}(x,y)| \leqslant \varepsilon, (x,y) \in G,$$

then the initial problem

$$\begin{cases} z' = \tilde{f}(x,z), \\ z(a) = \tilde{y}_0, \end{cases} \quad x \in [a,b]$$

has a solution $z(x)$ such that $|y(x) - z(x)| \leqslant k\varepsilon$ for any $x \in [a,b]$.

Theorem 8.1.2 The initial problem of (8.1.1) is well-posed.

Theorem 8.1.3 (Bellman inequality) Letting $\alpha \geqslant 0, \beta \geqslant 0, \varphi(x) \geqslant 0$, $\varphi(x) \in [a,b], \varphi(x)$ is continuous, if $\varphi(x) \leqslant \beta + \alpha \int_a^x \varphi(t) \mathrm{d}t, x \in [a,b]$, then

$$\varphi(x) \leq \beta e^{\alpha(x-a)}, \quad x \in [a,b].$$

Proof We consider the case of $\beta > 0$:
$$\psi(x) = \beta + \alpha \int_a^x \varphi(t) dt, \quad x \in [a,b],$$
since $\varphi(x)$ is continuous, then
$$\psi'(x) = \alpha \varphi(x) \leq \alpha \psi(x),$$
$$e^{-\alpha x} \psi'(x) \leq e^{-\alpha x} \alpha \psi(x),$$
$$\Rightarrow (\psi(x) e^{-\alpha x})' \leq 0.$$

Integral on $[a,x]$, we have
$$\psi(x) e^{-\alpha x} \leq \psi(a) e^{-\alpha a},$$
$$\Rightarrow \varphi(x) \leq \psi(x) \leq \beta e^{\alpha(x-a)}, \quad x \in [a,b].$$

Case: $\beta = 0$. $\forall \sigma > 0$, we have
$$\varphi(x) \leq \alpha \int_a^x \varphi(t) dt < \sigma + \alpha \int_a^x \varphi(t) dt,$$
$$\Rightarrow 0 \leq \varphi(x) \leq \sigma e^{\alpha(x-a)}, \quad x \in [a,b],$$
$$\Rightarrow \varphi(x) = 0.$$

Theorem 8.1.4 (**Discrete Bellman inequality**) If $\alpha \geq 0, \beta \geq 0, h > 0$, $\eta_0, \eta_1, \cdots, \eta_N \geq 0$ s.t.
$$\eta_m \leq \beta + \alpha h \sum_{j=0}^{m-1} \eta_j, \quad m = 0, 1, \cdots, N,$$
then
$$\eta_m \leq \beta e^{\alpha m h}, \quad m = 0, 1, \cdots, N.$$

Proof Letting $\xi_m = \beta + \alpha h \sum_{j=0}^{m-1} \eta_j, m = 0, 1, \cdots, N$, i.e. $\eta_m \leq \xi_m$, so
$$\xi_{m+1} - \xi_m = \alpha h \eta_m \leq \alpha h \xi_m.$$
That is,
$$\xi_{m+1} \leq (1 + \alpha h) \xi_m, \quad m = 0, 1, \cdots, N-1,$$
$$\Rightarrow \eta_m \leq \xi_m \leq (1 + \alpha h) \xi_{m-1} \leq \cdots \leq (1 + \alpha h)^m \xi_0 \leq \beta \cdot (e^{\alpha h})^m = \beta e^{\alpha m h}.$$

§8.2 Euler's Method

8.2.1 Euler's method

The initial problem:

Chapter 8   Numerical Solutions of Ordinary Differential Equations   177

$$\begin{cases} y' = f(x,y), & a \leqslant x \leqslant b, |y| < \infty, \\ y(a) = y_0, & y_0 \in \mathbf{R}. \end{cases} \tag{8.2.1}$$

Interval discrete:

$$a = x_0 < x_1 < x_2 < \cdots < x_N = b,$$

$h_m = x_{m+1} - x_m$ is called step size.

Find the approximate solution $y_1, \cdots, y_N$ at $x_1, \cdots, x_N$, write the equation (8.2.1) in the form of an equivalent integral equation

$$y(x+h) = y(x) + \int_x^{x+h} f(\tau, y(\tau)) d\tau.$$

Letting $x = x_m$, calculate, then

$$y(x_m + h) = y(x_m) + hf(x_m, y(x_m)) + R_m,$$

$$R_m = \int_{x_m}^{x_{m+1}} f(x, y(x)) dx - hf(x_m, y(x_m)),$$

R_m is called the remainder.

$$y(x_{m+1}) \approx y(x_m) + hf(x_m, y(x_m)),$$

$$y_{m+1} = y_m + hf(x_m, y_m),$$

$$y_{m+1} \approx y(x_{m+1}),$$

$$y_m \approx y(x_m),$$

then

$$\begin{cases} y_{m+1} = y_m + hf(x_m, y_m), & m = 0, 1, \cdots, N-1, \\ y(x_0) = y_0. \end{cases}$$

① Implicit Euler's method:

$$y_{m+1} = y_m + hf(x_{m+1}, y_{m+1}),$$

$$R_m = \int_{x_m}^{x_{m+1}} f(x, y(x)) dx - hf(x_{m+1}, y(x_{m+1})). \tag{8.2.2}$$

② Improved Euler's method:

$$y_{m+1} = y_m + h \frac{f(x_m, y_m) + f(x_{m+1}, y_{m+1})}{2},$$

$$R_m = \int_{x_m}^{x_{m+1}} f(x, y(x)) dx - h \frac{f(x_m, y(x_m)) + f(x_{m+1}, y(x_{m+1}))}{2}.$$

$$\tag{8.2.3}$$

Definition 8.2.1

Local truncation error: omitting R_m, i. e. assume that $y(x_m) = y_m$.

Global truncation error: $\varepsilon_m = y(x_m) - y_m$.

8.2.2 Error Analysis of Euler's Method

Suppose $|f(x_1,y_1) - f(x_2,y_2)| \leq k|x_1 - x_2|$,

then

$$|R_m| = \left|\int_{x_m}^{x_{m+1}} [f(x,y(x)) - f(x_m,y(x_m))]\,dx\right|$$

$$\leq \int_{x_m}^{x_{m+1}} |f(x,y(x)) - f(x_m,y(x))|\,dx$$

$$+ \int_{x_m}^{x_{m+1}} |f(x_m,y(x)) - f(x_m,y(x_m))|\,dx$$

$$\leq k\int_{x_m}^{x_{m+1}} |x - x_m|\,dx + L\int_{x_m}^{x_{m+1}} |y(x) - y(x_m)|\,dx$$

$$\leq k \cdot \frac{h^2}{2} + L\int_{x_m}^{x_{m+1}} |y'(x_m + \theta(x - x_m)) \cdot (x - x_m)|\,dx$$

$$\leq \frac{(k + LM)h^2}{2},$$

where $0 < \theta < 1$, k is Lipschitz constant, $M = \max\limits_{x \in [a,b]} |y'(x)| = \max\limits_{x \in [a,b]} |f(x,y(x))|$,
$|R_m| \leq R$ or $|R_m| = o(h^2)$.

$$y(x_{m+1}) = y(x_m) + hf(x_m,y(x_m)) + R_m,$$

$$y_{m+1} = y_m + hf(x_m,y_m),$$

$$\Rightarrow \varepsilon_{m+1} = \varepsilon_m + h[f(x_m,y(x_m)) - f(x_m,y_m)] + R_m.$$

Therefore, $m = 0,1,2,\cdots,N-1$, we have

$$|\varepsilon_{m+1}| \leq |\varepsilon_m| + hL|\varepsilon_m| + R, \quad m = 0,1,\cdots,N-1,$$

$$\Rightarrow |\varepsilon_m| \leq (1 + hL)|\varepsilon_{m-1}| + R$$

$$\leq (1 + hL)^2 |\varepsilon_{m-2}| + (1 + hL)R + R$$

$$\vdots$$

$$\leq (1 + hL)^m |\varepsilon_0| + R\sum_{j=0}^{m-1}(1 + hL)^j$$

$$\leq (1 + hL)^m |\varepsilon_0| + \frac{R}{hL}[(1 + hL)^m - 1]$$

$$\leq e^{hLm}|\varepsilon_0| + \frac{R}{hL}[e^{hLm} - 1]$$

$$\leq e^{L(b-a)}|\varepsilon_0| + \frac{R}{hL}[e^{L(b-a)} - 1].$$

So, we have
$$|\varepsilon_m| \le e^{L(b-a)} |\varepsilon_0| + \frac{h}{2}\left(M + \frac{k}{L}\right)[e^{L(b-a)} - 1]. \qquad (8.2.4)$$

Theorem 8.2.1 Suppose $|f(x_1,y) - f(x_2,y)| \le k |x_1 - x_2|$, and $y_0 \to y(a)$ as $h \to 0$, then $y_m \to y(x_m)$ and $|\varepsilon_m| \le e^{L(b-a)} |\varepsilon_0| + \frac{h}{2}\left(M + \frac{k}{L}\right)[e^{L(b-a)} - 1]$.

If $\varepsilon_0 = 0$, then the order of local error determine the order of the global truncation error.

The improved Euler's method:

$$y(x_{m+1}) = y(x_m) + \frac{h}{2}[f(x_m, y(x_m)) + f(x_{m+1}, y(x_{m+1}))] + R_m,$$

$$\int_{x_m}^{x_{m+1}} y'(x)\,\mathrm{d}x = \frac{h}{2}(y'(x_{m+1}) + y'(x_m)) - \frac{h^3}{12}y'''(x_m + \xi h), \quad 0 \le \xi \le 1,$$

$$R_m = -\frac{h^3}{12}y'''(x_m + \xi h).$$

The global error is $o(h^2)$.

Definition 8.2.2 Say Euler's method is stable, if $\exists c, h_0 > 0$, s.t. $\forall y_0, z_0$, satisfy

$$|y_m - z_m| \le c |y_0 - z_0|, \quad 0 < h < h_0, \quad mh < b - a.$$

Theorem 8.2.2 Under the conditions of the theorem 8.2.1, Euler's method is stable.

Proof

$$y_{m+1} = y_m + hf(x_m, y_m),$$
$$z_{m+1} = z_m + hf(x_m, z_m),$$

letting $e_m = y_m - z_m$, then

$$|e_{m+1}| \le |e_m| + h |f(x_m, y_m) - f(x_m, z_m)|$$
$$\le (1 + hL) |e_m|$$
$$\vdots$$
$$\le (1 + hL)^{m+1} |e_0|.$$

If $mh < b - a$, then $|e_{m+1}| \le e^{hL(m+1)} |e_0|$.

$$\therefore |e_m| \le e^{L(b-a)} |e_0|.$$

§8.3 Multistep Methods (I)

8.3.1 Difference Equation

Definition 8.3.1 $\sum_{j=0}^{k} a_j y_{m+j} = b_m, a_j, b_m \in C, m = 0,1,2,\cdots$ (8.3.1)

is called k order ordinary difference equation.

$\{y_m\}, m=0,1,\cdots$ is a solution of (8.3.1).

$$\sum_{j=0}^{k} a_j \xi^j = 0 \qquad (8.3.2)$$

is characteristic equation.

Theorem 8.3.1 Suppose (8.3.2) has k_0 ($k_0 \leq k$) roots: $\xi_1, \xi_2, \cdots, \xi_{k_0}$, the multiplicity of ξ_j is r_j.

If $a_0 \neq 0$, then $y_m = \sum_{j=1}^{k_0} \sum_{q=0}^{r_j-1} c_{jq} m^q \xi_j^m + \sum_{s=0}^{m-k} b_s y_{m-s-1}^* + \sum_{q=0}^{r_1-1} c_{1q} \delta_{mq} \cdot y_m^*$ satisfy

$$\begin{cases} \sum_{j=0}^{k} a_j y_{m+j} = 0, m = 0,1,2,\cdots, \\ y_0 = y_1 = \cdots = y_{k-2} = 0, y_{k-1} = \dfrac{1}{a_k}. \end{cases}$$

If $\delta_{ij} = 0\,(i \neq j)$ or $\delta_{ij} = 1\,(i=j)$, then c_{jq} is a constant.

8.3.2 Multistep Method

Euler's method or improved Euler's method is called one-step method. When solving y_{m+k}, the $y_{m+k-1}, y_{m+k-2}, \cdots, y_m$ are known as are $f(x_{m+k-1}, y_{m+k-1}), \cdots, f(x_m, y_m)$.

Linear k steps method: y_{m+k} is linearly determined by $y_{m+k-1}, \cdots, y_m$ and $f(x_{m+k-1}, y_{m+k-1}), \cdots, f(x_m, y_m)$.

Example 8.3.1 Linear 2 steps 3 orders multistep method.

Solution $y_{m+1} = \alpha_0 y_m + \alpha_1 y_{m-1} + h(\beta_0 f(x_m, y_m) + \beta_1 f(x_{m-1}, y_{m-1}))$.

Choose suitable $\alpha_0, \alpha_1, \beta_0, \beta_1$.

Taylor's formula:

$$y(x_{m+1}) = y(x_m) + y'(x_m)h + \frac{y''(x_m)}{2!}h^2 + \frac{y^{(3)}(x_m)}{3!}h^3 + \frac{y^{(4)}(\xi_1)}{4!}h^4,$$

$$y(x_{m-1}) = y(x_m) - y'(x_m)h + \frac{y''(x_m)}{2!}h^2 - \frac{y^{(3)}(x_m)}{3!}h^3 + \frac{y^{(4)}(\xi_2)}{4!}h^4,$$

$$y'(x_{m-1}) = y'(x_m) - y''(x_m)h + \frac{y^{(3)}(x_m)}{2!}h^2 - \frac{y^{(4)}(\xi_3)}{3!}h^3.$$

Local truncation error:
$$\begin{aligned}R_m &= y(x_{m+1}) - \alpha_0 y(x_m) - \alpha_1 y(x_{m-1}) - h(\beta_0 y'(x_m) + \beta_1 y'(x_{m-1}))\\ &= (1 - \alpha_0 - \alpha_1)y(x_m) + (1 + \alpha_1 - \beta_0 - \beta_1)hy'(x_m)\\ &\quad + \left(\frac{1}{2!} - \frac{1}{2!}\alpha_1 + \beta_1\right)y''(x_m)h^2 + \left(\frac{1}{3!} + \frac{\alpha_1}{3!} - \frac{\beta_1}{2!}\right)y'''(x_m)h^3\\ &\quad + \left(\frac{y^{(4)}(\xi_1)}{4!} - \frac{y^{(4)}(\xi_2)}{4!}\alpha_1 + \frac{y^{(4)}(\xi_3)}{3!}\beta_1\right)h^4.\end{aligned}$$

Letting
$$\begin{cases}1 - \alpha_0 - \alpha_1 = 0,\\ 1 + \alpha_1 - \beta_0 - \beta_1 = 0,\\ \dfrac{1}{2!} - \dfrac{1}{2!}\alpha_1 + \beta_1 = 0,\\ \dfrac{1}{3!} + \dfrac{\alpha_1}{3!} - \dfrac{\beta_1}{2!} = 0.\end{cases}$$

Then $\alpha_0 = -4, \alpha_1 = 5, \beta_0 = 4, \beta_1 = 2$.
$$\therefore R_m = o(h^4).$$
$$y_{m+1} = -4y_m + 5y_{m-1} + h(4f(x_m, y_m) + 2f(x_{m-1}, y_{m-1})).$$

k step method:
$$y(x_m), \cdots, y(x_m + kh),$$
$$hy'(x_m), \cdots, hy'(x_m + kh).$$

then
$$\Lambda[y(x_m);h] = \sum_{j=0}^{k}[\alpha_j y(x_m + jh) - \beta_j hy'(x_m + jh)],$$

$$\Lambda[y(x_m);h] = c_0 y(x_m) + c_1 hy'(x_m) + \cdots + c_q h^q y^q(x_m) + \cdots,$$

$$\begin{cases}c_0 = \sum_{j=0}^{k}\alpha_j,\\ \cdots\cdots\\ \sum_{j=0}^{k}\alpha_j y_{m+j} = h\sum_{j=0}^{k}\beta_j f(x_{m+j}, y_{m+j}).\end{cases}$$

k steps q orders method: $\sum_{j=0}^{k} \alpha_j y_{m+j} = h \sum_{j=0}^{k} \beta_j f_{m+j}$.

Gear's method: $\beta_j = 0, j = 0, 1, \cdots, k-1$.

k steps k orders method:

$$\sum_{j=0}^{k} \alpha_j y_{m+j} = h \beta_k f_{m+k}. \tag{8.3.3}$$

where $\alpha_k = 1$.

As $k = 1$, (8.3.3) is $\alpha_0 y_m + \alpha_1 y_{m+1} = h \beta_1 f_{m+1}$, then we have

$$\begin{cases} c_0 = \alpha_0 + 1 = 0, \\ c_1 = 1 - \beta_1 = 0 \end{cases} \Rightarrow \alpha_0 = -1, \beta_1 = 1.$$

One step one order Gear's method: $y_{m+1} = y_m + h f_{m+1}$.

The global truncation error: $e_m = y(x_m) - y_m, m = 0, 1, \cdots$.

Definition 8.3.2 (Convergent) When $h \to 0, y_0, y_1, \cdots, y_{k-1} \to y(a)$, then

$$\max_{mh \leq b-a} |y(x_m) - y_m| \to 0.$$

Definition 8.3.3 p order convergent: if $\max_{0 \leq j \leq k-1} |y(x_j) - y_j| = o(h^p), h \to 0$, then

$$\max_{mh \leq b-a} |y(x_m) - y_m| = o(h^p).$$

8.3.3 Numerical Stability

h is fixed, $m \to \infty$.

Absolute stability: $y' = \lambda y, \lambda \in C$.

If the initial is nonlinear, then $y' = Ay$, here $A = \dfrac{\partial f}{\partial y}$ is Jacobi Matrix.

If

$$Q^{-1} A Q = \Lambda = \text{diag}(\lambda_1, \cdots, \lambda_m),$$
$$y' = Ay \Rightarrow y' = Q \Lambda Q^{-1} y,$$
$$(Q^{-1} y)' = \Lambda Q^{-1} y.$$

Letting $Q^{-1} y = z$, then we have $\sum_{j=0}^{k} \alpha_j y_{m+j} = h \sum_{j=0}^{k} \beta_j f_{m+j}$.

As $f_{m+j} = y'(x_{m+j}) = \lambda y(x_{m+j})$,

so $\sum_{j=0}^{k} \alpha_j y_{m+j} = \lambda h \sum_{j=0}^{k} \beta_j y_{m+j}$.

Note $\bar{h} = \lambda h$, the constant coefficient linear difference equation,

Chapter 8 Numerical Solutions of Ordinary Differential Equations   183

$$\sum_{j=0}^{k} \alpha_j y_{m+j} = \bar{h} \sum_{j=0}^{k} \beta_j y_{m+j}. \quad (8.3.4)$$

Then, the characteristic polynomial of the difference equation is denoted as

$$\Pi(\xi, \bar{h}) = \sum_{j=0}^{k} \alpha_j \xi^j - \bar{h} \sum_{j=0}^{k} \beta_j \xi^j$$

$$= \rho(\xi) - \bar{h}\sigma(\xi).$$

Fix $h > 0$,

$$\sum_{j=0}^{k} \alpha_j y(x_m + jh) = \bar{h} \sum_{j=0}^{k} \beta_j y(x_m + jh) + \Lambda[y(x_m); h]. \quad (8.3.5)$$

Note $\varepsilon_m = y(x_m) - y_m$, let (8.3.5) - (8.3.4), we can have

$$\sum_{j=0}^{k} \alpha_j \varepsilon_{m+j} = \bar{h} \sum_{j=0}^{k} \beta_j \varepsilon_{m+j} + \Lambda[y(x_m); h].$$

$\Lambda[y(x_m); h]$ is called local truncation error.

Definition 8.3.4 For $\bar{h} \in C$, for every $|\xi| < 1$, then the method is called absolute stability, where ξ is root of $\Pi(\xi, \bar{h})$.

Absolute suable area: $S = \{\bar{h} \in C: |\xi_j(\bar{h})| < 1, j = 1, 2, \cdots, k\}$.

Example 8.3.2 The stable domain of the Euler's method.

Solution

$y_{m+1} = y_m + hf(x_m, y_m)$,

$y_{m+1} = y_m + \lambda h y_m$,

$\Pi(\xi, \bar{h}) = \xi - 1 - \bar{h}.$

As ξ is a solution of $\Pi(\xi, \bar{h})$, so

$\xi = 1 + \bar{h} = 1 + \lambda h.$

Letting $\bar{h} = a + bi$, $|\xi| < 1$, i. e.
$(1 + a)^2 + b^2 < 1$. The stable domain of the Euler's method is the disk on the complex plane, the center is $(-1, 0)$, and the radius is 1, as shown in the figure 8.3.1.

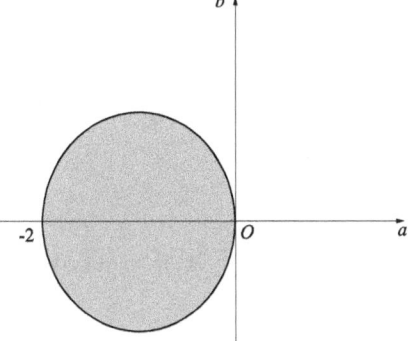

Figure 8.3.1 The stable domain of Euler's method

Example 8.3.3 The stable domian of the improved Euler's method:

$$y_{m+1} = y_m + \frac{h[f(x_m,y_m) + f(x_{m+1},y_{m+1})]}{2}.$$

Solution

$$y_{m+1} = y_m + \frac{\lambda h}{2}y_m + \frac{\lambda h}{2}y_{m+1},$$

$$\text{II}(\xi,\bar{h}) = \xi - 1 - \frac{\bar{h}}{2} - \frac{\bar{h}}{2}\xi = \left(1 - \frac{\bar{h}}{2}\right)\xi - 1 - \frac{\bar{h}}{2}.$$

So characteristic root is $\xi = \dfrac{2 + \bar{h}}{2 - \bar{h}}$.

Letting $\bar{h} = a + bi$, $|\xi| < 1$, i.e.
$$\sqrt{(2+a)^2 + b^2} < \sqrt{(2-a)^2 + b^2}$$
$$\Rightarrow a < 0.$$

So, The stable domain of the improved Euler's method on the complex plane as shown in the figure 8.3.2.

Definition 8.3.5 The method is called

A-stable, if $S \supset C_- = \{\bar{h} \in C \mid \operatorname{Re}\bar{h} < 0\}$;

$A(\alpha)$-stable: $S \supset \Omega_\alpha := \{\bar{h} \in \mathbb{C} \mid$

$|\arg \bar{h} - \pi| < \alpha\}$, where $\alpha \in (0, \pi(2))$.

$A(0)$-stable: $\exists \alpha > 0$, $A(\alpha)$-stable.

A_0-stable: $S \supset \{\bar{h}: a < 0\}$.

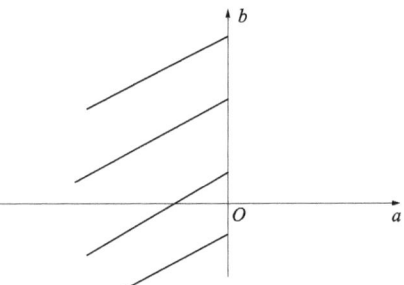

Figure 8.3.2 The stable domain of the improved Euler's method

§8.4 Multistep Methods (II)

8.4.1 The Initial Data

$y_0, y_1, \cdots, y_{k-1}$ are given, s.t. $\max\limits_{0 \leq j \leq k-1} |y(x_j) - y_j| = o(h^p)$, $h \to 0$.

①Using Euler's method to calculate the initial data, need h small enough.

②Taylor's series, k steps p orders method, initial value $y_0, y_1, \cdots, y_{k-1}$ satisfy the condition expand $y(x_0 + h)$ to be the Taylor formula at x_0, we have

$$y(x_0 + jh) - y_j = o(h^p).$$

$$y(x_0 + h) = y(x_0) + hy'(x_0) + \cdots + \frac{h^{p-1} y^{(p-1)}(x_0)}{(p-1)!} + o(h^p).$$

Denote $y_1 = y(x_0) + hy'(x_0) + \cdots + \dfrac{h^{p-1} y^{(p-1)}(x_0)}{(p-1)!}$, then

$$y_1 - y(x_0 + h) = o(h^p),$$

$$\begin{cases} y' = f, \\ y'' = f_x + f \cdot f_y \Rightarrow y_1, \\ \cdots\cdots \end{cases}$$

Similarly, calculate $y_2, y_3, \cdots, y_{k-1}$.

8.4.2 Richardson Extrapolation

$y(x;h)$ is approximate value of $y(x)$, step for h:

$$y(x;h) = y(x) + A_1 h + \cdots + A_p h^p + \cdots.$$

If step for $\dfrac{h}{2}$, then approximate value is $y\left(x;\dfrac{h}{2}\right)$:

$$y\left(x;\frac{h}{2}\right) = y(x) + \frac{1}{2}A_1 h + \cdots + \frac{1}{2^p}A_p h^p + \cdots.$$

$$2y\left(x;\frac{h}{2}\right) - y(x;h) = y(x) - \frac{1}{2}A_2 h^2 - \left(1 - \frac{1}{2^2}\right)A_3 h^3 + \cdots,$$

when the approximate value is $2y\left(x;\dfrac{h}{2}\right) - y(x;h)$, the error accuracy will be improved by one order, then

$$\bar{y}(x) = 2y\left(x;\frac{h}{2}\right) - y(x;h) = o(h^2),$$

$$\bar{y}(x) = \frac{1}{2^p - 1}\left[2^p y\left(x;\frac{h}{2}\right) - y(x;h)\right] = o(h^{p+1}).$$

Richardson extrapolation: $A_p h^p \approx \dfrac{2^p}{2^p - 1}\left[y(x;h) - y\left(x;\dfrac{h}{2}\right)\right]$.

8.4.3 Implicit Formula

Explicit formula:

$$y_{m+k} = -\sum_{j=0}^{k-1} \alpha_j y_{m+j} + h \sum_{j=0}^{k-1} \beta_j f(x_{m+j}, y_{m+j}),$$

need $y_{m+k-1}, \cdots, y_m$. To calculate y_{m+k},

$$y_{m+k} + \sum_{j=0}^{k-1} \alpha_j y_{m+j} = h\beta_k f(x_{m+k}, y_{m+k}) + h\sum_{j=0}^{k-1} \beta_j f(x_{m+j}, y_{m+j}),$$

$$\Rightarrow y_{m+k} - h\beta_k f(x_{m+k}, y_{m+k}) + \omega_m = 0,$$

where $\omega_m = \sum_{j=0}^{k-1} \alpha_j y_{m+j} - h\sum_{j=0}^{k-1} \beta_j f(x_{m+j}, y_{m+j}).$

The iterative formula is

$$\begin{cases} y_{m+k}^{(n+1)} - h\beta_k f(x_{m+k}, y_{m+k}^{(n)}) + \omega_m = 0, \\ y_{m+k}^{(0)}, \end{cases}$$

$$y_{m+k}^{*} - h\beta_k f(x_{m+k}, y_{m+k}^{*}) + \omega_m = 0,$$

$$|y_{m+k}^{(n+1)} - y_{m+k}^{*}| \le h|\beta_k| L |y_{m+k}^{(n)} - y_{m+k}^{*}|$$

$$\le (h|\beta_k| L)^{n+1} |y_{m+k}^{(0)} - y_{m+k}^{*}|,$$

$$|h\beta_k L| < 1 \Rightarrow h < \frac{1}{|\beta_k| L}.$$

Newton's method:

$$y_{m+k}^{(n+1)} = y_{m+k}^{(n)} - [1 - h\beta_k f_y(x_{m+k}, y_{m+k}^{(n)})]^{-1} \cdot [y_{m+k}^{(n)} - h\beta_k f(x_{m+k}, y_{m+k}^{(n)}) + \omega_m].$$

8.4.4 Predictor Corrector Method

How to calculate $y_{m+k}^{[0]}$?

Predictor corrector method:

$$\begin{cases} y_{m+k}^{(0)} + \sum_{j=0}^{k-1} \alpha_j^{*} y_{m+j} = h\sum_{j=0}^{k-1} \beta_j^{*} f(x_{m+j}, y_{m+j}), \\ y_{m+k}^{(n+1)} - h\beta_k f(x_{m+k}, y_{m+k}^{(n)}) + \omega_m = 0. \end{cases}$$

P: $y_{m+k}^{(0)} + \sum_{j=0}^{k-1} \alpha_j^{*} y_{m+j}^{(N)} = h\sum_{j=0}^{k-1} \beta_j^{*} f_{m+j}^{(N-1)}$;

E: $f_{m+k}^{(n)} = f(x_{m+k}, y_{m+k}^{(n)})$;

C: $y_{m+k}^{(n+1)} + \sum_{j=0}^{k-1} \alpha_j y_{m+j}^{(N)} = h\beta_k f_{m+k}^{(n)} + h\sum_{j=0}^{k-1} \beta_j f_{m+j}^{(N-1)}, n = 0, 1, \cdots, N-1,$

where $f_{m+j}^{(N-1)} = f(x_{m+j}, y_{m+j}^{(n-1)}), j = 0, 1, \cdots, k-1.$

The simplest PC method:

$$\begin{cases} y_{m+1}^{(0)} = y_m + hf(x_m, y_m), \\ y_{m+1}^{(n+1)} = y_m + \dfrac{h}{2}(f(x_m, y_m) + f(x_{m+1}, y_{m+1}^{(n)})), \end{cases} n = 0, 1, \cdots, N-1.$$

Adams 3 steps 4 orders PECE:

$$P: y_{m+4} - y_{m+3} = \frac{h(55f_{m+3} - 59f_{m+2} + 37f_{m+1} - 9f_m)}{24}.$$

$$C: y_{m+4} - y_{m+3} = \frac{h(9f_{m+4} + 19f_{m+3} - 5f_{m+2} + f_{m+1})}{24}.$$

§8.5　Runge-Kutta Method

8.5.1　Runge-Kutta Method

Explicit scheme:

Difference quotient $\dfrac{y(x_{m+1}) - y(x_m)}{h} = y'(\xi)$, $\exists \xi, x_m < \xi < x_{m+1}$,

i.e. $y(x_{m+1}) = y(x_m) + hf(\xi, y(\xi))$.

Letting $k = f(\xi, y(\xi))$,

then $y(x_{m+1}) = y(x_m) + hk$.

Euler's method:　$k_1 = f(x_m, y_m)$.

Improved Euler's scheme:

$$\begin{cases} y_{m+1} = y_m + \dfrac{h}{2}(k_1 + k_2), \\ k_1 = f(x_m, y_m), \\ k_2 = f(x_{m+1}, y_m + hk_1). \end{cases}$$

Runge-Kutta method:

$$y_{m+1} = y_m + h\sum_{i=1}^{s} b_i k_i,$$

where b_i is weight factor, the number of slopes is s,

$$k_i = f(x_m + c_i h, y_m + h\sum_{j=1}^{i-1} a_{ij} k_j), \quad i = 1, 2, \cdots, s,$$

and $c_1 = 0$, $c_i = \sum\limits_{j=1}^{i-1} a_{ij}$, $i = 2, 3, \cdots, s$.

Taylor's formula:
$$y(x_m + h) = y(x_m) + hy'(x_m) + \cdots + o(h^4)$$
$$= y(x_m) + hf + \cdots,$$
$$k_1 = f(x_m, y_m),$$
$$k_2 = f(x_m + c_2 h, y_m + ha_{21} k_1)$$
$$= f(x_m, y_m) + h(c_2 f_x + a_{21} f \cdot f_y) + o(h^2).$$
$$\begin{cases} b_1 + b_2 = 1, \\ b_2 c_2 = \dfrac{1}{2}, \\ b_2 a_{21} = \dfrac{1}{2}. \end{cases}$$

If
$$c_2 = \frac{1}{2}, \frac{2}{3}, 1,$$

so
$$(b_1, b_2, a_{21}) = \left(0, 1, \frac{1}{2}\right), \left(\frac{1}{4}, \frac{3}{4}, \frac{2}{3}\right), \left(\frac{1}{2}, \frac{1}{2}, 1\right).$$

2 order Runge-Kutta method:
$$y_{m+1} = y_m + hf\left(x_m + \frac{h}{2}, y_m + \frac{hf_m}{2}\right),$$
$$y_{m+1} = y_m + \frac{h}{4}\left[f(x_m, y_m) + 3f\left(x_m + \frac{2h}{3}, y_m + \frac{2h}{3} f_m\right)\right],$$
$$y_{m+1} = y_m + \frac{h}{2}[f(x_m, y_m) + f(x_m + h, y_m + hf_m)],$$

where $f_m = f(x_m, y_m)$.

3 order Runge-Kutta method:
$$\begin{cases} y_{m+1} = y_m + \dfrac{h}{4}(k_1 + 3k_3), \\ k_1 = f(x_m, y_m), \\ k_2 = f\left(x_m + \dfrac{h}{3}, y_m + \dfrac{k_1 h}{3}\right), \\ k_3 = f\left(x_m + \dfrac{2h}{3}, y_m + \dfrac{2k_2 h}{3}\right). \end{cases}$$

Heun:

$$\begin{cases} y_{m+1} - y_m = \dfrac{h}{6}(k_1 + 4k_2 + k_3), \\ k_1 = f(x_m, y_m), \\ k_2 = f\left(x_m + \dfrac{h}{2}, y_m + \dfrac{k_1 h}{2}\right), \\ k_3 = f(x_m + h, y_m - hk_1 + 2hk_2). \end{cases}$$

8.5.2 Stability of Runge-Kutta Method

One step method: $y_{m+1} = y_m + h\phi(x_m, y_m, h)$.

Similar to Euler's method: $y_{m+1} = y_m + hf(x_m, y_m)$.

Euler's method:

$$R(h) = 1 + h\lambda,$$
$$|1 + h\lambda| < 1 \Rightarrow -2 < h\lambda < 0.$$

2 order Runge-Kutta method:

$$y_{n+1} = \left[1 + h\lambda + \dfrac{(h\lambda)^2}{2}\right] y_n.$$

§8.6 Stiff Problem

8.6.1 First Order ODEs

Similar to the method of ODE, we can give the Euler's method (or other methods) ODEs:

$$\begin{cases} \dfrac{dy_1}{dx} = f_1(x, y_1, y_2, \cdots, y_n), \\ \cdots\cdots \\ \dfrac{dy_n}{dx} = f_n(x, y_1, y_2, \cdots, y_n), \\ y_1(a) = y_{10}, \cdots, y_n(a) = y_{n0}. \end{cases}$$

$$Y = (y_1, y_2, \cdots, y_n)^T,$$
$$\begin{cases} Y'(x) = f(x, Y), \\ Y(a) = Y_0. \end{cases}$$

Euler's method:
$$Y_{m+1} = Y_m + hf_m,$$
$$f_m = (f_{1m}, \cdots, f_{nm})^T.$$

8.6.2 Stiff Problem

Definition 8.6.1 $\dfrac{dY}{dx} = JY + f(x)$ is stiff, if $\operatorname{Re}\lambda_i < 0, i = 1, 2, \cdots, n$, and $\max_j |\operatorname{Re}\lambda_j| \gg \min_j |\operatorname{Re}\lambda_j|$.

As for the stiff problem, one should use implicit Runge-Kutta method.

§8.7 Numerical Solution for Boundary-value Problem

Boundary-value Problem:
$$y''(x) = f(x, y, y'), \quad a \leqslant x \leqslant b, \quad |y| < \infty. \tag{8.7.1}$$

The first boundary-value conditions: $y(a) = \alpha, y(b) = \beta$.
The second boundary-value conditions: $y'(a) = \alpha, y'(b) = \beta$.
The third boundary-value conditions: $y'(a) - a_0 y(a) = \alpha_1, y'(b) + \beta_0 y(b) = \beta_1$.

8.7.1 Difference Method

Divide the interval $[a, b]$ into N equal parts, x_i as a node, since Taylor formula, we have

$$a = x_0, x_1 = a + h, \cdots, x_N = a + Nh, h = \frac{b-a}{N},$$

$$y''(x_m) = \frac{y(x_{m+1}) - 2y(x_m) + y(x_{m-1})}{h^2} + \frac{h^2}{12} y^{(4)}(\xi_m),$$

$$h^2 y''(x_m) \approx y(x_{m+1}) - 2y(x_m) + y(x_{m-1}).$$

Taking $2hy' \approx y(x_{m+1}) - y(x_{m-1})$, then $(8.7.1) \Rightarrow$

$$y_{m+1} - 2y_m + y_{m-1} - h^2 f\left(x_m, y_m, \frac{y_{m+1} - y_{m-1}}{2h}\right) = 0, \quad m = 1, 2, \cdots, N-1.$$

Discretization of boundary conditions:
1st BC: $y_0 = \alpha, y_N = \beta$.

2nd BC:
$$y_0' = \frac{y_1 - y_0}{h}, \quad y_N' = \frac{y_N - y_{N-1}}{h}.$$

or
$$\begin{cases} 2hy'_0 = -y_2 + 4y_1 - 3y_0, \\ 2hy'_N = 3y_N - 4y_{N-1} + y_{N-2}. \end{cases}$$

3rd BC:
$$-y_2 + 4y_1 - 3y_0 - 2h\alpha_0 y_0 = 2h\alpha_1,$$
$$3y_N - 4y_{N-1} + y_{N-2} + 2h\beta_0 y_N = 2h\beta_1.$$

8.7.2 Finite Difference Method

$$y_{m+1} - 2y_m + y_{m-1} - h^2\left[r_m + q_m y_m + p_m \frac{y_{m+1} - y_{m-1}}{2h}\right] = 0,$$

$$-\left(1 + \frac{h}{2}p_m\right)y_{m-1} + (2 + h^2 q_m)y_m - \left(1 - \frac{h}{2}p_m\right)y_{m+1} = -h^2 r_m,$$

$$m = 1, 2, \cdots, N-1.$$

Letting $a_m = -\left(1 + \frac{h}{2}p_m\right), d_m = (2 + h^2 q_m), c_m = -\left(1 - \frac{h}{2}p_m\right), b_m = -h^2 r_m,$

then
$$a_m y_{m-1} + d_m y_m + c_m y_{m+1} = b_m.$$

The difference equation of the first boundary value problem can be written as

$$\begin{cases} d_1 y_1 + c_1 y_2 = b_1 - a_1 \alpha, \\ a_m y_{m-1} + d_m y_m + c_m y_{m+1} = b_m, \quad 2 \leqslant m \leqslant N-2. \\ a_{N-1} y_{N-2} + d_{N-1} y_{N-1} = b_{N-1} - c_{N-1}\beta, \end{cases}$$

$$\begin{pmatrix} d_1 & c_1 & & & \\ a_2 & d_2 & c_2 & & \\ & \ddots & \ddots & \ddots & \\ & & a_{N-2} & d_{N-2} & c_{N-2} \\ & & & a_{N-1} & d_{N-1} \end{pmatrix} \begin{pmatrix} y_1 \\ y_2 \\ \vdots \\ y_{N-2} \\ y_{N-1} \end{pmatrix} = \begin{pmatrix} b_1 - a_1 \alpha \\ b_2 \\ \vdots \\ b_{N-2} \\ b_{N-1} - c_{N-1}\beta \end{pmatrix}.$$

8.7.3 The Shooting Method

Convert the boundary value problem to the initial value problem.
$$y(a) = \alpha.$$
Given $y'(a) = t, y(x,t), y(b,t) = \beta$ or $|y(b,t) - \beta| < \varepsilon$. suppose $y(x)$ is the solution to the boundary value problem,
$$\begin{cases} y'' = f(x, y, y'), \ x \in [a, b], \ |y| < +\infty, \\ y(a) = \alpha, y'(a) = t_0. \end{cases}$$

$$y(x,t_0), y(b,t_0) = \beta_0.$$

If $\beta_0 = \beta$ or $|\beta_0 - \beta| < \varepsilon$, then ok.

$y(x,t_k)$ is approximated to $y(x)$.

How to choose $\{t_k\}$?

$$y(b,t) - \beta = 0,$$

$$t_k = t_{k-1} - \frac{(y(b,t_{k-1}) - \beta)(t_{k-1} - t_{k-2})}{y(b,t_{k-1}) - y(b,t_{k-2})}, \quad k = 2, 3, \cdots.$$

Shooting method for linear problem:

$$\begin{cases} y'' = p(x)y' + q(x)y + r(x), \\ y(a) = \alpha, y(b) = \beta, \end{cases}$$

suppose $t = t_1, t_2$, then

$$\begin{cases} y'' = p(x)y' + q(x)y + r(x), \\ y(a) = \alpha, y'(a) = t. \end{cases}$$

The solution are $y(x,t_1), y(x,t_2)$,

Letting $z(x) = \lambda y(x,t_1) + (1-\lambda)y(x,t_2)$, satisfies

$$\begin{cases} z'' = p(x)z' + q(x)z + r(x), \\ z(a) = \alpha, \end{cases}$$

since $z(b) = \beta$, then

$$\lambda y(b,t_1) + (1-\lambda)y(b,t_2) = \beta,$$

$$\Rightarrow \lambda = \frac{\beta - y(b,t_2)}{y(b,t_1) - y(b,t_2)}$$

$$\Leftrightarrow \begin{cases} y'' = p(x)y' + q(x)y + r(x), \\ y(a) = \alpha, y'(a) = 0 \end{cases} \Rightarrow y_1(x).$$

And

$$\begin{cases} y'' = p(x)y' + q(x)y + r(x), \\ y(a) = \alpha, y'(a) = 1 \end{cases} \Rightarrow y_2(x).$$

So $y(x) = \lambda y_1(x) + (1-\lambda)y_2(x)$, $\lambda = \dfrac{\beta - y_2(b)}{y_1(b) - y_2(b)}.$

Excises 8

8.1 The solution of the initial value problem $\begin{cases} \dfrac{dy}{dx} = -y, \\ y(0) = 1 \end{cases}$ is $y(x) = e^{-x}$, $y(0.01) = 0.99049833$. Let $h = 0.01$, use the Euler's method, the implicit Euler's method, the trapezoidal method and the improved Euler's method to calculate the approximation of $y(0.01)$ each step.

8.2 Use the Euler's method, the improved Euler's method and the trapezoidal method to solve the initial value problem

$$\begin{cases} \dfrac{dy}{dx} = -y + x + 1, \\ y(0) = 1. \end{cases}$$

Take $h = 0.1$, calculate to $x = 0.5$.

8.3 Use the Euler's method (taking $h = 0.025$), the improved Euler's method (taking $h = 0.05$) and the classical fourth-order Runge-Kutta method (taking $h = 0.1$) to solve initial value problem $\dfrac{dy}{dx} = -y + 1, y(0) = 0$.

8.4 The trapezoidal method of solving the initial value problem is

$$y_{n+1} = y_n + \frac{h}{2}[f(x_n, y_n) + f(x_{n+1}, y_{n+1})], \quad n = 0, 1, 2, \cdots.$$

Each step of solving y_{n+1} is to solve an y_{n+1} equation, if the Euler's method of calculation results as the initial value, the construction of the iterative method.

(1) Try to prove: if the iteration convergence, which L satisfied

$$\left| \frac{\partial f}{\partial y}(x, y) \right| \leq L, \quad \forall (x, y) \in \{(x, y) \mid x \in [x_0, h], y \in \mathbf{R}\}.$$

(2) Select the step size h for the initial value problem

$$\begin{cases} y' = e^x \sin(xy), & x \in (0, 1], \\ y(0) = 1. \end{cases}$$

8.5 Derivative the order, local truncation error and the main expression of the Euler's method, trapezoidal method and improved Euler's method.

8.6 If a two-level Runge-Kutta method

$$y_{n+1} = y_n + h[c_1 f(x_n, y_n) + c_2 f(x_n + a_2 h, y_n + hb_{21} f(x_n, y_n))]$$

is first or second order, what the coefficient should meet?

8.7 If the improved Euler's method is used to solve the initial value problem

$$\begin{cases} \dfrac{dy}{dx} = -2ax, \\ y(0) = 1. \end{cases}$$

Find that the numerical solution $y_1, y_2, \cdots$ and the true solution $y(x_1), y(x_2), \cdots$ are in full compliance (regardless of the rounding error), try to explain the reason.

8.8 Let $a > 0$, use the trapezoidal method to solve the initial value problem

$$\begin{cases} \dfrac{dy}{dx} = -ay, & x \in (0, b], \\ y(0) = y_0. \end{cases}$$

Try to prove that

(1) $|y_n| < |y_0|, n = 1, 2, \cdots$.

(2) $y_n = \left(\dfrac{2 - ah}{2 + ah}\right)^n y_0$, and when $h \to 0$, y_n converges to exact solution $y(x)$ of the initial value problem for the fixed $x = x_n = nh$ ($h \to 0, n \to \infty$).

8.9 A single step approach $y_{n+1} = y_n + h\phi(x_n, y_n; h)$ to the initial value problem

$$\begin{cases} \dfrac{dy}{dx} = f(x, y), & x \in [x_0, b], \\ y(x_0) = y_0 \end{cases}$$

is the p-order method. The incremental function $\phi(x, y; h)$ satisfies the Lipschitz condition for y, that is, there is a $L > 0$, such that

$$|\phi(x, y; h) - \phi(x, \bar{y}; h)| \leq L |y - \bar{y}|, \quad \forall y, \bar{y} \in \mathbf{R}.$$

Prove that this method is convergent, and the overall truncation error is

$$y(x_n) - y_n = O(h^p).$$

8.10 Explain the meaning of absolute stability.

8.11 Try to derive the absolute stability conditions and absolute stability intervals of first and second order explicit Runge-Kutta method and trapezoidal method.

8.12 For initial value problem

$$\begin{cases} \dfrac{dy}{dx} = -20y, & x \in (0,1], \\ y(0) = 1. \end{cases}$$

(1) Calculate it with the classic fourth order Runge-Kutta method, taking $h = 0.1$ and 0.2 respectively, give the calculation errors and analysis results.

(2) If the Euler's method is used to calculate, what the value of h should take to make the method stable?

8.13 Derive the two-step Adams explicit and implicit formula by numerical integration.

8.14 Take $h = 0.1$, and use the fourth order explicit and implicit Adams method to solve the initial problem

$$\begin{cases} \dfrac{dy}{dx} = -y + x + 1, & 0 < x \leqslant 1, \\ y(0) = 1. \end{cases}$$

8.15 For linear multistep method $\sum_{j=0}^{k} \alpha_j y_{n+j} = h \sum_{j=0}^{k} \beta_j f_{n+j}$, define λ polynomial

$$\rho(\lambda) = \sum_{j=0}^{k} \alpha_j \lambda^j, \quad \sigma(\lambda) = \sum_{j=0}^{k} \beta_j \lambda^j.$$

If the operator $L[y(x);h] = \sum_{j=0}^{k} [\alpha_j y(x+jh) - h\beta_j y'(x+jh)]$ is unfolded

$$L[y(x);h] = c_0 y(x) + c_1 h y'(x) + \cdots + c_l h^l y^{(l)}(x) + \cdots,$$

try to prove

$$c_0 = \rho(1), \quad c_1 = \rho'(1) - \sigma(1),$$

and write the expression of c_l ($l = 2, 3, \cdots$).

8.16 Derive the explicit linear two-step method and obtain the local truncation error.

8.17 Analysis the order of Hamming method

$$y_{n+3} = \frac{1}{8}(9y_{n+2} - y_n) + \frac{3}{8}h(f_{n+3} + 2f_{n+2} - f_{n+1})$$

and find its local truncation error.

8.18 Determine the parameters $\beta_1, \beta_2, \beta_3$, such that the steps of the multistep method

$$y_{n+4} = y_n + h(\beta_1 f_{n+1} + \beta_2 f_{n+2} + \beta_3 f_{n+3})$$

are as high as possible.

8. 19 Prove linear two-step method

$$y_{n+2} + (b-1)y_{n+1} - by_n = \frac{1}{4}h[(b+3)f_{n+2} + (3b+1)f_n]$$

is a second-order method when $b \neq 1$ and a third-order method when $b = -1$.

8. 20 The fourth-order Adams explicit method (four-step) and the fourth-order Adams implicit method (three-steps) form an estimate-correction scheme and is used to solve the initial problem

$$\begin{cases} \dfrac{dy}{dx} = -y + x + 1, & 0 < x \leqslant 1, \\ y(0) = 1, \end{cases}$$

Compare their errors.

References

[1] 胡祖炽,林源渠. 数值分析. 北京:高等教育出版社,1986.
[2] 黄云清,舒适,陈艳萍,等. 数值计算方法. 北京:科学出版社,2009.
[3] 徐翠薇,孙绳武. 计算方法引论.2版. 北京:高等教育出版社,2002.
[4] Richard L. Burden, J. Douglas Faires. Numerical Analysis(Seventh Edition). Boston:Thomson Learning,2001.
[5] John H. Mathews, Kurtis D. Fink. Numerical Methods Using MATLAB (Third Edition). Englewood:Prentice Hall,2001.
[6] 蔡大用,白峰杉. 高等数值分析. 北京:清华大学出版社,1997.
[7] 陈公宁,沈嘉骥. 计算方法导引.3版. 北京:北京师范大学出版社,2009.
[8] 冯康. 数值计算方法. 北京:国防工业出版社,1978.
[9] 冯果忱,刘经伦. 数值代数基础. 长春:吉林大学出版社,1991.
[10] 封建湖,车刚明,聂玉峰. 数值分析原理. 北京:科学出版社,2001.
[11] 关治,陈景良. 数值计算方法. 北京:清华大学出版社,1990.
[12] 蒋尔雄,赵风光,苏仰锋. 数值逼近.2版. 上海:复旦大学出版社,2008.
[13] 李庆扬,王能超,易大义. 数值分析.5版. 北京:清华大学出版社,2008.
[14] 李荣华,冯果忱. 微分方程数值解法.3版. 北京:高等教育出版社,1996.
[15] 林成森. 数值计算方法.2版. 北京:科学出版社,2005.
[16] 王仁宏. 数值逼近. 北京:高等教育出版社,1999.
[17] 王德人,杨忠华. 数值逼近引论. 北京:高等教育出版社,1990.
[18] 王能超. 数值分析简明教程. 北京:高等教育出版社,1984.
[19] 魏毅强,张建国,张洪斌,等. 数值计算方法. 北京:科学出版社,2004.
[20] 徐树方,高立,张平文. 数值线性代数.2版. 北京:北京大学出版社,2013.
[21] 张平文,李铁军. 数值分析. 北京:北京大学出版社,2007.